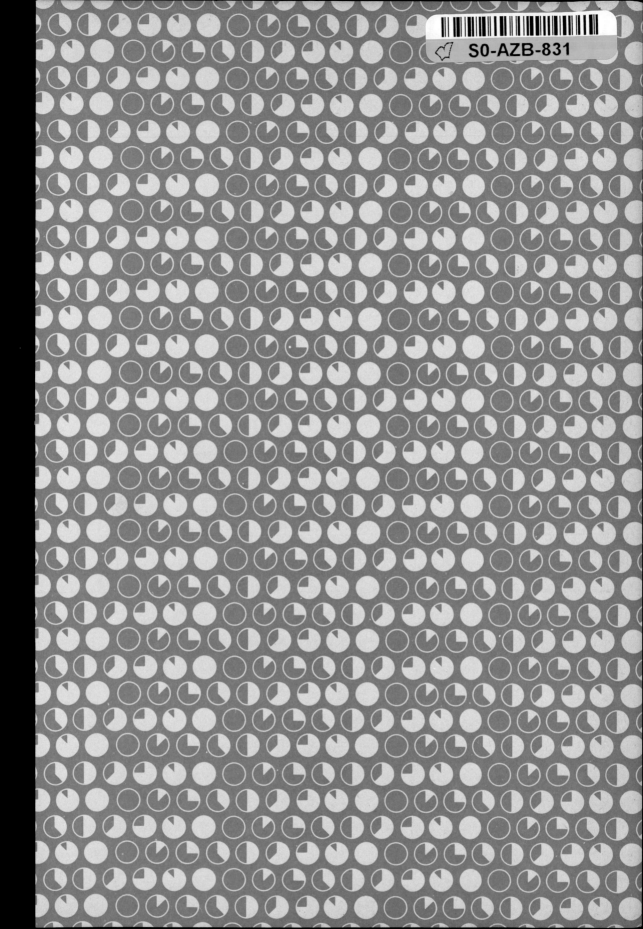

THE NEW STATE OF THE WORLD ATLAS

THE NEW
STATE OF THE WORLD
ATLAS

4th edition

Michael Kidron and Ronald Segal

A Pluto Project

A TOUCHSTONE BOOK

Published by Simon & Schuster Inc
New York

Simon and Schuster/Touchstone Books
Published by Simon & Schuster Inc.
Simon & Schuster Building
Rockefeller Center
1230 Avenue of the Americas
New York NY 10020

SIMON AND SCHUSTER, TOUCHSTONE and colophons
are registered trademarks of Simon & Schuster Inc.

Published in Great Britain by
Simon & Schuster Ltd., London

Edited and coordinated for
Swanston Publishing Limited, Derby and London by
Anne Benewick
with Pamela Hopkinson, David Pratt, George Wilkes

Maps and text created for
Swanston Graphics Limited, Derby by
Isabelle Lewis
with Andrea Fairbrass, Jeanne Radford and Malcolm Swanston

Design by Grundy & Northedge, London

Produced by Mandarin Offset
Printed and bound in Hong Kong

10 9 8 7 6 5 4 3 2 1
10 9 8 7 6 5 4 3 2 1 Pbk

Library of Congress Cataloging-in-Publication Data

Kidron, Michael,
    The new state of the world atlas/Michael Kidron and Ronald Segal. – 4th ed.
        p.   cm.
    "Maps copyright by Swanston Publishing Limited, ... Artwork for
maps by Swanston Graphics Limited" – CIP t.p. verso.
        "Published in Great Britain by TK" – CIP t.p. verso.
        "A Touchstone book."
        "A Pluto Press project"
        Includes bibliographical reference and index,
        ISBN 0-671-74639-1: $27.95. – ISBN 0-671-74556-5 (pbk.): $14.95
        I. Atlases   2.   Economic geogaphy – Maps.   3. Social problems – Maps.   4. World politics – 1945-   –Maps.
    I. Segal, Ronald, 1932-   II. Swanston Graphics Limited.   III. Title.
    G1021.K46   1991   <G&M>
    912–dc20   91-6798
                                                                                                          CIP
                                                                                                          MAP

CONTENTS

INTRODUCTION

'I wish it! I command it! Let my will take the place of reason!'

If anything, the powerful have become more powerful, their behaviour more capricious, their effect on the powerless more devastating in the 1900 years since Juvenal. And the poor are poorer, the excluded more redundant, the refugee, the ailing, the neglected, more hapless – and vastly more numerous.

Yet, even in the blink of time since the last edition of this atlas, 1987, a few cracks have appeared in our confinement.

One crack runs through the integrity of the state. It is deepening as nationalism, sub-nationalism and supra-nationalism beat against the state's borders – in the USSR, in great parts of Europe, in the Middle East, most of Africa, Asia, Latin America and in Canada. Another crack divides the state from the market system. It too is deepening as the markets extend to encompass the entire world and the state remains frozen.

The crack that separates society at large from the system is also deepening as populations grow faster than the system extends. And so too is the crack between society and nature as the human species demands more than the finite sphere that is our current home can offer.

As yet these are hairline cracks barely visible to the unpractised eye. They do not threaten to ground the world as we know it. But they indicate where the stresses are, and hint at what might happen if they are not dealt with.

This edition of the atlas rests, like its predecessors, on the enduring features of the world of states: its political composition, the concen-tration of economic, social and cultural power within each state and amongst them. All of the content has been reviewed and updated, most of it has been rethought, much of it is new.

In one, domestic, respect this edition is different from its prede-cessors. To the regret of us both, Ronald Segal was unable to play an active part in its planning or preparation. (He is engaged on a major work, *The Black Diaspora*, to be published in 1993 by Farrar, Straus & Giroux in New York and Faber & Faber in London). Many readers will feel the loss, but none so keenly as the remaining author, deprived of the glee, the outrageousness and the balance of true partnership. If there is any comfort to be drawn from this loss it is that the reader may blame any deficiency that he or she detects on his absence rather than on my continued presence.

This is a work of cartojournalism. It displays through maps the background to a prodigious variety of commonly-observed events. Many people have contributed, willingly or not, to it. Where that contribution was specific I have acknowledged it in the notes to each map. But some contributions cannot be so confined. Anne Benewick and her supporting team at Swanston Publishing transformed austere lists and occasionally outlandish suggestions into comprehensible maps – speedily, efficiently and pleasantly. Isabelle Lewis at Swanston Graphics acquired new computer skills under pressure and, with Malcolm Swanston, breathed new life into symbols and graphics.

Then there are the knowledge curators, the librarians, without whose general ethos and generous help works like this would not be possible. Although they lean towards modest anonymity, there are some whose cover I am able to break: they are Maggie Julian, Jenny Foreman, Lis Parcell and John Peel at the Royal Institute of International Affairs, London; John Pinfold at the British Library of Political and Economic Sciences (at the London School of Economics); John Montgomery at the Royal United Services, London; Martin Watton at the United Nations Information Office, London; Carolyn Wells, Sue Baker and Hilary Oakley at the International Institute for Strategic Studies. Those whose cover I have not succeeded in breaking are the librarians at the Royal Geographical Society and at the Kensington & Chelsea Borough Library, especially its North Kensington branch.

Finally there are the people who have helped me towards an understanding, edgy though it remains, with my computer and its peripherals, without which this book would have been far more difficult to compile than it has proved to be. They are Roc Sandford, Rob Somerville and Doron Swade.

Michael Kidron

London
23 April 1991

GREENLAND
(Den)

ICELAND

CANADA

IRELAND
UNITED
KINGDOM
DENMA
NETH
GERM
BEL

UNITED STATES
OF AMERICA

FRANCE

SPAIN

PORTUGAL

ST PIERRE & MIQUELON
(Fr)

AZORES (Port)

TUN

MOROCCO

BERMUDA

MEXICO

ATLANTIC
OCEAN

ALGERIA

WESTERN SAHARA

BAHAMAS

CUBA

BELIZE
GUATEMALA
EL SALVADOR
HONDURAS
NICARAGUA
COSTA RICA
PANAMA

HAITI
JAMAICA

DOMINICAN REPUBLIC
PUERTO RICO (US)
GUADELOUPE (Fr)

GRENADA

BARBADOS
TRINIDAD & TOBAGO

VENEZUELA

GUYANA
SURINAME
FRENCH GUIANA (Fr)

CAPE VERDE

MAURITANIA

MALI

NIG

SENEGAL
GAMBIA
GUINEA-BISSAU
GUINEA
SIERRA LEONE
IVORY
COAST

BURKINA
FASO
BENIN
GHANA
TOGO

NIGERIA

CA

REVILLA GIGEDO
ISLANDS (Mex)

GALAPAGOS ISLANDS ECUADOR

COLOMBIA

LIBERIA

SAO TOME & PRINCIPE

GAB

PACIFIC
OCEAN

PERU

BRAZIL

EQUATORIAL GUINEA

ASCENSION ISLAND
(UK)

ST HELENA

BOLIVIA

PARAGUAY

THE STATE INVADES ANTARCTICA

CLAIMS AND OVERLAPPING CLAIMS 1990
Belgium, Japan, Poland, South Africa, the USA and the
USSR do not recognize any of the claims on Antarctica.
The USA and the
USSR reserve
the right to
claim.

BORDER DISPUTES

SOVEREIGN STATES 1990

- states with unresolved
  jurisdictional dispute(s)

- no current dispute

- privileged zone (extended
  economic zone or
  exclusive fishing zone)
  schematic

- states whose jurisdictional
  disputes have led to
  armed clashes 1950-90

CHILE

URUGUAY

ARGENTINA

FRANCE

NEW
ZEALAND

AUSTRALIA

ANTARCTICA

Pacific sector

60°

NORWAY

CHILE

Sources: Border and Territorial Disputes;
Buzan; CIA; Times Atlas of the
Oceans; Maritime Affairs

FALKLAND ISLANDS
(UK)

BRITAIN

ARGENTINA

Sources: Earthscan; SCAR Bulletin

To exist at all, states must recognize each other. In practice their jurisdictions nearly always clash.

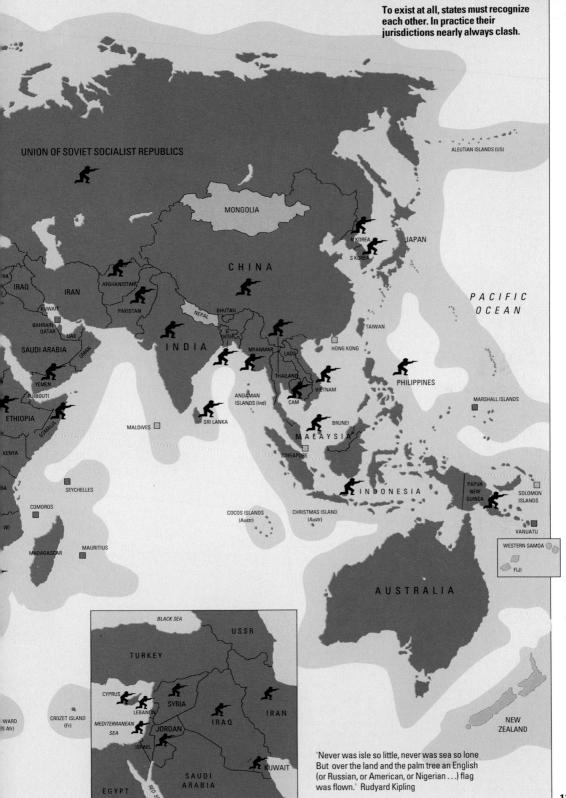

'Never was isle so little, never was sea so lone
But over the land and the palm tree an English
(or Russian, or American, or Nigerian . . .) flag
was flown.' Rudyard Kipling

Copyright © Swanston Publishing Limited

ICELAND

NOR

CANADA

IRELAND

UNITED
KINGDOM

DENMARK

UNITED STATES
OF
AMERICA

BEL— N

FRANCE

GERMANY

AUS

ITALY

BAHAMAS

MONACO

MEXICO

SPAIN

PORTUGAL

CUBA

GUATEMALA

DOMINICAN
REPUBLIC

EL SALVADOR

HAITI

TUNISIA

HONDURAS

PUERTO RICO (US)

MOROCCO

ALGERIA

LIBYA

EGYP

NICARAGUA

ANTIGUA

COSTA RICA

DOMINICA

MALI

NIGER

CHAD

SUDA

PANAMA

GUYANA

MARTINIQUE (Fr)

SENEGAL

MAURITANIA

TRINIDAD & TOBAGO

GUINEA
BISSAU

GUINEA

BURKINA
FASO

CAPE VERDE

COLOMBIA

VENEZUELA

SURINAME

SIERRA
LEONE

LIBERIA

IVORY
COAST

GHANA

TOGO

BENIN

NIGERIA

C A R

ECUADOR

B R A Z I L

EQUATORIAL GUINEA

CAM

CONGO

ETHIC

SAO TOME & PRINCIPE

GABON

UG

PERU

ZAIRE

ANGOLA

ZAMBIA

PARAGUAY

ZIM

MAL

BOLIVIA

URUGUAY

NAMIBIA

BOTS

CHILE

ARGENTINA

SOUTH AFRIC

Sources: CIA; Foreign and
Commonwealth Office

THE CLAIMS

TERRITORIAL AND OTHER CLAIMS,
1990
Proportion of total world surface,
percentages

=1.0%

=0.1%

TOTAL CLAIM COMPARED WITH
TERRITORIAL CLAIM *1990*

ten times

three times

twice

one and a half times

the same

includes major inhabited
dependencies and
associated territories

States claim exclusive territorial rights to
149 million square kilometres of land and
inland waters, and to 8 million square
kilometres of seas and oceans.
They also claim exclusive economic
privileges in a further 125 million square
kilometres of ocean. Altogether they lay
claim to 54 percent of the world's surface.

States divide among themselves the earth and the waters thereof; they also divide the waters and the riches thereof.

JAPAN

N KOREA

S KOREA

N OF SOVIET SOCIALIST REPUBLICS

MONGOLIA

CHINA

AFGHANISTAN

B-DESH

NEPAL

PAKISTAN

MYANMAR

LAOS

THAILAND

VIETNAM

INDIA

TAIWAN

CAM

MALDIVES

SRI LANKA

MALAYSIA

P H I L I P P I N E S

BRUNEI

EYCHELLES

KIRIBATI

SOLOMON ISLANDS

W SAMOA

I N D O N E S I A

PAPUA NEW GUINEA

MAURITIUS

VANUATU

FIJI

TONGA

REUNION

AGASCAR

AUSTRALIA

NEW ZEALAND

29 OTHER INDEPENDENT STATES

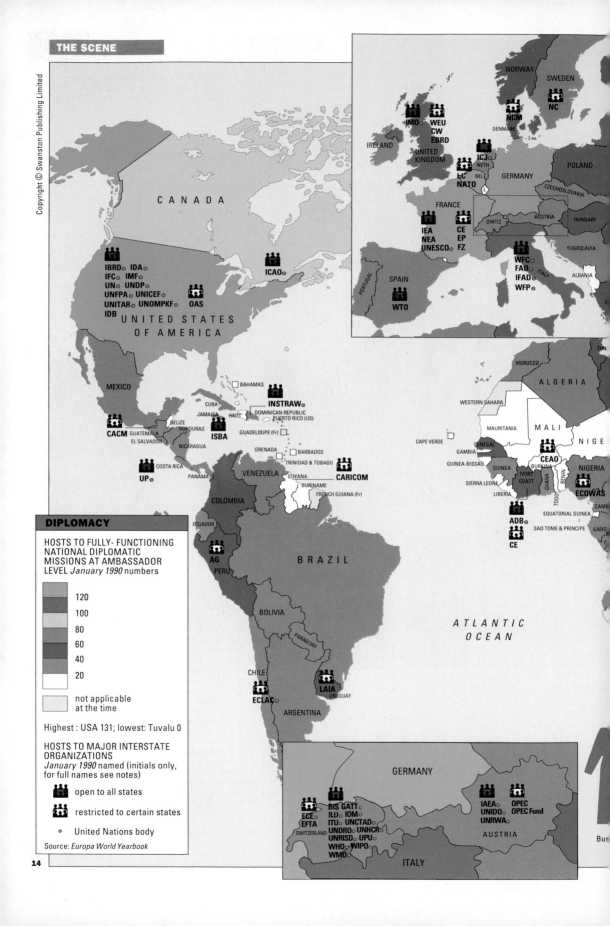

DIPLOMACY

HOSTS TO FULLY- FUNCTIONING NATIONAL DIPLOMATIC MISSIONS AT AMBASSADOR LEVEL *January 1990* numbers

120
100
80
60
40
20

not applicable at the time

Highest : USA 131; lowest: Tuvalu 0

HOSTS TO MAJOR INTERSTATE ORGANIZATIONS
January 1990 named (initials only, for full names see notes)

open to all states

restricted to certain states

United Nations body

Source: *Europa World Yearbook*

14

Among states, too, there are stars and wallflowers, steadies and one-night stands.

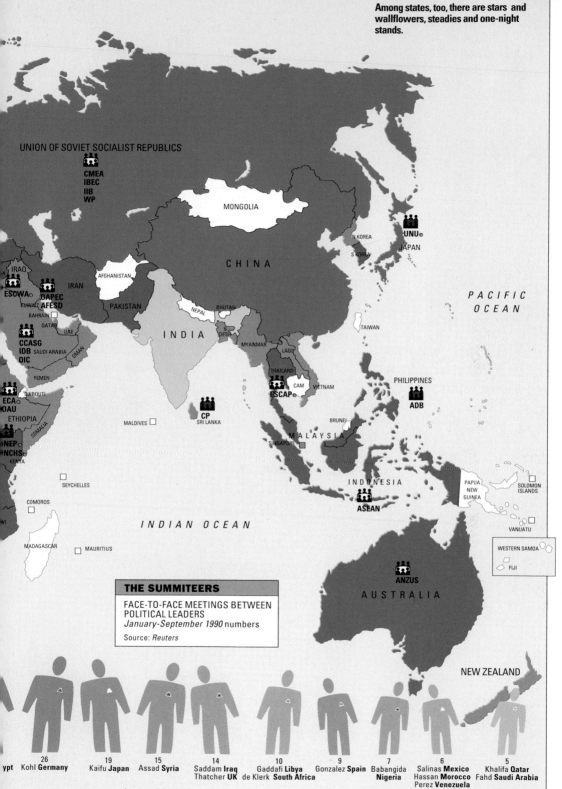

UNION OF SOVIET SOCIALIST REPUBLICS

CMEA
IBEC
IIB
WP

MONGOLIA

N KOREA
S KOREA

UNU©
JAPAN

CHINA

PACIFIC OCEAN

IRAQ
ESCWA
DAPEC
AFESD
IRAN
AFGHANISTAN
PAKISTAN
KUWAIT
BAHRAIN
QATAR
UAE
CCASG
IDB
OIC
SAUDI ARABIA
OMAN
YEMEN

INDIA

NEPAL
BHUTAN
B'DESH
MYANMAR
LAOS
THAILAND
ESCAP
CAM
VIETNAM

TAIWAN

PHILIPPINES
ADB

DJIBOUTI
ECA
OAU
ETHIOPIA
SOMALIA
NEP
NCHS
KENYA

MALDIVES

CP
SRI LANKA

BRUNEI

MALAYSIA
SINGAPORE

SEYCHELLES

COMOROS

INDIAN OCEAN

INDONESIA

ASEAN

PAPUA NEW GUINEA

SOLOMON ISLANDS

MADAGASCAR
MAURITIUS

VANUATU

WESTERN SAMOA
FIJI

ANZUS

AUSTRALIA

THE SUMMITEERS

FACE-TO-FACE MEETINGS BETWEEN POLITICAL LEADERS
January-September 1990 numbers

Source: *Reuters*

NEW ZEALAND

| ypt | 26 Kohl **Germany** | 19 Kaifu **Japan** | 15 Assad **Syria** | 14 Saddam **Iraq** Thatcher **UK** | 10 Gaddafi **Libya** de Klerk **South Africa** | 9 Gonzalez **Spain** | 7 Babangida **Nigeria** | 6 Salinas **Mexico** Hassan **Morocco** Perez **Venezuela** | 5 Khalifa **Qatar** Fahd **Saudi Arabia** |

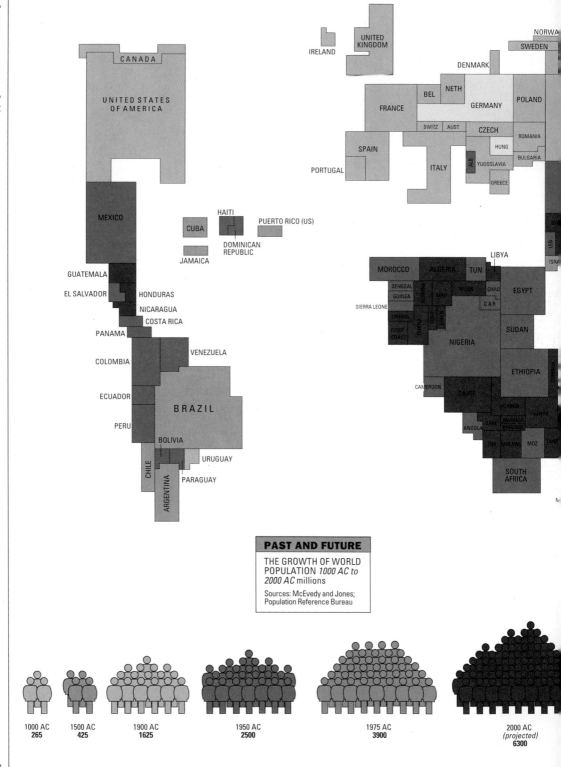

CANADA

UNITED STATES
OF AMERICA

MEXICO

CUBA

HAITI

PUERTO RICO (US)

DOMINICAN
REPUBLIC

JAMAICA

GUATEMALA

EL SALVADOR

HONDURAS

NICARAGUA

COSTA RICA

PANAMA

VENEZUELA

COLOMBIA

ECUADOR

BRAZIL

PERU

BOLIVIA

URUGUAY

CHILE

PARAGUAY

ARGENTINA

IRELAND

UNITED
KINGDOM

NORWA

SWEDEN

DENMARK

BEL NETH

FRANCE

GERMANY

POLAND

SWITZ AUST

CZECH

ROMANIA

HUNG

SPAIN

BULGARIA

PORTUGAL

ITALY

ALB YUGOSLAVIA

GREECE

LIBYA

MOROCCO

ALGERIA

TUN

SENEGAL

GUINEA

NIGER

CHAD

EGYPT

SIERRA LEONE

MALI

CAR

LIBERIA

IVORY
COAST

NIGERIA

SUDAN

CAMEROON

ZAIRE

ETHIOPIA

SOMALIA

UGANDA

KENYA

ANGOLA

ZAM

RWANDA

BURUNDI

ZIM

MALAWI

MOZ

TANZ

SOUTH
AFRICA

PAST AND FUTURE

THE GROWTH OF WORLD
POPULATION *1000 AC* to
2000 AC millions

Sources: McEvedy and Jones;
Population Reference Bureau

1000 AC	1500 AC	1900 AC	1950 AC	1975 AC	2000 AC
265	**425**	**1625**	**2500**	**3900**	*(projected)* **6300**

There are 5321 million people on earth and many more on the way.

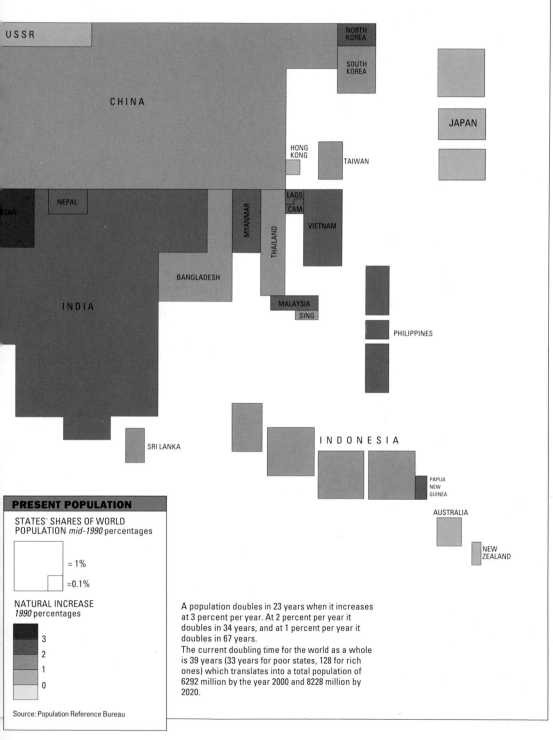

USSR

NORTH KOREA

SOUTH KOREA

CHINA

JAPAN

HONG KONG

TAIWAN

TAN

NEPAL

LAOS

CAM

MYANMAR

THAILAND

VIETNAM

BANGLADESH

INDIA

MALAYSIA

SING

PHILIPPINES

SRI LANKA

I N D O N E S I A

PAPUA NEW GUINEA

AUSTRALIA

NEW ZEALAND

PRESENT POPULATION

STATES' SHARES OF WORLD POPULATION *mid-1990* percentages

= 1%

=0.1%

NATURAL INCREASE
1990 percentages

3
2
1
0

Source: Population Reference Bureau

A population doubles in 23 years when it increases at 3 percent per year. At 2 percent per year it doubles in 34 years, and at 1 percent per year it doubles in 67 years.
The current doubling time for the world as a whole is 39 years (33 years for poor states, 128 for rich ones) which translates into a total population of 6292 million by the year 2000 and 8228 million by 2020.

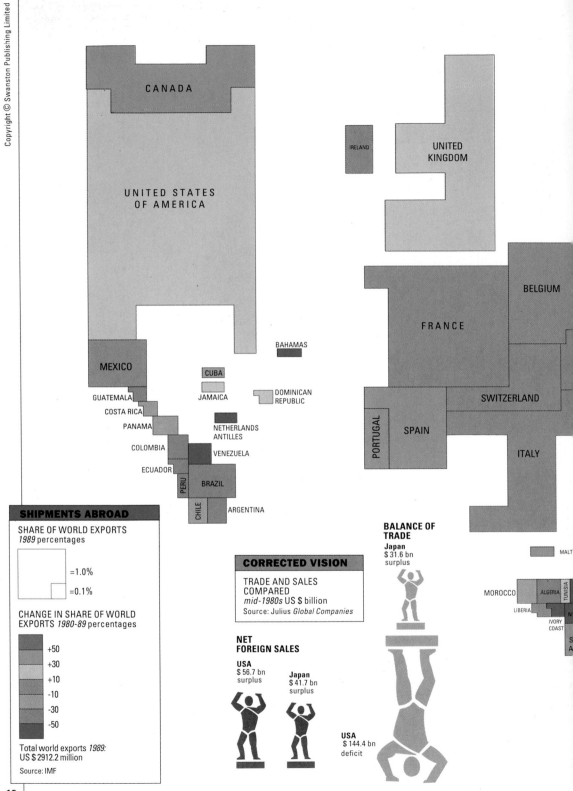

CANADA

UNITED STATES
OF AMERICA

IRELAND

UNITED
KINGDOM

BELGIUM

FRANCE

BAHAMAS

MEXICO

CUBA

JAMAICA

DOMINICAN
REPUBLIC

SWITZERLAND

GUATEMALA

COSTA RICA

PANAMA

COLOMBIA

NETHERLANDS
ANTILLES

VENEZUELA

PORTUGAL

SPAIN

ITALY

ECUADOR

PERU

BRAZIL

CHILE

ARGENTINA

SHIPMENTS ABROAD

SHARE OF WORLD EXPORTS
1989 percentages

=1.0%

=0.1%

CHANGE IN SHARE OF WORLD
EXPORTS *1980-89* percentages

+50

+30

+10

-10

-30

-50

Total world exports *1989*:
US $ 2912.2 million

Source: IMF

CORRECTED VISION

TRADE AND SALES
COMPARED
mid-1980s US $ billion
Source: Julius *Global Companies*

NET
FOREIGN SALES

USA
$ 56.7 bn
surplus

Japan
$ 41.7 bn
surplus

BALANCE OF
TRADE

Japan
$ 31.6 bn
surplus

USA
$ 144.4 bn
deficit

MALT

MOROCCO

ALGERIA

TUNISIA

LIBERIA

IVORY
COAST

N

S
A

More than half recorded exports come from just seven states. Their businesses sell abroad four times as much as they ship from home.

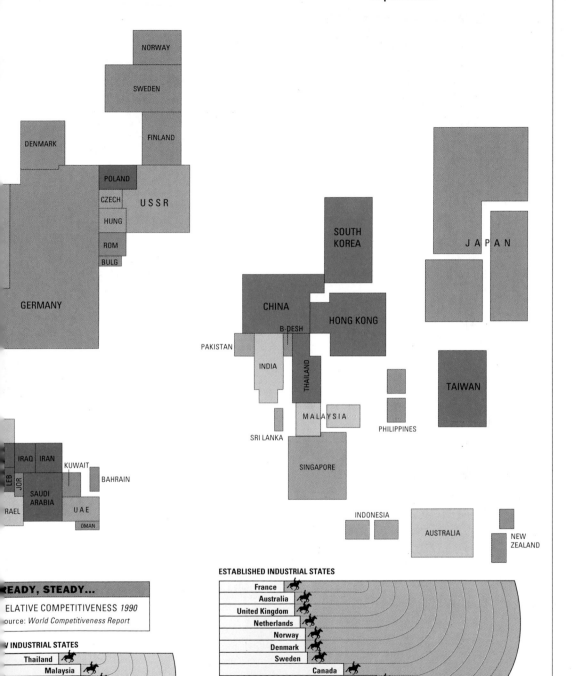

NORWAY

SWEDEN

FINLAND

DENMARK

POLAND

CZECH

HUNG

ROM

BULG

USSR

GERMANY

SOUTH KOREA

CHINA

B-DESH

PAKISTAN

HONG KONG

INDIA

THAILAND

J A P A N

TAIWAN

MALAYSIA

SRI LANKA

PHILIPPINES

IRAQ IRAN KUWAIT

LEB

JOR

BAHRAIN

SAUDI ARABIA

RAEL

U A E

OMAN

SINGAPORE

INDONESIA

AUSTRALIA

NEW ZEALAND

READY, STEADY...

RELATIVE COMPETITIVENESS *1990*
ource: *World Competitiveness Report*

W INDUSTRIAL STATES

Thailand
Malaysia
Korea
Hong Kong
Taiwan
Singapore

ESTABLISHED INDUSTRIAL STATES

France
Australia
United Kingdom
Netherlands
Norway
Denmark
Sweden
Canada
Germany
USA
Switzerland
Japan

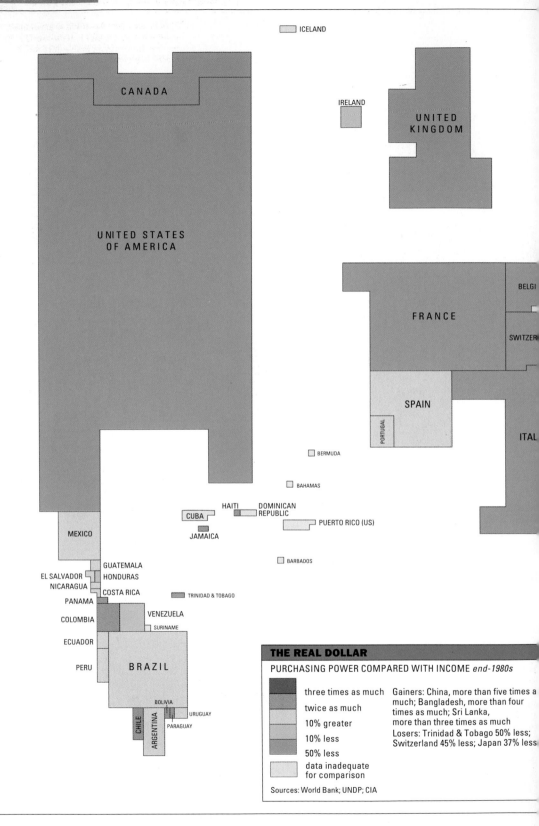

ICELAND

CANADA

IRELAND

UNITED
KINGDOM

UNITED STATES
OF AMERICA

FRANCE

BELGI

SWITZER

SPAIN

PORTUGAL

BERMUDA

ITAL

BAHAMAS

HAITI   DOMINICAN
          REPUBLIC

CUBA

PUERTO RICO (US)

JAMAICA

MEXICO

BARBADOS

GUATEMALA

EL SALVADOR   HONDURAS
NICARAGUA
              COSTA RICA

PANAMA   TRINIDAD & TOBAGO

COLOMBIA   VENEZUELA

                SURINAME

ECUADOR

PERU   BRAZIL

BOLIVIA

                          URUGUAY
CHILE   ARGENTINA
                PARAGUAY

THE REAL DOLLAR

PURCHASING POWER COMPARED WITH INCOME *end-1980s*

- three times as much
- twice as much
- 10% greater
- 10% less
- 50% less
- data inadequate for comparison

Gainers: China, more than five times a
much; Bangladesh, more than four
times as much; Sri Lanka,
more than three times as much
Losers: Trinidad & Tobago 50% less;
Switzerland 45% less; Japan 37% less

Sources: World Bank; UNDP; CIA

20

Three states with 9 percent of the world's population account for half the world's income, and for more than a third of the world's purchasing power.

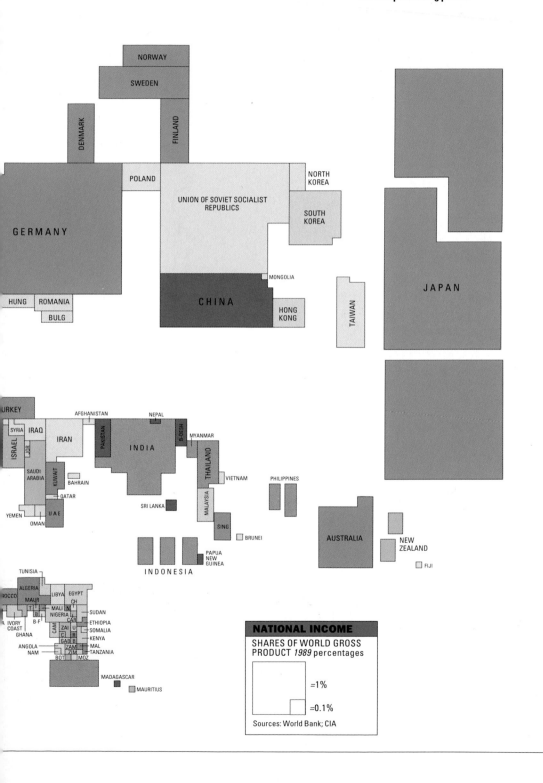

NORWAY

SWEDEN

DENMARK

FINLAND

POLAND

NORTH KOREA

UNION OF SOVIET SOCIALIST REPUBLICS

SOUTH KOREA

GERMANY

MONGOLIA

HUNG | ROMANIA

BULG

CHINA

HONG KONG

TAIWAN

JAPAN

URKEY

AFGHANISTAN

NEPAL

SYRIA | IRAQ

IRAN

PAKISTAN

B-DESH

MYANMAR

ISRAEL | JOR

INDIA

THAILAND

SAUDI ARABIA | KUWAIT

BAHRAIN

VIETNAM

PHILIPPINES

QATAR

YEMEN | U A E

OMAN

SRI LANKA

MALAYSIA

SING

BRUNEI

AUSTRALIA

NEW ZEALAND

FIJI

INDONESIA

PAPUA NEW GUINEA

TUNISIA

ALGERIA

LIBYA | EGYPT

ROCCO

MAUR

CH

MALI

SUDAN

N

NIGERIA

IVORY COAST

B-F

CAR

ETHIOPIA

CAM | ZAI

U

SOMALIA

GHANA

C | R

KENYA

GAB | B.

ANGOLA

ZAM

MAL

NAM

ZIM

TANZANIA

BOT | MOZ

MADAGASCAR

MAURITIUS

NATIONAL INCOME

SHARES OF WORLD GROSS PRODUCT *1989* percentages

=1%

=0.1%

Sources: World Bank; CIA

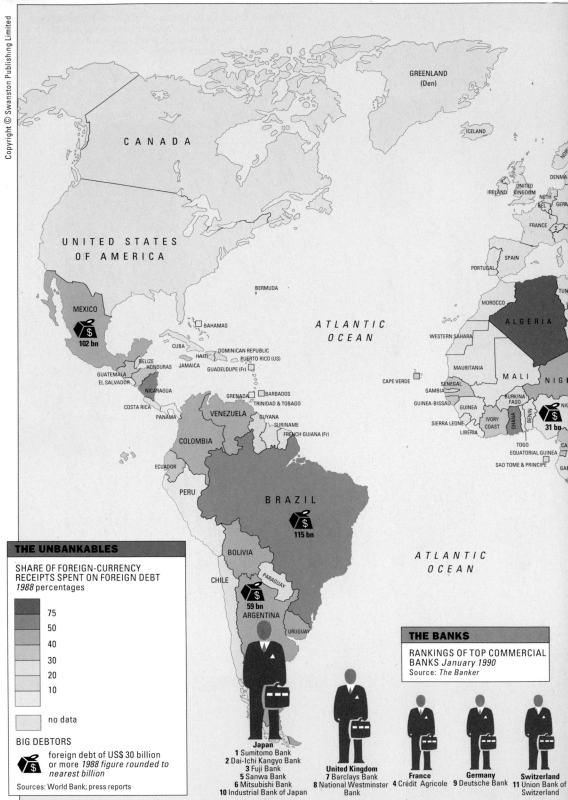

Copyright © Swanston Publishing Limited

GREENLAND
(Den)

ICELAND

CANADA

UNITED STATES
OF AMERICA

IRELAND
UNITED KINGDOM
NETH
BEL
GERM
FRANCE

BERMUDA

SPAIN
PORTUGAL

MEXICO
102 bn

BAHAMAS

ATLANTIC
OCEAN

MOROCCO

TUN

ALGERIA

WESTERN SAHARA

CUBA
HAITI
DOMINICAN REPUBLIC
PUERTO RICO (US)
BELIZE
HONDURAS
JAMAICA
GUADELOUPE (Fr)
GUATEMALA
EL SALVADOR
NICARAGUA
GRENADA
BARBADOS
TRINIDAD & TOBAGO
COSTA RICA
PANAMA

CAPE VERDE

MAURITANIA

MALI

NIG

GAMBIA
SENEGAL
GUINEA-BISSAU
GUINEA
SIERRA LEONE
LIBERIA
IVORY
COAST
GHANA
BURKINA
FASO
BENIN
NIG
NI
31 bn

VENEZUELA
GUYANA
SURINAME
FRENCH GUIANA (Fr)

COLOMBIA

ECUADOR

PERU

BRAZIL
115 bn

BOLIVIA

CHILE

PARAGUAY

59 bn
ARGENTINA

URUGUAY

TOGO
EQUATORIAL GUINEA
SAO TOME & PRINCIPE
CA
GA

ATLANTIC
OCEAN

THE UNBANKABLES

SHARE OF FOREIGN-CURRENCY
RECEIPTS SPENT ON FOREIGN DEBT
1988 percentages

75
50
40
30
20
10

no data

BIG DEBTORS

foreign debt of US$ 30 billion
or more *1988 figure rounded to
nearest billion*

Sources: World Bank; press reports

THE BANKS

RANKINGS OF TOP COMMERCIAL
BANKS *January 1990*
Source: *The Banker*

Japan
1 Sumitomo Bank
2 Dai-Ichi Kangyo Bank
3 Fuji Bank
5 Sanwa Bank
6 Mitsubishi Bank
10 Industrial Bank of Japan

United Kingdom
7 Barclays Bank
8 National Westminster
Bank

France
4 Crédit Agricole

Germany
9 Deutsche Bank

Switzerland
11 Union Bank of
Switzerland

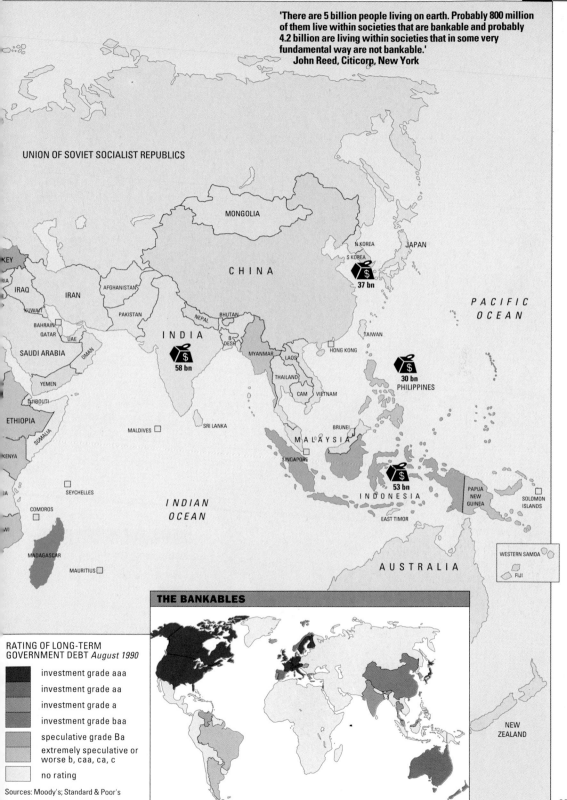

'There are 5 billion people living on earth. Probably 800 million of them live within societies that are bankable and probably 4.2 billion are living within societies that in some very fundamental way are not bankable.'
John Reed, Citicorp, New York

UNION OF SOVIET SOCIALIST REPUBLICS

MONGOLIA

CHINA

N.KOREA

JAPAN

S.KOREA

37 bn

PACIFIC OCEAN

KEY

IRAQ

IRAN

AFGHANISTAN

KUWAIT

PAKISTAN

NEPAL

BHUTAN

BAHRAIN

QATAR

UAE

OMAN

INDIA

B.
DESH

TAIWAN

SAUDI ARABIA

MYANMAR

LAOS

HONG KONG

58 bn

THAILAND

YEMEN

CAM

VIETNAM

30 bn
PHILIPPINES

DJIBOUTI

ETHIOPIA

SOMALIA

MALDIVES

SRI LANKA

BRUNEI

MALAYSIA

KENYA

SINGAPORE

SEYCHELLES

53 bn

INDONESIA

PAPUA
NEW
GUINEA

SOLOMON
ISLANDS

COMOROS

INDIAN
OCEAN

EAST TIMOR

WESTERN SAMOA

MADAGASCAR

MAURITIUS

AUSTRALIA

FIJI

THE BANKABLES

RATING OF LONG-TERM
GOVERNMENT DEBT *August 1990*

- investment grade aaa
- investment grade aa
- investment grade a
- investment grade baa
- speculative grade Ba
- extremely speculative or worse b, caa, ca, c
- no rating

NEW
ZEALAND

Sources: Moody's; Standard & Poor's

23

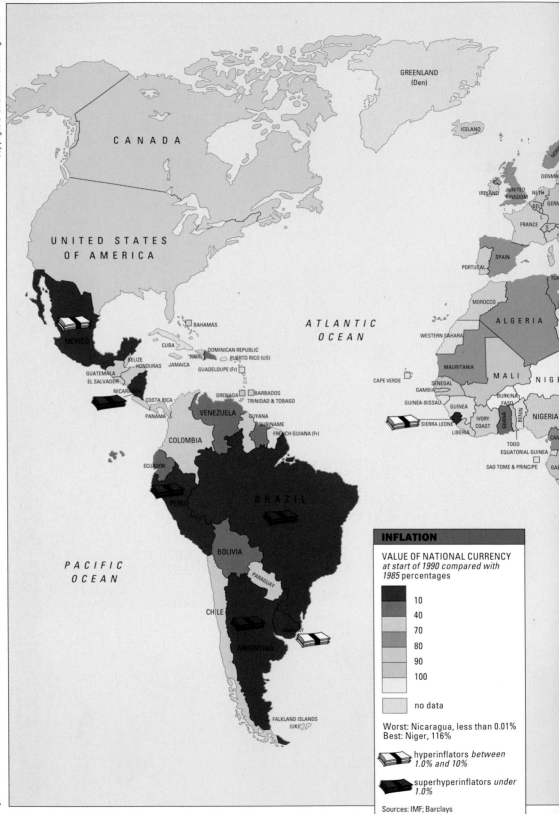

Copyright © Swanston Publishing Limited

GREENLAND
(Den)

ICELAND

C A N A D A

NORW

DENMAR

IRELAND UNITED NETH
KINGDOM GERM
BEL
L
FRANCE

UNITED STATES
OF AMERICA

SPAIN

PORTUGAL

TUN

MOROCCO

A T L A N T I C
O C E A N

ALGERIA

BAHAMAS

WESTERN SAHARA

CUBA

DOMINICAN REPUBLIC

MAURITANIA

MALI NIGE

MEXICO

BELIZE
HAITI PUERTO RICO (US)
HONDURAS JAMAICA
GUADELOUPE (Fr)

CAPE VERDE

SENEGAL
GAMBIA

GUATEMALA
EL SALVADOR
NICARAGUA GRENADA BARBADOS
TRINIDAD & TOBAGO

GUINEA-BISSAU

BURKINA
FASO

NIGERIA

COSTA RICA

PANAMA VENEZUELA GUYANA
SURINAME
FRENCH GUIANA (Fr)

GUINEA
SIERRA LEONE
LIBERIA

IVORY
COAST GHANA BENIN

CAM

COLOMBIA

TOGO
EQUATORIAL GUINEA
SAO TOME & PRINCIPE GAB

ECUADOR

B R A Z I L

PERU

PACIFIC
OCEAN

BOLIVIA

PARAGUAY

CHILE

ARGENTINA

FALKLAND ISLANDS
(UK)

INFLATION

VALUE OF NATIONAL CURRENCY
*at start of 1990 compared with
1985* percentages

10
40
70
80
90
100

no data

Worst: Nicaragua, less than 0.01%
Best: Niger, 116%

hyperinflators *between
1.0% and 10%*

superhyperinflators *under
1.0%*

Sources: IMF; Barclays

24

In the five years between 1985 and 1990,
money lost one third of its value
worldwide on average.

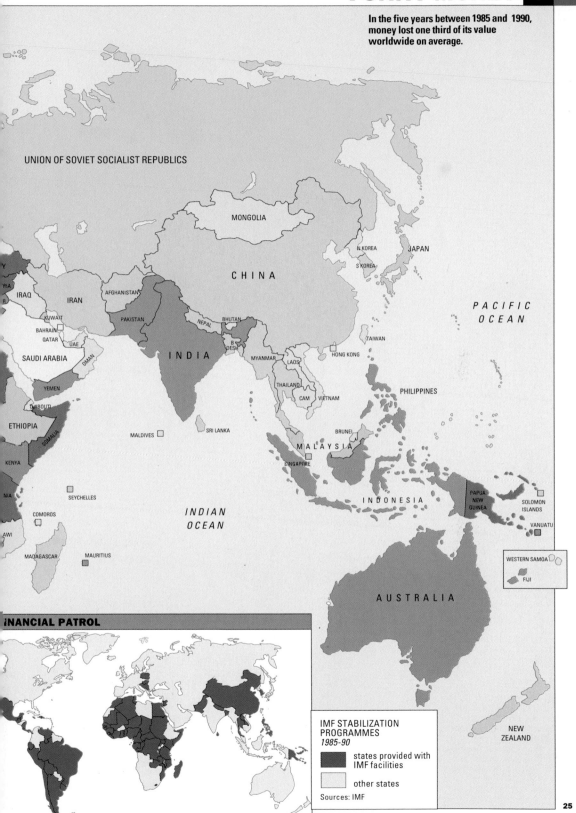

UNION OF SOVIET SOCIALIST REPUBLICS

MONGOLIA

N.KOREA   JAPAN

S.KOREA

CHINA

PACIFIC
OCEAN

IRAQ   IRAN   AFGHANISTAN

KUWAIT   PAKISTAN   NEPAL   BHUTAN

BAHRAIN

QATAR   UAE

B

SAUDI ARABIA   OMAN   INDIA   DESH

MYANMAR   LAOS   HONG KONG   TAIWAN

YEMEN   THAILAND

DJIBOUTI   CAM   VIETNAM   PHILIPPINES

ETHIOPIA   SOMALIA   SRI LANKA

KENYA   MALDIVES   BRUNEI

MALAYSIA

SINGAPORE

NIA   SEYCHELLES

COMOROS   INDONESIA   PAPUA
NEW
GUINEA   SOLOMON
ISLANDS

AWI   INDIAN
OCEAN   VANUATU

MADAGASCAR   MAURITIUS

WESTERN SAMOA

FIJI

AUSTRALIA

INANCIAL PATROL

IMF STABILIZATION
PROGRAMMES
1985-90

states provided with
IMF facilities

other states

Sources: IMF

NEW
ZEALAND

ENERGY

DOMESTIC ENERGY PRODUCTION COMPARED WITH ENERGY USE
1988

- three times as much
- twice as much
- the same
- three quarters
- a half
- a quarter
- no data

Highest: Iraq 14 times;
Angola 12 times; Oman 10 times;
Kuwait, Congo 7 times;
Brunei 6 times; Libya, Saudi Arabia,
Gabon 5 times

traditional fuels (wood, animal wastes etc) provide half or more of domestic energy use

Source: UN

HEAT EXCHANGE

THE TOP TEN NET EXPORTERS AND IMPORTERS OF ENERGY
1988 thousand terajoules

EXPORTERS

USSR	11,453
Saudi Arabia	8805
Mexico	6150
Iraq	5034
Canada	3295
Venezuela	3209
UAE	3189
Norway	3124
Iran	3029
Algeria	2843

IMP

13,19
12,85
6860
4773
4349
2281
2125
1544
1543
1086

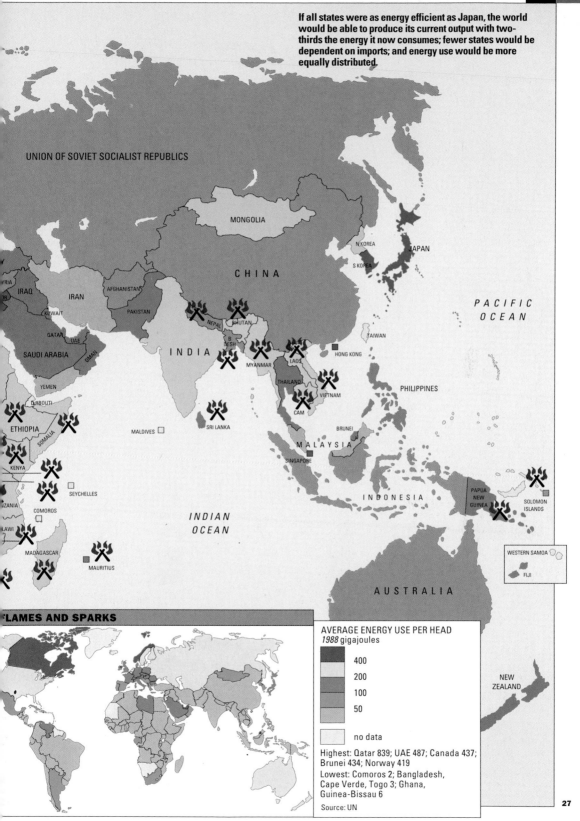

If all states were as energy efficient as Japan, the world would be able to produce its current output with two-thirds the energy it now consumes; fewer states would be dependent on imports; and energy use would be more equally distributed.

UNION OF SOVIET SOCIALIST REPUBLICS

MONGOLIA

N KOREA

JAPAN

S KOREA

CHINA

PACIFIC OCEAN

SYRIA

IRAQ

IRAN

AFGHANISTAN

KUWAIT

PAKISTAN

NEPAL

BHUTAN

QATAR

UAE

B'DESH

SAUDI ARABIA

OMAN

INDIA

MYANMAR

LAOS

TAIWAN

HONG KONG

YEMEN

THAILAND

VIETNAM

PHILIPPINES

DJIBOUTI

CAM

ETHIOPIA

SOMALIA

MALDIVES

SRI LANKA

BRUNEI

KENYA

SEYCHELLES

MALAYSIA

SINGAPORE

TANZANIA

COMOROS

INDONESIA

PAPUA NEW GUINEA

SOLOMON ISLANDS

INDIAN OCEAN

MALAWI

MADAGASCAR

MAURITIUS

WESTERN SAMOA

FIJI

AUSTRALIA

FLAMES AND SPARKS

NEW ZEALAND

AVERAGE ENERGY USE PER HEAD
1988 gigajoules

- 400
- 200
- 100
- 50

no data

Highest: Qatar 839; UAE 487; Canada 437; Brunei 434; Norway 419

Lowest: Comoros 2; Bangladesh, Cape Verde, Togo 3; Ghana, Guinea-Bissau 6

Source: UN

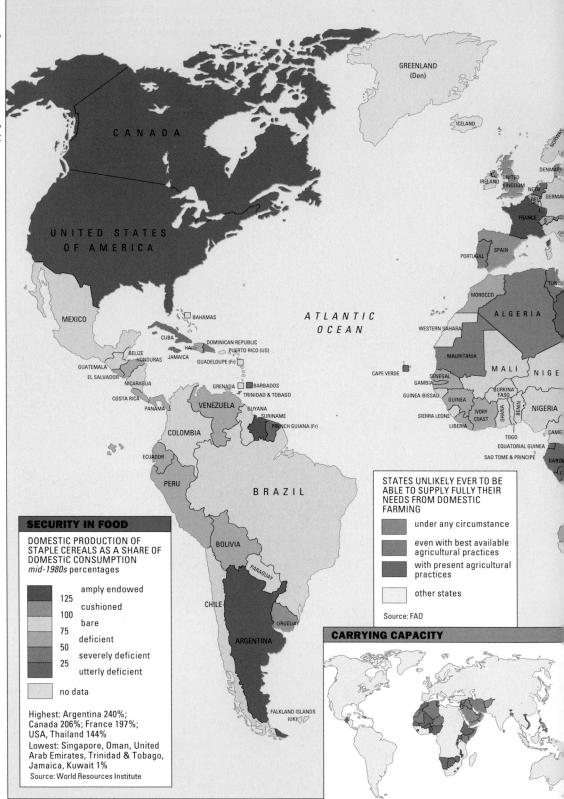

GREENLAND
(Den)

ICELAND

NORWAY

C A N A D A

DENMARK

IRELAND · UNITED
KINGDOM

NETH
BEL · GERMA

UNITED STATES
OF AMERICA

FRANCE · S

PORTUGAL · SPAIN

MEXICO

ATLANTIC
OCEAN

MOROCCO

TUNIS

WESTERN SAHARA

ALGERIA

BAHAMAS

CUBA

DOMINICAN REPUBLIC
HAITI · PUERTO RICO (US)

BELIZE
HONDURAS · JAMAICA · GUADELOUPE (Fr)

GUATEMALA

EL SALVADOR

NICARAGUA

COSTA RICA

PANAMA

GRENADA · BARBADOS

TRINIDAD & TOBAGO

VENEZUELA · GUYANA
SURINAME
FRENCH GUIANA (Fr)

COLOMBIA

ECUADOR

PERU

B R A Z I L

CAPE VERDE

MAURITANIA

MALI · NIGE

SENEGAL

GAMBIA · BURKINA
FASO · BENIN · NIGERIA

GUINEA-BISSAU · GUINEA

SIERRA LEONE · IVORY
COAST · GHANA

LIBERIA · TOGO

EQUATORIAL GUINEA
SAO TOME & PRINCIPE · GABO

CAME

SECURITY IN FOOD

DOMESTIC PRODUCTION OF
STAPLE CEREALS AS A SHARE OF
DOMESTIC CONSUMPTION
mid-1980s percentages

125	amply endowed
	cushioned
100	
	bare
75	
	deficient
50	
	severely deficient
25	
	utterly deficient
	no data

Highest: Argentina 240%;
Canada 206%; France 197%;
USA, Thailand 144%
Lowest: Singapore, Oman, United
Arab Emirates, Trinidad & Tobago,
Jamaica, Kuwait 1%
Source: World Resources Institute

BOLIVIA

PARAGUAY

CHILE

URUGUAY

ARGENTINA

FALKLAND ISLANDS
(UK)

STATES UNLIKELY EVER TO BE
ABLE TO SUPPLY FULLY THEIR
NEEDS FROM DOMESTIC
FARMING

	under any circumstance
	even with best available
agricultural practices
	with present agricultural
practices
	other states

Source: FAO

CARRYING CAPACITY

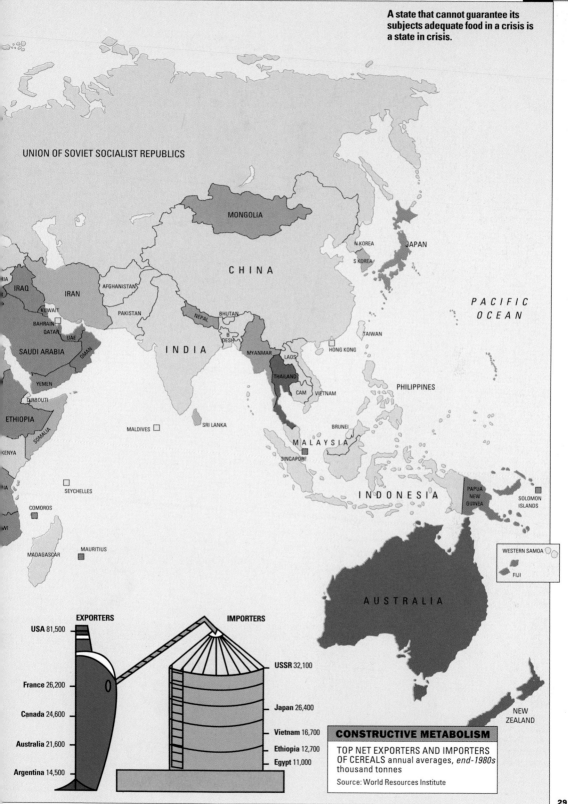

A state that cannot guarantee its subjects adequate food in a crisis is a state in crisis.

UNION OF SOVIET SOCIALIST REPUBLICS

MONGOLIA

CHINA

N KOREA

JAPAN

S KOREA

IRAQ

IRAN

AFGHANISTAN

KUWAIT

PAKISTAN

NEPAL

BHUTAN

BAHRAIN

QATAR

UAE

B DESH

PACIFIC OCEAN

SAUDI ARABIA

OMAN

INDIA

MYANMAR

LAOS

TAIWAN

HONG KONG

YEMEN

THAILAND

DJIBOUTI

CAM

VIETNAM

PHILIPPINES

ETHIOPIA

MALDIVES

SRI LANKA

SOMALIA

BRUNEI

KENYA

MALAYSIA

SINGAPORE

SEYCHELLES

COMOROS

INDONESIA

PAPUA NEW GUINEA

SOLOMON ISLANDS

MADAGASCAR

MAURITIUS

WESTERN SAMOA

FIJI

AUSTRALIA

NEW ZEALAND

EXPORTERS

USA 81,500

France 26,200

Canada 24,600

Australia 21,600

Argentina 14,500

IMPORTERS

USSR 32,100

Japan 26,400

Vietnam 16,700

Ethiopia 12,700

Egypt 11,000

CONSTRUCTIVE METABOLISM

TOP NET EXPORTERS AND IMPORTERS OF CEREALS annual averages, *end-1980s* thousand tonnes

Source: World Resources Institute

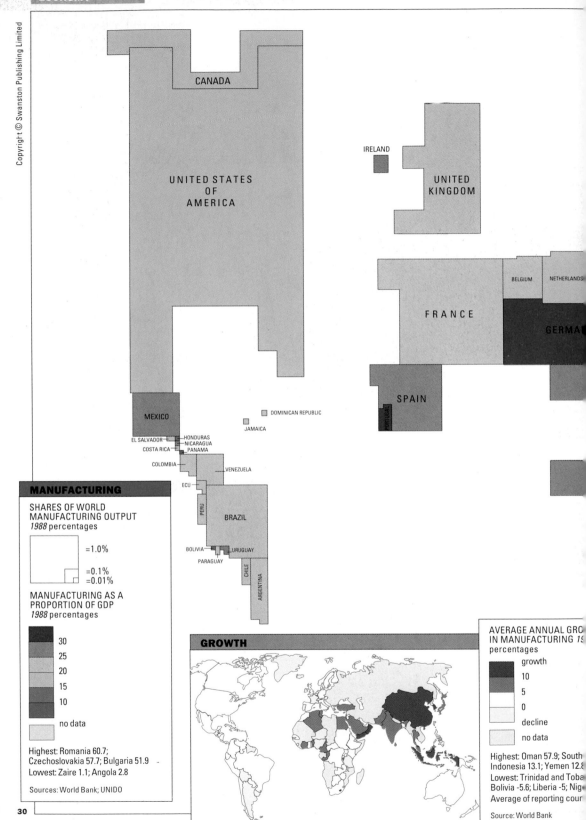

Copyright © Swanston Publishing Limited

CANADA

UNITED STATES
OF
AMERICA

IRELAND

UNITED
KINGDOM

BELGIUM   NETHERLANDS

FRANCE   GERMA

SPAIN

PORTUGAL

MEXICO

DOMINICAN REPUBLIC

JAMAICA

EL SALVADOR — HONDURAS
NICARAGUA
COSTA RICA — PANAMA

COLOMBIA

VENEZUELA

ECU

PERU

BRAZIL

BOLIVIA — URUGUAY
PARAGUAY

CHILE
ARGENTINA

MANUFACTURING

SHARES OF WORLD
MANUFACTURING OUTPUT
1988 percentages

     =1.0%

     =0.1%
     =0.01%

MANUFACTURING AS A
PROPORTION OF GDP
1988 percentages

- 30
- 25
- 20
- 15
- 10
- no data

Highest: Romania 60.7;
Czechoslovakia 57.7; Bulgaria 51.9
Lowest: Zaire 1.1; Angola 2.8

Sources: World Bank; UNIDO

GROWTH

AVERAGE ANNUAL GRO
IN MANUFACTURING *19*
percentages

     growth
- 10
- 5
- 0
- decline
- no data

Highest: Oman 57.9; South
Indonesia 13.1; Yemen 12.8
Lowest: Trinidad and Toba
Bolivia -5.6; Liberia -5; Nig
Average of reporting coun

Source: World Bank

Manufacturing is still the primary source of state power. Four states produce three-quarters of all manufactures.

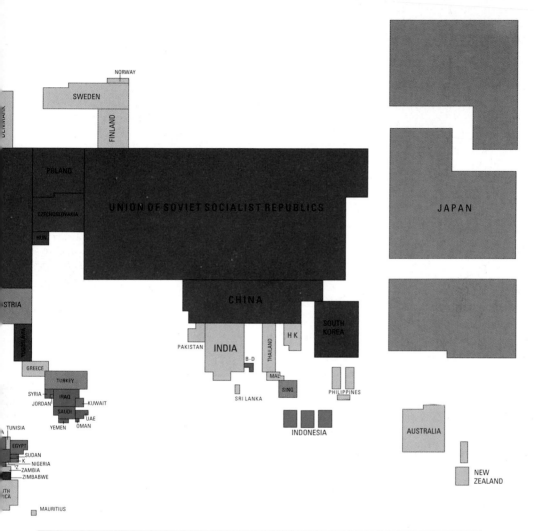

NORWAY

SWEDEN

FINLAND

DENMARK

POLAND

CZECHOSLOVAKIA

HUN.

UNION OF SOVIET SOCIALIST REPUBLICS

JAPAN

STRIA

CHINA

SOUTH KOREA

PAKISTAN INDIA THAILAND H K

B-D

GREECE

TURKEY

SYRIA IRAQ KUWAIT

JORDAN

SAUDI

UAE

TUNISIA YEMEN OMAN

MAL

SING

SRI LANKA

PHILIPPINES

EGYPT

SUDAN

K NIGERIA

TZ ZAMBIA

ZIMBABWE

UTH ICA

MAURITIUS

INDONESIA

AUSTRALIA

NEW ZEALAND

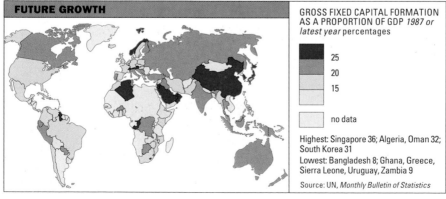

FUTURE GROWTH

GROSS FIXED CAPITAL FORMATION AS A PROPORTION OF GDP *1987 or latest year* percentages

- 25
- 20
- 15

no data

Highest: Singapore 36; Algeria, Oman 32; South Korea 31

Lowest: Bangladesh 8; Ghana, Greece, Sierra Leone, Uruguay, Zambia 9

Source: UN, *Monthly Bulletin of Statistics*

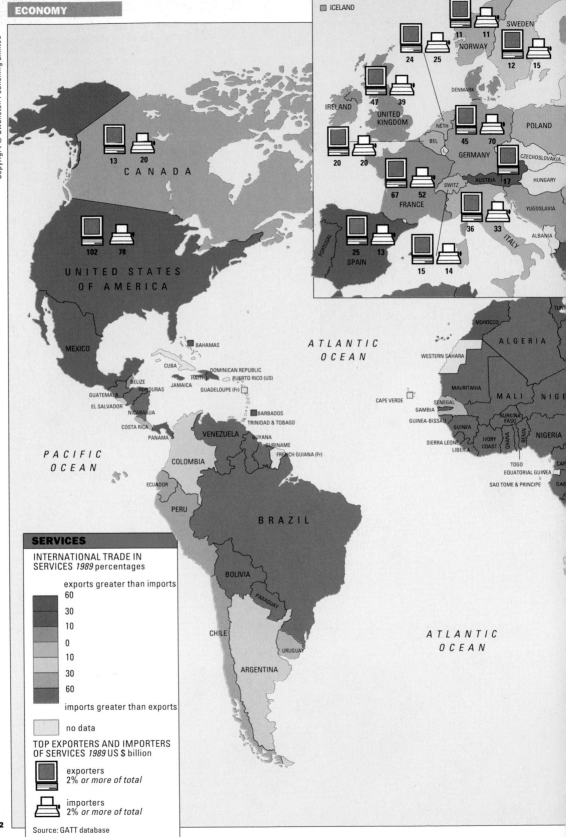

ICELAND

SWEDEN

11 11
NORWAY

24 25

12 15

DENMARK

47 39

IRELAND

UNITED
KINGDOM

POLAND

NETH.

20 20

BEL

45 70

GERMANY

CZECHOSLOVAKIA

SWITZ AUSTRIA 17 HUNGARY

67 52

FRANCE

YUGOSLAVIA

36 33 ITALY ALBANIA

PORTUGAL

25 13
SPAIN

15 14

13 20

C A N A D A

102 78

U N I T E D   S T A T E S
O F   A M E R I C A

MEXICO

BAHAMAS

ATLANTIC
OCEAN

MOROCCO

TUN

ALGERIA

WESTERN SAHARA

CUBA

DOMINICAN REPUBLIC

BELIZE

HAITI PUERTO RICO (US)

JAMAICA

GUADELOUPE (Fr)

MAURITANIA

MALI NIGE

GUATEMALA

HONDURAS

EL SALVADOR

NICARAGUA

CAPE VERDE

SENEGAL

GAMBIA

GUINEA-BISSAU

BARBADOS

TRINIDAD & TOBAGO

BURKINA
FASO

COSTA RICA

PANAMA

VENEZUELA

GUYANA

SURINAME

FRENCH GUIANA (Fr)

GUINEA

SIERRA LEONE

IVORY
COAST

GHANA

BENIN

NIGERIA

LIBERIA

PACIFIC
OCEAN

COLOMBIA

ECUADOR

TOGO

EQUATORIAL GUINEA

SAO TOME & PRINCIPE

CA

GAB

PERU

B R A Z I L

BOLIVIA

PARAGUAY

CHILE

URUGUAY

ATLANTIC
OCEAN

ARGENTINA

SERVICES

INTERNATIONAL TRADE IN
SERVICES *1989* percentages

exports greater than imports

60
30
10
0
10
30
60

imports greater than exports

no data

TOP EXPORTERS AND IMPORTERS
OF SERVICES *1989* US $ billion

exporters
2% *or more of total*

importers
2% *or more of total*

Source: GATT database

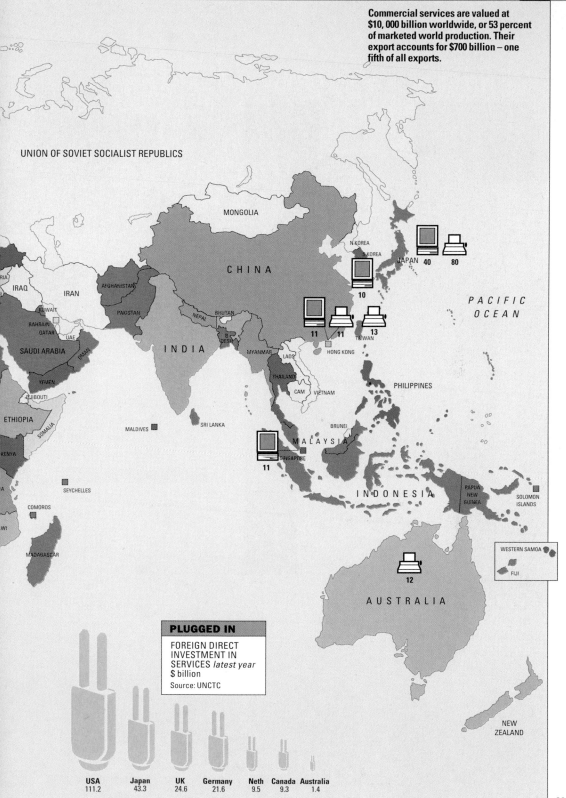

Commercial services are valued at $10, 000 billion worldwide, or 53 percent of marketed world production. Their export accounts for $700 billion – one fifth of all exports.

UNION OF SOVIET SOCIALIST REPUBLICS

MONGOLIA

N.KOREA
S.KOREA

JAPAN 40 80

CHINA

10

PACIFIC OCEAN

RIA
IRAQ
IRAN
AFGHANISTAN
KUWAIT
BAHRAIN
QATAR
UAE
PAKISTAN
NEPAL
BHUTAN
B.DESH
OMAN
SAUDI ARABIA
YEMEN
DJIBOUTI

INDIA

MYANMAR
LAOS
THAILAND
CAM
VIETNAM

11 11   13
TAIWAN

HONG KONG

PHILIPPINES

ETHIOPIA
SOMALIA
KENYA

MALDIVES

SRI LANKA

BRUNEI

MALAYSIA

SINGAPORE
11

SEYCHELLES
COMOROS
WI

INDONESIA

PAPUA NEW GUINEA

SOLOMON ISLANDS

MADAGASCAR

WESTERN SAMOA

FIJI

12

AUSTRALIA

NEW ZEALAND

PLUGGED IN

FOREIGN DIRECT INVESTMENT IN SERVICES *latest year* $ billion
Source: UNCTC

USA	Japan	UK	Germany	Neth	Canada	Australia
111.2	43.3	24.6	21.6	9.5	9.3	1.4

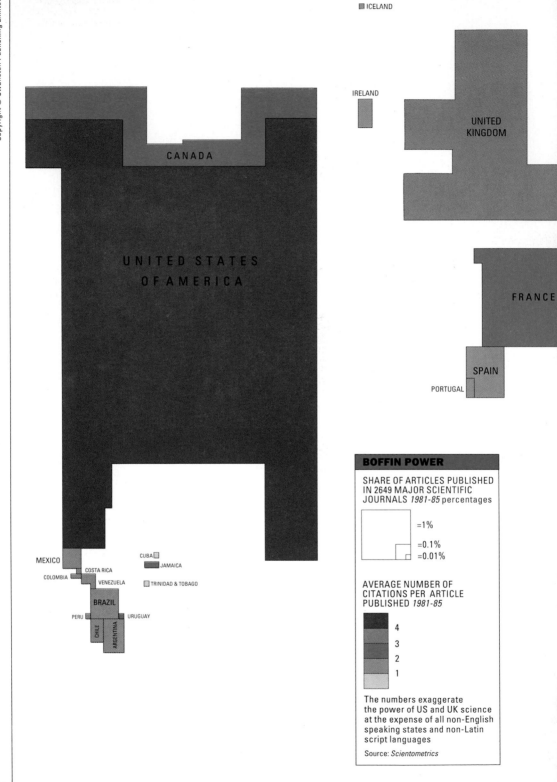

ICELAND

IRELAND

UNITED KINGDOM

CANADA

UNITED STATES OF AMERICA

FRANCE

SPAIN

PORTUGAL

MEXICO

COSTA RICA

COLOMBIA

VENEZUELA

CUBA

JAMAICA

TRINIDAD & TOBAGO

BRAZIL

PERU

URUGUAY

CHILE

ARGENTINA

BOFFIN POWER

SHARE OF ARTICLES PUBLISHED IN 2649 MAJOR SCIENTIFIC JOURNALS *1981-85* percentages

=1%

=0.1%

=0.01%

AVERAGE NUMBER OF CITATIONS PER ARTICLE PUBLISHED *1981-85*

4

3

2

1

The numbers exaggerate the power of US and UK science at the expense of all non-English speaking states and non-Latin script languages

Source: *Scientometrics*

Science is a rich state's preoccupation. Just six states produce between three-fifths and three-quarters of all science.

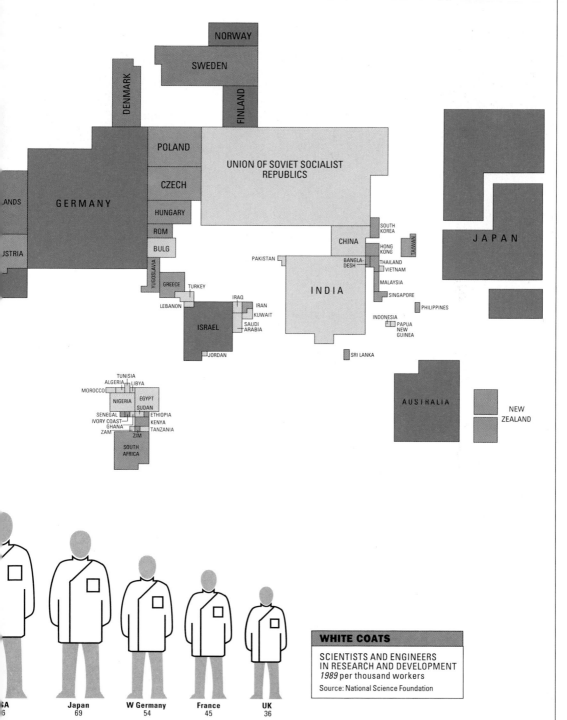

NORWAY
SWEDEN
DENMARK
FINLAND
POLAND
UNION OF SOVIET SOCIALIST REPUBLICS
CZECH
GERMANY
HUNGARY
ROM
BULG
ANDS
USTRIA
YUGOSLAVIA
GREECE
TURKEY
LEBANON
IRAQ
IRAN
KUWAIT
ISRAEL
SAUDI ARABIA
JORDAN
SOUTH KOREA
CHINA
HONG KONG
TAIWAN
PAKISTAN
BANGLA-DESH
THAILAND
VIETNAM
MALAYSIA
SINGAPORE
INDIA
PHILIPPINES
INDONESIA
PAPUA NEW GUINEA
SRI LANKA
JAPAN
AUSTRALIA
NEW ZEALAND

TUNISIA
ALGERIA
LIBYA
MOROCCO
NIGERIA
EGYPT
SUDAN
SENEGAL
IVORY COAST
GHANA
ZAM
ETHIOPIA
KENYA
TANZANIA
ZIM
SOUTH AFRICA

WHITE COATS

SCIENTISTS AND ENGINEERS
IN RESEARCH AND DEVELOPMENT
1989 per thousand workers
Source: National Science Foundation

USA	Japan	W Germany	France	UK
6	69	54	45	36

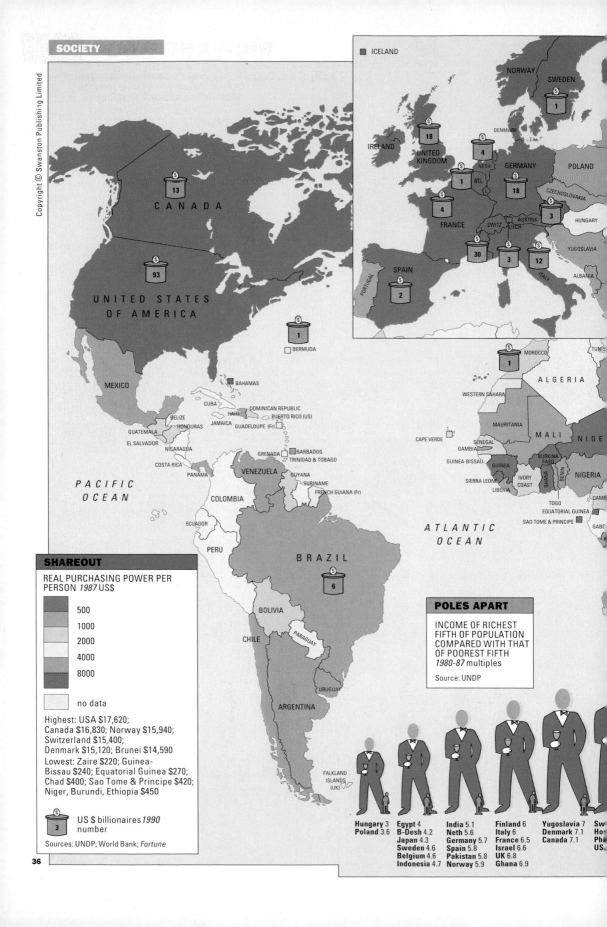

ICELAND

NORWAY

SWEDEN

$ 1

IRELAND

DENMARK

UNITED KINGDOM

$ 18

$ 4

NETH.

GERMANY

POLAND

$ 1

BEL.

$ 18

CZECHOSLOVAKIA

FRANCE

SWITZ.

AUSTRIA

$ 3

HUNGARY

$ 4

LIECH.

$ 30

$ 3

$ 12

ITALY

YUGOSLAVIA

SPAIN

ALBANIA

PORTUGAL

$ 2

CANADA

$ 13

UNITED STATES
OF AMERICA

$ 93

MEXICO

BERMUDA

$ 1

MOROCCO

$ 1

ALGERIA

BAHAMAS

WESTERN SAHARA

CUBA

DOMINICAN REPUBLIC

HAITI

PUERTO RICO (US)

BELIZE

JAMAICA

GUADELOUPE (Fr)

MAURITANIA

MALI

NIGE

GUATEMALA

HONDURAS

CAPE VERDE

SENEGAL

EL SALVADOR

NICARAGUA

GAMBIA

GUINEA-BISSAU

BURKINA
FASO

COSTA RICA

GRENADA

BARBADOS

TRINIDAD & TOBAGO

GUINEA

BENIN

NIGERIA

PANAMA

VENEZUELA

GUYANA

SIERRA LEONE

IVORY
COAST

GHANA

COLOMBIA

SURINAME

LIBERIA

FRENCH GUIANA (Fr)

TOGO

EQUATORIAL GUINEA

GABO

ECUADOR

ATLANTIC
OCEAN

SAO TOME & PRINCIPE

CAM

PACIFIC
OCEAN

PERU

BRAZIL

$ 6

BOLIVIA

CHILE

PARAGUAY

URUGUAY

ARGENTINA

FALKLAND
ISLANDS
(UK)

SHAREOUT

REAL PURCHASING POWER PER
PERSON *1987* US$

	500
	1000
	2000
	4000
	8000
	no data

Highest: USA $17,620;
Canada $16,830; Norway $15,940;
Switzerland $15,400;
Denmark $15,120; Brunei $14,590
Lowest: Zaire $220; Guinea-
Bissau $240; Equatorial Guinea $270;
Chad $400; Sao Tome & Principe $420;
Niger, Burundi, Ethiopia $450

$ 3 US $ billionaires *1990*
number

Sources: UNDP; World Bank; *Fortune*

POLES APART

INCOME OF RICHEST
FIFTH OF POPULATION
COMPARED WITH THAT
OF POOREST FIFTH
1980-87 multiples

Source: UNDP

Hungary 3
Poland 3.6

Egypt 4
B-Desh 4.2
Japan 4.3
Sweden 4.6
Belgium 4.6
Indonesia 4.7

India 5.1
Neth 5.6
Germany 5.7
Spain 5.8
Pakistan 5.8
Norway 5.9

Finland 6
Italy 6
France 6.5
Israel 6.6
UK 6.8
Ghana 6.9

Yugoslavia 7
Denmark 7.1
Canada 7.1

Sw
Ho
Phi
US

It may be that the poor will inherit the earth one day. Meanwhile the rich are in profitable possession. 257 billionaires receive $47 billion a year in income – 2.5 percent of world income, or as much as is earned by all the people in China and Indonesia combined (one quarter of the world's population).

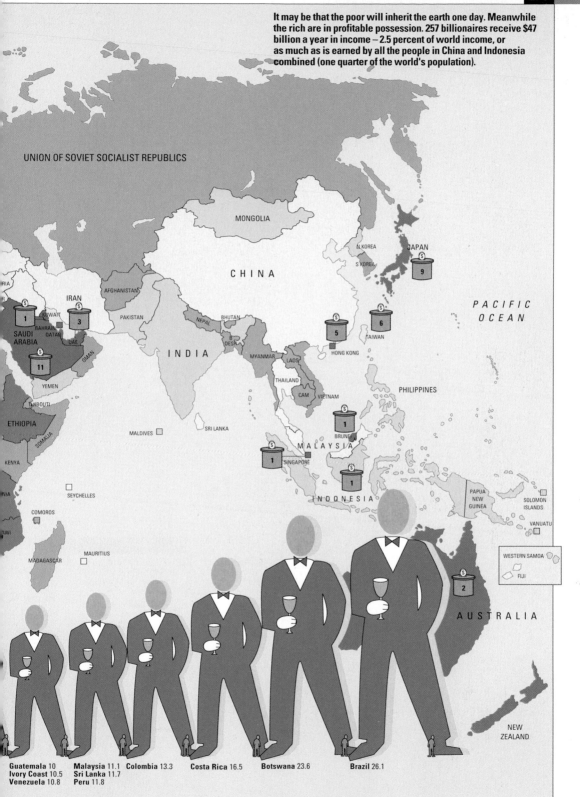

Guatemala 10
Ivory Coast 10.5
Venezuela 10.8

Malaysia 11.1
Sri Lanka 11.7
Peru 11.8

Colombia 13.3

Costa Rica 16.5

Botswana 23.6

Brazil 26.1

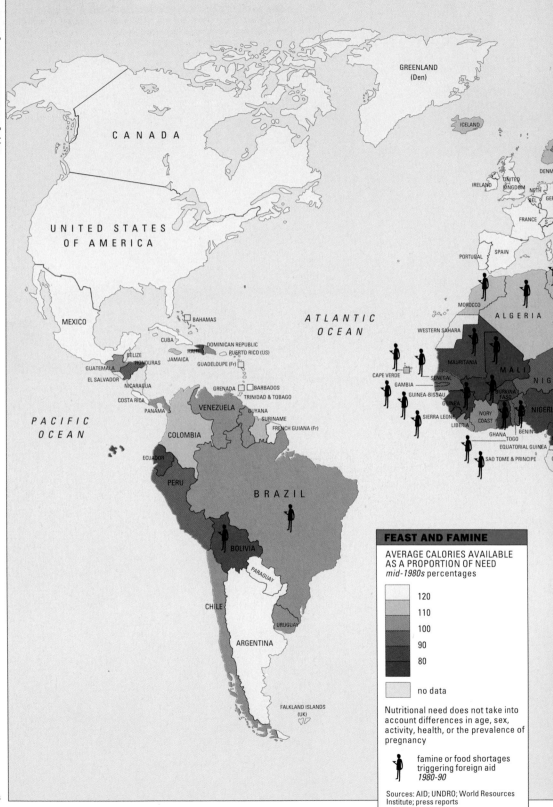

GREENLAND
(Den)

ICELAND

NORWA

DENMAR

IRELAND UNITED
KINGDOM NETH GERM
BEL
FRANCE S
ITA

PORTUGAL SPAIN

C A N A D A

U N I T E D   S T A T E S
O F   A M E R I C A

MOROCCO ALGERIA

WESTERN SAHARA

A T L A N T I C
O C E A N

MEXICO

BAHAMAS

CUBA
BELIZE DOMINICAN REPUBLIC
HONDURAS JAMAICA HAITI PUERTO RICO (US)
GUATEMALA GUADELOUPE (Fr)
EL SALVADOR
NICARAGUA GRENADA BARBADOS
COSTA RICA TRINIDAD & TOBAGO
PANAMA

CAPE VERDE
GAMBIA
SENEGAL
GUINEA-BISSAU
GUINEA

MAURITANIA
MALI NIGE

BURKINA
FASO
SIERRA LEONE IVORY NIGERIA
COAST
LIBERIA
GHANA BENIN
TOGO
EQUATORIAL GUINEA GAB
SAO TOME & PRINCIPE

VENEZUELA
GUYANA
SURINAME
FRENCH GUIANA (Fr)
COLOMBIA

P A C I F I C
O C E A N

ECUADOR

PERU

B R A Z I L

BOLIVIA

PARAGUAY

CHILE

URUGUAY

ARGENTINA

FALKLAND ISLANDS
(UK)

FEAST AND FAMINE

AVERAGE CALORIES AVAILABLE
AS A PROPORTION OF NEED
mid-1980s percentages

- 120
- 110
- 100
- 90
- 80

no data

Nutritional need does not take into
account differences in age, sex,
activity, health, or the prevalence of
pregnancy

famine or food shortages
triggering foreign aid
1980-90

Sources: AID; UNDRO; World Resources
Institute; press reports

More than 500 million people suffer from chronic malnutrition. Each year some 40 million die from hunger and hunger-related diseases—the equivalent of over 300 jumbo-jet crashes a day with no survivors. Half the passengers are children.

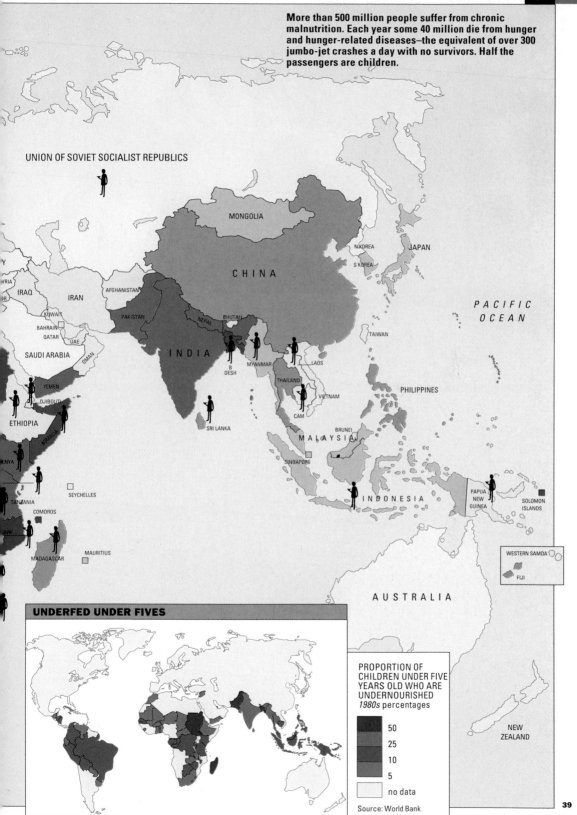

UNION OF SOVIET SOCIALIST REPUBLICS

MONGOLIA

N.KOREA JAPAN
S.KOREA

CHINA

PACIFIC
OCEAN

Y

SYRIA

IRAQ   IRAN   AFGHANISTAN

KUWAIT
BAHRAIN   PAKISTAN   NEPAL   BHUTAN
QATAR   UAE
OMAN   INDIA   TAIWAN
SAUDI ARABIA

B
DESH   MYANMAR   LAOS

YEMEN   THAILAND

DJIBOUTI   VIETNAM

ETHIOPIA   CAM

PHILIPPINES

SRI LANKA
KENYA   BRUNEI
                          MALAYSIA
TANZANIA   SEYCHELLES   SINGAPORE

COMOROS   INDONESIA   PAPUA
                                              NEW   SOLOMON
                                              GUINEA   ISLANDS

MADAGASCAR   MAURITIUS

WESTERN SAMOA

FIJI

AUSTRALIA

UNDERFED UNDER FIVES

**PROPORTION OF
CHILDREN UNDER FIVE
YEARS OLD WHO ARE
UNDERNOURISHED**
1980s percentages

50
25
10
5
no data

NEW
ZEALAND

Source: World Bank

ICELAND

NORWAY

SWEDEN

DENMARK

IRELAND

UNITED
KINGDOM

NETH

POLAND

BEL

GERMANY

CZECHOSLOVAKIA

FRANCE

AUSTRIA

HUNGARY

L

SWITZ

YUGOSLAVIA

ITALY

ALBANIA

PORTUGAL

SPAIN

C A N A D A

UNITED STATES
OF AMERICA

MEXICO

BAHAMAS

CUBA

DOMINICAN REPUBLIC

BELIZE

HAITI

PUERTO RICO (US)

GUATEMALA

HONDURAS

JAMAICA

EL SALVADOR

NICARAGUA

COSTA RICA

PANAMA

BARBADOS

TRINIDAD & TOBAGO

VENEZUELA

GUYANA

SURINAME

FRENCH GUIANA (Fr)

COLOMBIA

ECUADOR

PERU

B R A Z I L

BOLIVIA

PARAGUAY

CHILE

URUGUAY

ARGENTINA

FALKLAND ISLANDS
(UK)

ATLANTIC
OCEAN

PACIFIC
OCEAN

MOROCCO

ALGERIA

WESTERN SAHARA

MAURITANIA

MALI

NIGE

CAPE VERDE

SENEGAL

GAMBIA

BURKINA
FASO

GUINEA-BISSAU

GUINEA

NIGERIA

SIERRA LEONE

IVORY
COAST

GHANA

BENIN

LIBERIA

CAME

TOGO

EQUATORIAL GUINEA

GAB

TUN

LIFE EXPECTANCY

AVERAGE LIFE EXPECTANCY AT BIRTH
1985-90 years

75

65

55

45

no data

Highest: Japan 77.2; Iceland 77.1; Sweden
76.8; Switzerland 76.5; Norway 76.4;
Canada 76.3; Australia 75.7; France, Italy
75.2; Israel 75.1; Spain, USA 75

Lowest: Sierra Leone 36; Gambia 37.9;
Afghanistan 39

states claiming universal
access to medical care

Least access to medical care amongst
reporting states, percentage of
population: Mali 15; Benin 18; Rwanda 27

Sources: UNDP; World Bank;
World Resources Institute

40

Lives are longer where water is safe to drink and health care available to all.

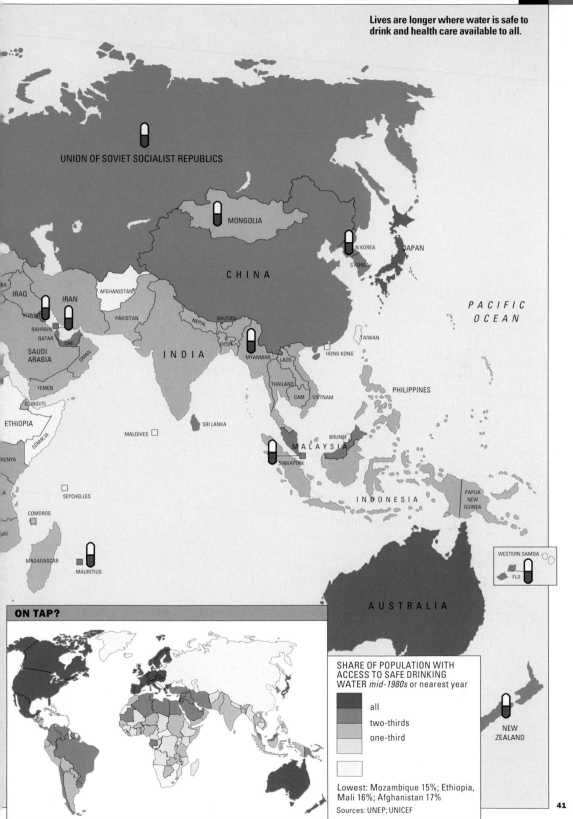

UNION OF SOVIET SOCIALIST REPUBLICS

MONGOLIA

N KOREA

JAPAN

S KOREA

CHINA

IRAQ

IRAN

AFGHANISTAN

KUWAIT

PAKISTAN

BAHRAIN

NEPAL

BHUTAN

QATAR

UAE

B
DESH

SAUDI
ARABIA

OMAN

INDIA

MYANMAR

LAOS

HONG KONG

PACIFIC
OCEAN

TAIWAN

YEMEN

THAILAND

DJIBOUTI

CAM

VIETNAM

PHILIPPINES

ETHIOPIA

SRI LANKA

SOMALIA

MALDIVES

KENYA

BRUNEI

MALAYSIA

SINGAPORE

SEYCHELLES

INDONESIA

PAPUA
NEW
GUINEA

COMOROS

WESTERN SAMOA

MADAGASCAR

FIJI

MAURITIUS

AUSTRALIA

ON TAP?

SHARE OF POPULATION WITH
ACCESS TO SAFE DRINKING
WATER *mid-1980s* or nearest year

- all
- two-thirds
- one-third

Lowest: Mozambique 15%; Ethiopia,
Mali 16%; Afghanistan 17%

Sources: UNEP; UNICEF

NEW
ZEALAND

ICELAND

NORWAY   SWEDEN

DENMARK

IRELAND

3798   **1456**

UNITED
KINGDOM

NETH.   **5402**   POLAND

BEL.   GERMANY
WEST & EAST   CZECHOSLOVAKIA

FRANCE   AUSTRIA   HUNGARY

9718   SWITZ.

1497   ITALY   YUGOSLAVIA

7576   ALBANIA

PORTUGAL   SPAIN

7047

C A N A D A

4427

U N I T E D   S T A T E S
O F   A M E R I C A

152,231

BERMUDA

A T L A N T I C
O C E A N

TUN

MOROCCO

5113

MEXICO

BAHAMAS

ALGERIA

CUBA

2456   **1423**

WESTERN SAHARA

DOMINICAN REPUBLIC

HAITI   PUERTO RICO (US)

BELIZE   JAMAICA

GUATEMALA   HONDURAS

GUADELOUPE (Fr)

EL SALVADOR   NICARAGUA

MAURITANIA   M A L I   NIG

CAPE VERDE

GRENADA   BARBADOS

SENEGAL

COSTA RICA   TRINIDAD & TOBAGO

GAMBIA   GUINEA   BURKINA
FASO

PANAMA   VENEZUELA   GUYANA

GUINEA-BISSAU   BENIN

COLOMBIA   SURINAME

GUINEA   IVORY
COAST   GHANA   NIGERIA

FRENCH GUIANA (Fr)

SIERRA LEONE   TOGO

PACIFIC
OCEAN

LIBERIA

ECUADOR

1732   **3647**   EQUATORIAL GUINEA

TOGO

PERU   SAO TOME & PRINCIPE   GA

1940

B R A Z I L

12,402

A T L A N T I C
O C E A N

BOLIVIA

PARAGUAY

AIDS REPORT

CASES OF AIDS REPORTED TO THE WORLD
HEALTH ORGANIZATION
1989 rate per 100,000 population

CHILE

20

10

1.0

0.1

URUGUAY

ARGENTINA

no cases reported

12,402   number of cases reported to
30 November 1990 *1000 and above*

World Health Organization estimates total
number of cases to September 1990 at
1.2 million cases as against 280,000 reported

FALKLAND ISLANDS
(UK)

Source: *WHO Update*

REAPERS OF THE RICH

Causes of death in rich countries
late 1980s percentages

Source: WHO

heart
attacks
24   cancers
23

strokes
15   respiratory
diseases
9   other
21

violent
causes
8

Aids is a recent social killer. It is not the
only one. In 1990, 17.5 million people died
before their time – a third of all deaths.

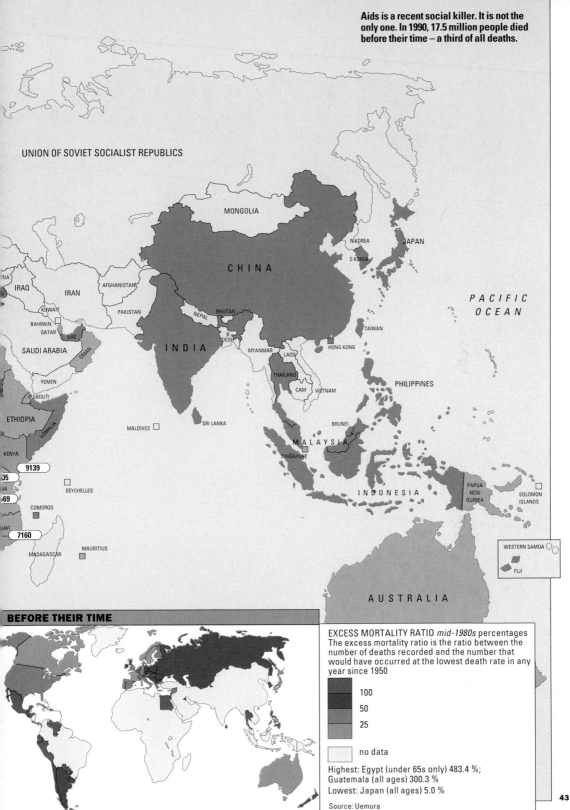

UNION OF SOVIET SOCIALIST REPUBLICS

MONGOLIA

N.KOREA

JAPAN

S.KOREA

CHINA

PACIFIC
OCEAN

RIA

IRAQ

IRAN

AFGHANISTAN

KUWAIT

PAKISTAN

NEPAL

BHUTAN

BAHRAIN

QATAR

UAE

B
DESH

TAIWAN

SAUDI ARABIA

OMAN

INDIA

MYANMAR

LAOS

HONG KONG

YEMEN

THAILAND

DJIBOUTI

CAM

VIETNAM

PHILIPPINES

ETHIOPIA

SOMALIA

KENYA

MALDIVES

SRI LANKA

BRUNEI

9139

MALAYSIA

SINGAPORE

05

SEYCHELLES

IA

69

COMOROS

INDONESIA

PAPUA
NEW
GUINEA

SOLOMON
ISLANDS

7160

MAURITIUS

MADAGASCAR

WESTERN SAMOA

FIJI

AUSTRALIA

BEFORE THEIR TIME

EXCESS MORTALITY RATIO *mid-1980s* percentages
The excess mortality ratio is the ratio between the
number of deaths recorded and the number that
would have occurred at the lowest death rate in any
year since 1950

- 100
- 50
- 25

no data

Highest: Egypt (under 65s only) 483.4 %;
Guatemala (all ages) 300.3 %
Lowest: Japan (all ages) 5.0 %

Source: Uemura

43

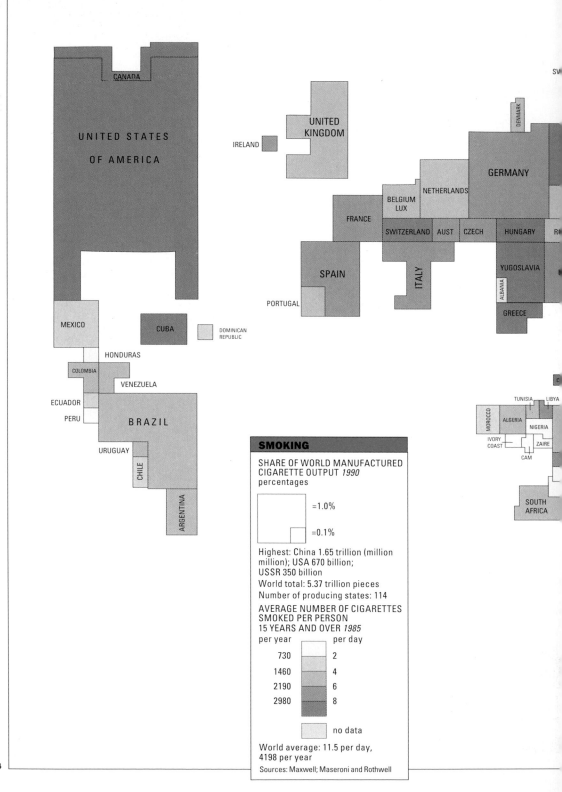

CANADA

UNITED STATES

OF AMERICA

IRELAND

UNITED KINGDOM

DENMARK

GERMANY

NETHERLANDS

BELGIUM LUX

FRANCE

SWITZERLAND | AUST | CZECH | HUNGARY

SPAIN

ITALY

YUGOSLAVIA

ALBANIA

PORTUGAL

GREECE

MEXICO

CUBA

DOMINICAN REPUBLIC

HONDURAS

COLOMBIA

VENEZUELA

ECUADOR

PERU

BRAZIL

URUGUAY

CHILE

ARGENTINA

TUNISIA | LIBYA

MOROCCO | ALGERIA

NIGERIA

IVORY COAST

ZAIRE

CAM

SOUTH AFRICA

SMOKING

SHARE OF WORLD MANUFACTURED
CIGARETTE OUTPUT *1990*
percentages

=1.0%

=0.1%

Highest: China 1.65 trillion (million
million); USA 670 billion;
USSR 350 billion

World total: 5.37 trillion pieces

Number of producing states: 114

AVERAGE NUMBER OF CIGARETTES
SMOKED PER PERSON
15 YEARS AND OVER *1985*

per year		per day
730		2
1460		4
2190		6
2980		8

no data

World average: 11.5 per day,
4198 per year

Sources: Maxwell; Maseroni and Rothwell

44

Nicotine is the most widely used of all drugs. More is spent on it than on any other. And it is more dangerous — more than alcohol, more than heroin, cocaine, marijuana, tranquillizers, amphetamines, LSD, designer drugs, glue. Each day, over 1.3 billion adults (36 percent of all adults) smoke 14.7 billion manufactured cigarettes, uncounted roll-your-owns, cigars and pipes. Some chew tobacco and inhale snuff.

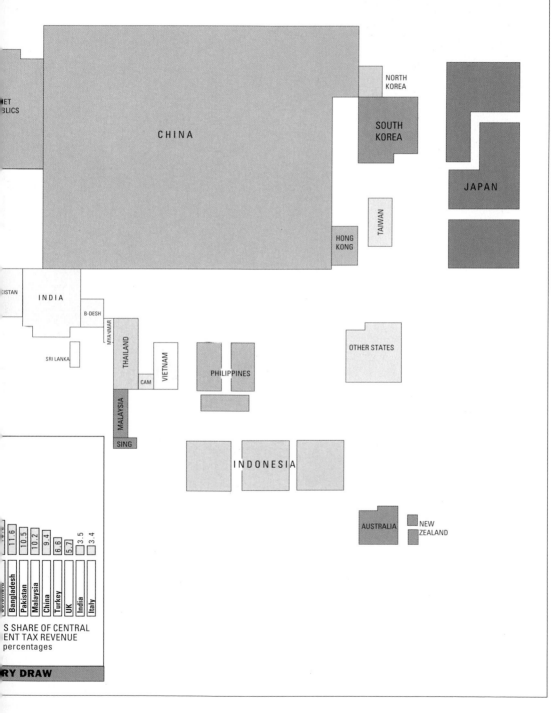

SOVIET
PUBLICS

CHINA

NORTH
KOREA

SOUTH
KOREA

JAPAN

TAIWAN

HONG
KONG

PAKISTAN

INDIA

B-DESH

SRI LANKA

MYANMAR

THAILAND

VIETNAM

CAM

PHILIPPINES

OTHER STATES

MALAYSIA

SING

INDONESIA

AUSTRALIA

NEW
ZEALAND

	11.6	10.5	10.2	9.4	6.6	5.7	3.5	3.4
Bangladesh	Pakistan	Malaysia	China	Turkey	UK	India	Italy	

S SHARE OF CENTRAL
ENT TAX REVENUE
percentages

RY DRAW

Copyright © Swanston Publishing Limited

NORWAY
SWEDEN
DENMARK
IRELAND
UNITED KINGDOM
London
NETH
BEL
POLAND
Warsaw
GERMANY
CZECHOSLOVAKIA
Berlin
Paris
FRANCE
AUSTRIA
HUNGARY
SWITZ
Milan
ITALY
YUGOSLAVIA
PORTUGAL
SPAIN
Madrid
Barcelona
Rome
Naples
ALBANIA

C A N A D A

San Francisco
Los Angeles
UNITED STATES
OF AMERICA
Detroit
Chicago
Philadelphia
Toronto
New York

MEXICO
Mexico City

BAHAMAS
CUBA
BELIZE
GUATEMALA
HONDURAS
EL SALVADOR
NICARAGUA
COSTA RICA
PANAMA
JAMAICA
HAITI
DOMINICAN REPUBLIC
PUERTO RICO (US)
GUADELOUPE (Fr)
BARBADOS
TRINIDAD & TOBAGO

A T L A N T I C
O C E A N

MOROCCO
ALGERIA
WESTERN SAHARA
TUN
CAPE VERDE
MAURITANIA
MALI
NIG
SENEGAL
GAMBIA
GUINEA-BISSAU
GUINEA
BURKINA FASO
BENIN
NIGER
SIERRA LEONE
IVORY COAST
GHANA
LIBERIA
TOGO
Lagos
CA
EQUATORIAL GUINEA
SAO TOME & PRINCIPE
GA

P A C I F I C
O C E A N

Caracas
VENEZUELA
GUYANA
SURINAME
FRENCH GUIANA (Fr)
Bogota
COLOMBIA
ECUADOR
PERU
Lima
BRAZIL
Belo Horizonte
Rio de Janeiro
São Paulo
BOLIVIA
PARAGUAY
CHILE
ARGENTINA
URUGUAY
Santiago
Buenos Aires

CITIES

URBAN POPULATION AS A
PROPORTION OF TOTAL
POPULATION *1990* percentages

- 80
- 60
- 40
- 20

no data

urban areas with 3 million
or more inhabitants

Highest: Belgium 96.9; Kuwait 95.6;
UK 92.5
Lowest: Bhutan 5.3; Burundi 7.3;
Rwanda 7.7

Sources: UNDP; UNESCO; World Bank

CRORE CITIES

THE BIGGEST DOZEN
end-1980s millions
Source: UNEP

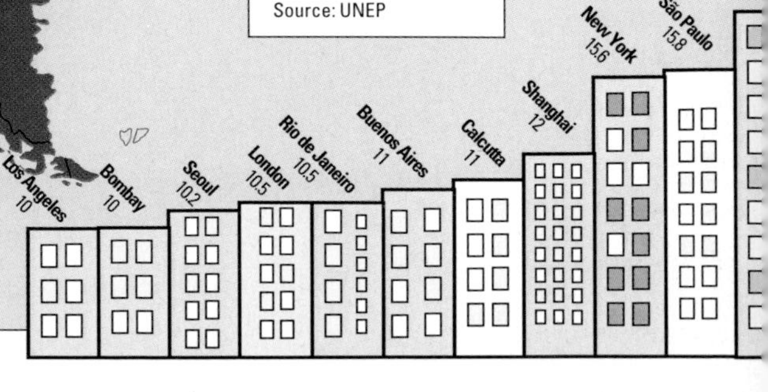

Mexico City 17
São Paulo 15.8
New York 15.6
Shanghai 12
Calcutta 11
Buenos Aires 11
Rio de Janeiro 10.5
London 10.5
Seoul 10.2
Bombay 10
Los Angeles 10

46

More than two out of five people live in cities. Their number is growing almost twice as fast as their country cousins'.

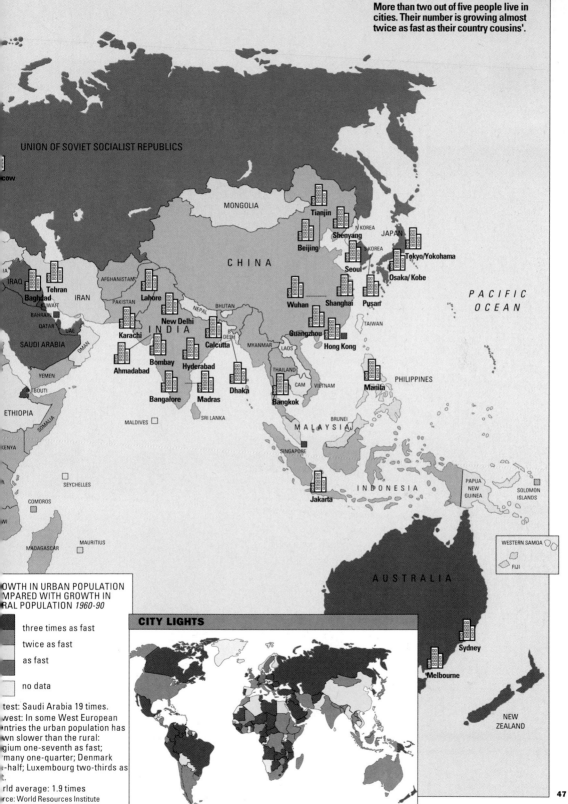

UNION OF SOVIET SOCIALIST REPUBLICS

cow

MONGOLIA

Tianjin

Shenyang

N KOREA

JAPAN

Beijing

S.KOREA

Tokyo/Yokohama

CHINA

Seoul

Osaka/ Kobe

Pusan

PACIFIC OCEAN

IA

IRAQ

Tehran

Baghdad

KUWAIT

IRAN

AFGHANISTAN

BAHRAIN

QATAR

PAKISTAN

Lahore

NEPAL

BHUTAN

Wuhan

Shanghai

UAE

New Delhi

INDIA

B'DESH

Guangzhou

TAIWAN

SAUDI ARABIA

OMAN

Karachi

Calcutta

MYANMAR

Hong Kong

YEMEN

Bombay

Hyderabad

LAOS

THAILAND

Ahmadabad

CAM

VIETNAM

DJIBOUTI

Bangalore

Madras

Dhaka

Manila

PHILIPPINES

ETHIOPIA

Bangkok

SRI LANKA

MALDIVES

BRUNEI

MALAYSIA

KENYA

SEYCHELLES

SINGAPORE

INDONESIA

PAPUA NEW GUINEA

SOLOMON ISLANDS

COMOROS

Jakarta

MADAGASCAR

MAURITIUS

WESTERN SAMOA

FIJI

AUSTRALIA

GROWTH IN URBAN POPULATION COMPARED WITH GROWTH IN RURAL POPULATION *1960-90*

- three times as fast
- twice as fast
- as fast
- no data

Sydney

Melbourne

NEW ZEALAND

test: Saudi Arabia 19 times.

west: In some West European ntries the urban population has wn slower than the rural: gium one-seventh as fast; many one-quarter; Denmark -half; Luxembourg two-thirds as

rld average: 1.9 times

rce: World Resources Institute

CITY LIGHTS

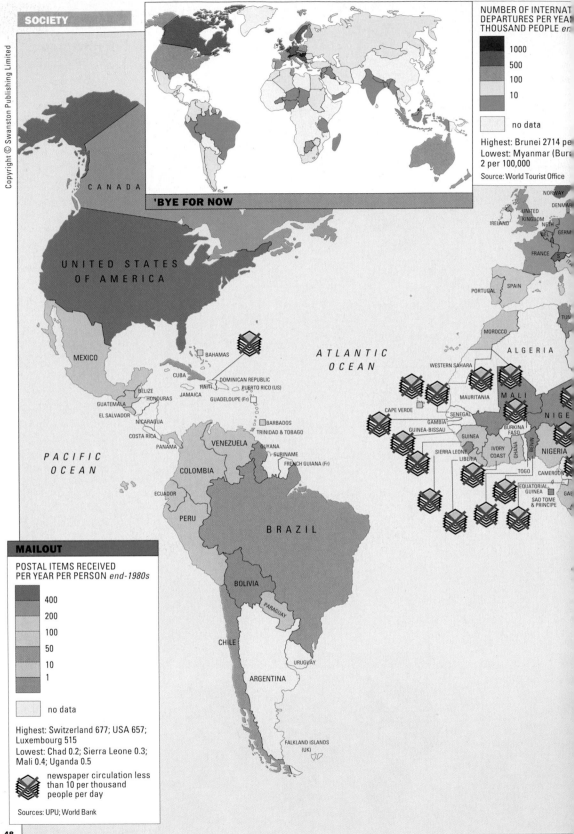

NUMBER OF INTERNAT
DEPARTURES PER YEAR
THOUSAND PEOPLE *er*

1000
500
100
10

no data

Highest: Brunei 2714 pe
Lowest: Myanmar (Burr
2 per 100,000

Source: World Tourist Office

'BYE FOR NOW

NORWAY
DENMAR
UNITED
KINGDOM
IRELAND
NETH
BEL GERM
FRANCE
ITA
PORTUGAL SPAIN
TUN
MOROCCO
ALGERIA
WESTERN SAHARA
MAURITANIA MALI
NIGE
CAPE VERDE
GAMBIA
GUINEA-BISSAU BURKINA
FASO
GUINEA BENIN NIGERIA
SIERRA LEONE IVORY
LIBERIA COAST GHANA TOGO
CAMEROON
EQUATORIAL
GUINEA GAB
SAO TOME
& PRINCIPE

CANADA

UNITED STATES
OF AMERICA

MEXICO

BAHAMAS

CUBA
DOMINICAN REPUBLIC
HAITI PUERTO RICO (US)
BELIZE JAMAICA
HONDURAS GUADELOUPE (Fr)
GUATEMALA
EL SALVADOR
NICARAGUA BARBADOS
COSTA RICA TRINIDAD & TOBAGO
PANAMA
VENEZUELA
GUYANA
COLOMBIA SURINAME
FRENCH GUIANA (Fr)

ATLANTIC
OCEAN

ECUADOR

PACIFIC
OCEAN

PERU

BRAZIL

BOLIVIA

PARAGUAY

CHILE

URUGUAY

ARGENTINA

FALKLAND ISLANDS
(UK)

MAILOUT

POSTAL ITEMS RECEIVED
PER YEAR PER PERSON *end-1980s*

400
200
100
50
10
1

no data

Highest: Switzerland 677; USA 657;
Luxembourg 515
Lowest: Chad 0.2; Sierra Leone 0.3;
Mali 0.4; Uganda 0.5

newspaper circulation less
than 10 per thousand
people per day

Sources: UPU; World Bank

Some people see the world as their
village; some the village as their world;
most are in between. What they see
depends on their income and on state
policy.

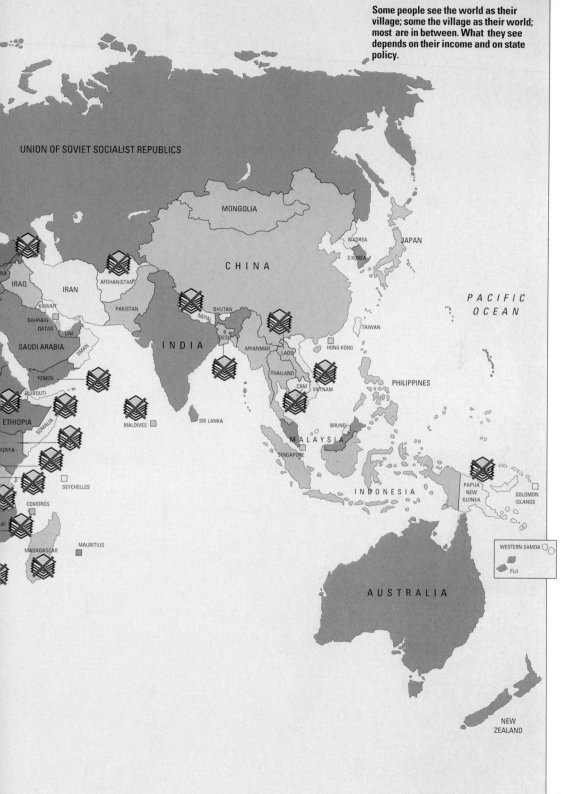

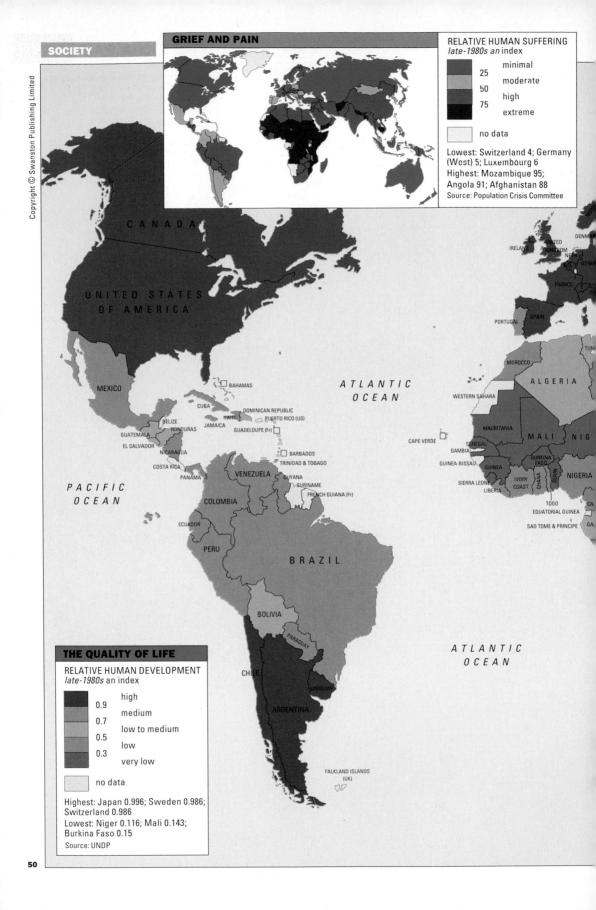

GRIEF AND PAIN

RELATIVE HUMAN SUFFERING
late-1980s an index

25	minimal
50	moderate
	high
75	extreme

no data

Lowest: Switzerland 4; Germany
(West) 5; Luxembourg 6
Highest: Mozambique 95;
Angola 91; Afghanistan 88
Source: Population Crisis Committee

CANADA

UNITED STATES
OF AMERICA

MEXICO

BAHAMAS

CUBA
HAITI
DOMINICAN REPUBLIC
PUERTO RICO (US)

BELIZE
HONDURAS
JAMAICA
GUATEMALA
GUADELOUPE (Fr)
EL SALVADOR
NICARAGUA
BARBADOS
COSTA RICA
TRINIDAD & TOBAGO
PANAMA
VENEZUELA
GUYANA
SURINAME
COLOMBIA
FRENCH GUIANA (Fr)

ECUADOR

PERU

BRAZIL

BOLIVIA

PARAGUAY

CHILE

URUGUAY

ARGENTINA

*ATLANTIC
OCEAN*

*PACIFIC
OCEAN*

*ATLANTIC
OCEAN*

FALKLAND ISLANDS
(UK)

IRELAND
UNITED
KINGDOM
DENM
NETH
BEL
GERM
FRANCE
S

PORTUGAL
SPAIN

TUN
MOROCCO

ALGERIA

WESTERN SAHARA

CAPE VERDE

MAURITANIA
MALI
NIG

SENEGAL
GAMBIA
BURKINA
FASO
BENIN
GUINEA-BISSAU
GUINEA
NIGERIA
SIERRA LEONE
IVORY
COAST
GHANA
LIBERIA
TOGO
CA
EQUATORIAL GUINEA
SAO TOME & PRINCIPE
GA

THE QUALITY OF LIFE

RELATIVE HUMAN DEVELOPMENT
late-1980s an index

0.9	high
0.7	medium
0.5	low to medium
0.3	low
	very low

no data

Highest: Japan 0.996; Sweden 0.986;
Switzerland 0.986
Lowest: Niger 0.116; Mali 0.143;
Burkina Faso 0.15
Source: UNDP

Strung out between Eden and Gehenna,
most people live in fear yet fear to die.

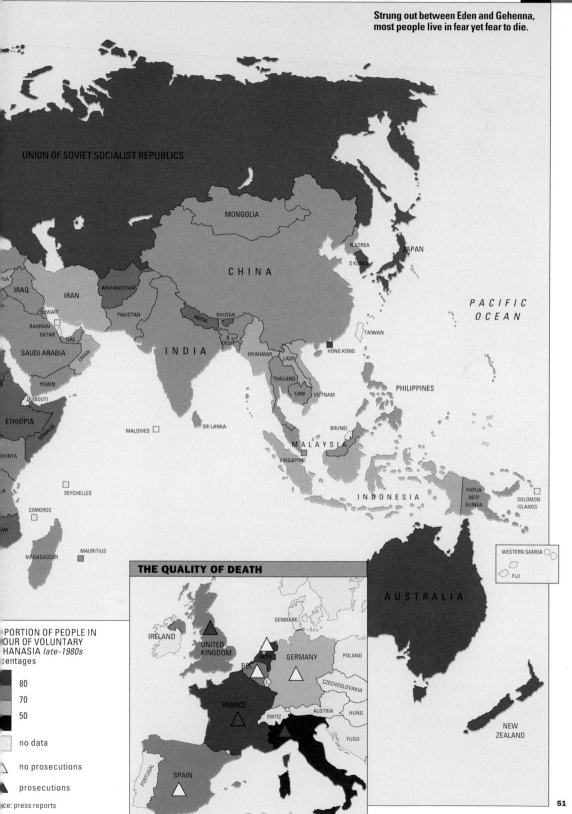

UNION OF SOVIET SOCIALIST REPUBLICS

MONGOLIA

N.KOREA

JAPAN

S KOREA

CHINA

RIA

IRAQ

IRAN

AFGHANISTAN

KUWAIT

PAKISTAN

BAHRAIN

QATAR

UAE

NEPAL   BHUTAN

TAIWAN

SAUDI ARABIA

OMAN

B DESH

INDIA

MYANMAR

HONG KONG

LAOS

YEMEN

THAILAND

DJIBOUTI

CAM   VIETNAM

PHILIPPINES

ETHIOPIA

SOMALIA

MALDIVES

SRI LANKA

BRUNEI

KENYA

MALAYSIA

SINGAPORE

SEYCHELLES

INDONESIA

PAPUA
NEW
GUINEA

SOLOMON
ISLANDS

COMOROS

PACIFIC
OCEAN

MAURITIUS

MADAGASCAR

WESTERN SAMOA

FIJI

AUSTRALIA

THE QUALITY OF DEATH

DENMARK

IRELAND

UNITED
KINGDOM

GERMANY

POLAND

NETH

BEL

CZECHOSLOVAKIA

FRANCE

AUSTRIA   HUNG

SWITZ

YUGO

PORTUGAL

SPAIN

NEW
ZEALAND

PORTION OF PEOPLE IN
OUR OF VOLUNTARY
HANASIA *late-1980s*
centages

80

70

50

no data

no prosecutions

prosecutions

ce: press reports

51

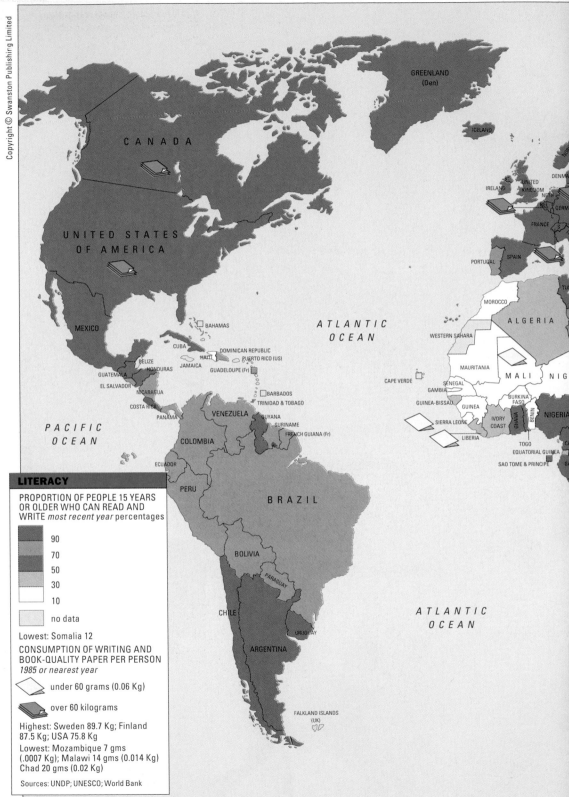

GREENLAND
(Den)

ICELAND

IRELAND
UNITED
KINGDOM
DENMA
NETH
BEL
GERM
FRANCE

PORTUGAL
SPAIN

MOROCCO
ALGERIA
TU

C A N A D A

U N I T E D   S T A T E S
O F   A M E R I C A

MEXICO

BAHAMAS

CUBA
DOMINICAN REPUBLIC
HAITI
PUERTO RICO (US)
JAMAICA
GUADELOUPE (Fr)
BELIZE
HONDURAS
GUATEMALA
EL SALVADOR
NICARAGUA
COSTA RICA
PANAMA

BARBADOS
TRINIDAD & TOBAGO

VENEZUELA
GUYANA
SURINAME
FRENCH GUIANA (Fr)
COLOMBIA
ECUADOR

PERU

BRAZIL

BOLIVIA

PARAGUAY

CHILE

URUGUAY

ARGENTINA

A T L A N T I C
O C E A N

P A C I F I C
O C E A N

WESTERN SAHARA

MAURITANIA

MALI
NIG

CAPE VERDE

SENEGAL
GAMBIA
GUINEA-BISSAU
GUINEA
SIERRA LEONE

BURKINA
FASO
IVORY
COAST
GHANA
BENIN
LIBERIA

NIGERIA

TOGO
EQUATORIAL GUINEA
SAO TOME & PRINCIPE
GA

A T L A N T I C
O C E A N

FALKLAND ISLANDS
(UK)

LITERACY

PROPORTION OF PEOPLE 15 YEARS
OR OLDER WHO CAN READ AND
WRITE *most recent year* percentages

90
70
50
30
10

no data

Lowest: Somalia 12

CONSUMPTION OF WRITING AND
BOOK-QUALITY PAPER PER PERSON
1985 or nearest year

under 60 grams (0.06 Kg)

over 60 kilograms

Highest: Sweden 89.7 Kg; Finland
87.5 Kg; USA 75.8 Kg
Lowest: Mozambique 7 gms
(.0007 Kg); Malawi 14 gms (0.014 Kg)
Chad 20 gms (0.02 Kg)

Sources: UNDP; UNESCO; World Bank

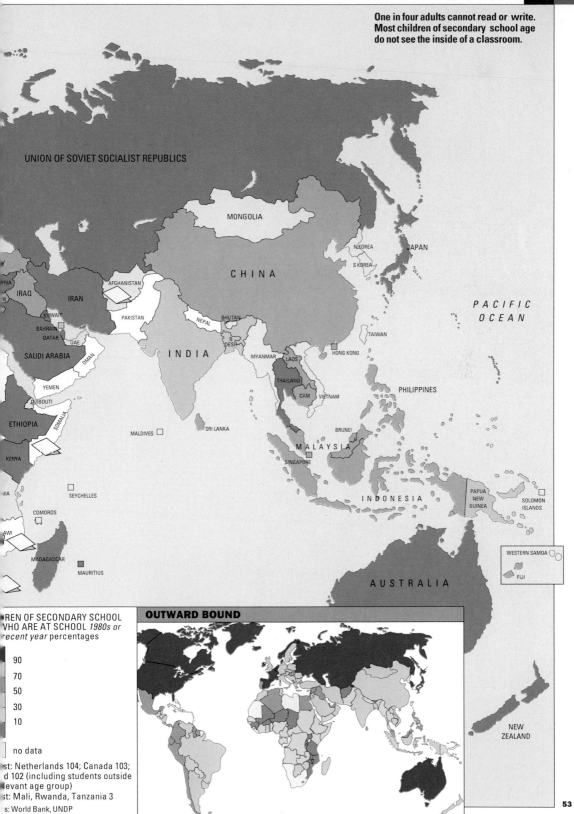

One in four adults cannot read or write.
Most children of secondary school age
do not see the inside of a classroom.

UNION OF SOVIET SOCIALIST REPUBLICS

MONGOLIA

CHINA

N.KOREA   JAPAN

S KOREA

PACIFIC
OCEAN

AFGHANISTAN

IRAQ   IRAN

KUWAIT

BAHRAIN

QATAR

UAE   OMAN

PAKISTAN   NEPAL   BHUTAN

B.DESH

TAIWAN

SAUDI ARABIA

INDIA   MYANMAR   LAOS   HONG KONG

YEMEN

DJIBOUTI

SOMALIA

ETHIOPIA

THAILAND

CAM   VIETNAM

PHILIPPINES

MALDIVES   SRI LANKA   BRUNEI

KENYA

MALAYSIA

SINGAPORE

SEYCHELLES

INDONESIA

PAPUA
NEW
GUINEA

SOLOMON
ISLANDS

COMOROS

MADAGASCAR

MAURITIUS

WESTERN SAMOA

FIJI

AUSTRALIA

NEW
ZEALAND

REN OF SECONDARY SCHOOL
WHO ARE AT SCHOOL *1980s or
recent year* percentages

90
70
50
30
10

no data

st: Netherlands 104; Canada 103;
d 102 (including students outside
evant age group)
st: Mali, Rwanda, Tanzania 3
s: World Bank, UNDP

OUTWARD BOUND

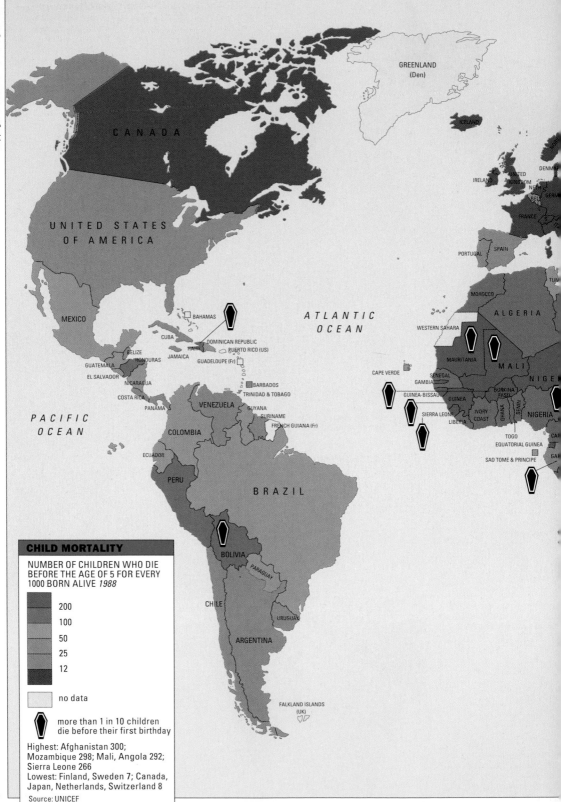

GREENLAND
(Den)

ICELAND

C A N A D A

DENMARK

IRELAND
UNITED
KINGDOM

NETH
GER

BEL

FRANCE

UNITED STATES
OF AMERICA

PORTUGAL

SPAIN

TUN

MOROCCO

ALGERIA

MEXICO

ATLANTIC
OCEAN

WESTERN SAHARA

BAHAMAS

CUBA

DOMINICAN REPUBLIC

BELIZE
HONDURAS
JAMAICA
HAITI
PUERTO RICO (US)

GUADELOUPE (Fr)

MAURITANIA

MALI

NIGER

GUATEMALA

EL SALVADOR

CAPE VERDE

SENEGAL

GAMBIA

BARBADOS

NICARAGUA

TRINIDAD & TOBAGO

GUINEA-BISSAU

GUINEA

BURKINA
FASO

BENIN

COSTA RICA

VENEZUELA

GUYANA

SIERRA LEONE

IVORY
COAST

GHANA

NIGERIA

PANAMA

SURINAME

LIBERIA

PACIFIC
OCEAN

COLOMBIA

FRENCH GUIANA (Fr)

TOGO

EQUATORIAL GUINEA

CAM

ECUADOR

SAO TOME & PRINCIPE

GAB

PERU

B R A Z I L

BOLIVIA

PARAGUAY

CHILE

URUGUAY

ARGENTINA

FALKLAND ISLANDS
(UK)

CHILD MORTALITY

NUMBER OF CHILDREN WHO DIE
BEFORE THE AGE OF 5 FOR EVERY
1000 BORN ALIVE *1988*

200

100

50

25

12

no data

more than 1 in 10 children
die before their first birthday

Highest: Afghanistan 300;
Mozambique 298; Mali, Angola 292;
Sierra Leone 266
Lowest: Finland, Sweden 7; Canada,
Japan, Netherlands, Switzerland 8

Source: UNICEF

Mankind owes to the child the best it has to give... The child shall enjoy special protection and shall be given opportunities and facilities, by law and by other means, to enable him to develop physically, mentally and in conditions of freedom and dignity... The child shall be protected against all forms of neglect, cruelty and exploitation.

United Nations Declaration of the Rights of the Child *1959*

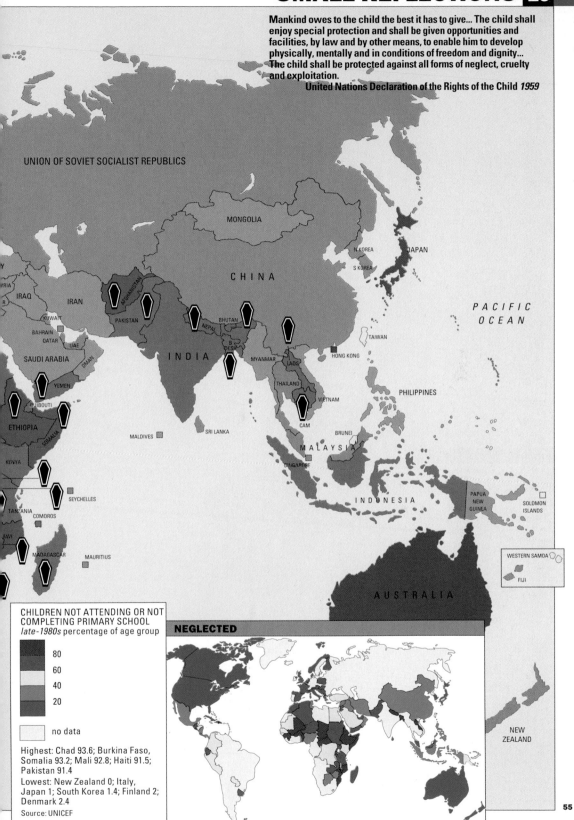

UNION OF SOVIET SOCIALIST REPUBLICS

MONGOLIA

N.KOREA

JAPAN

S.KOREA

CHINA

PACIFIC OCEAN

IRAQ

IRAN

KUWAIT

AFGHANISTAN

PAKISTAN

BHUTAN

NEPAL

B DESH

TAIWAN

BAHRAIN

QATAR

UAE

OMAN

SAUDI ARABIA

INDIA

MYANMAR

LAOS

HONG KONG

YEMEN

THAILAND

DJIBOUTI

VIETNAM

PHILIPPINES

ETHIOPIA

SOMALIA

MALDIVES

SRI LANKA

CAM

BRUNEI

KENYA

MALAYSIA

SINGAPORE

SEYCHELLES

TANZANIA

COMOROS

INDONESIA

PAPUA NEW GUINEA

SOLOMON ISLANDS

MADAGASCAR

MAURITIUS

WESTERN SAMOA

FIJI

AUSTRALIA

CHILDREN NOT ATTENDING OR NOT COMPLETING PRIMARY SCHOOL
late-1980s percentage of age group

NEGLECTED

80

60

40

20

no data

Highest: Chad 93.6; Burkina Faso, Somalia 93.2; Mali 92.8; Haiti 91.5; Pakistan 91.4

Lowest: New Zealand 0; Italy, Japan 1; South Korea 1.4; Finland 2; Denmark 2.4

Source: UNICEF

NEW ZEALAND

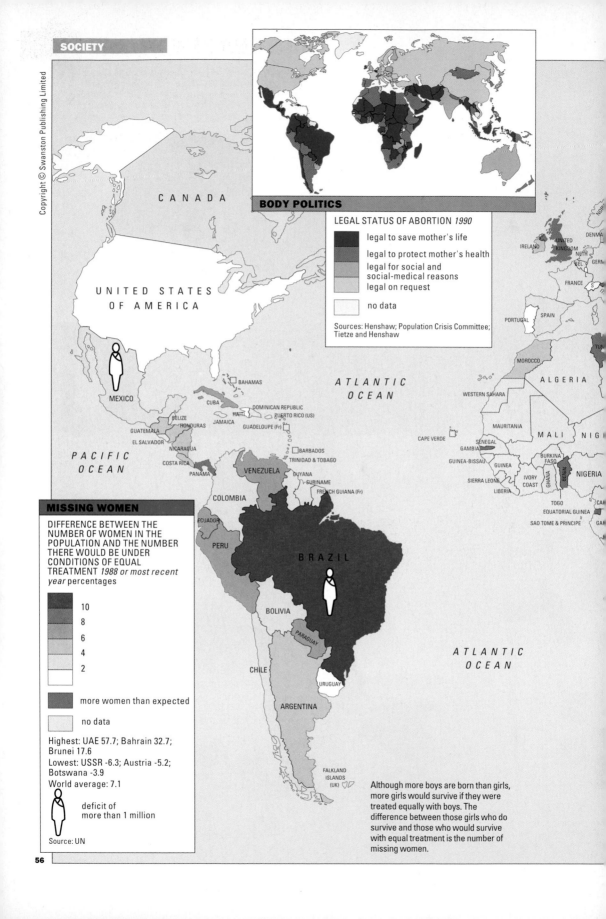

CANADA

UNITED STATES
OF AMERICA

MEXICO

BAHAMAS

CUBA
BELIZE
HONDURAS
JAMAICA
GUATEMALA
EL SALVADOR
NICARAGUA
COSTA RICA
PANAMA

DOMINICAN REPUBLIC
PUERTO RICO (US)
GUADELOUPE (Fr)

BARBADOS
TRINIDAD & TOBAGO

ATLANTIC
OCEAN

PACIFIC
OCEAN

VENEZUELA
GUYANA
SURINAME
FRENCH GUIANA (Fr)

COLOMBIA

ECUADOR

PERU

B R A Z I L

BOLIVIA

PARAGUAY

CHILE

URUGUAY

ARGENTINA

FALKLAND
ISLANDS
(UK)

ATLANTIC
OCEAN

NOR

IRELAND
UNITED
KINGDOM
DENMA

NETH
BEL
GERM

FRANCE

PORTUGAL
SPAIN

TUN

MOROCCO

ALGERIA

WESTERN SAHARA

MAURITANIA

MALI

NIG

CAPE VERDE

SENEGAL
GAMBIA
GUINEA-BISSAU
GUINEA

BURKINA
FASO
BENIN

NIGERIA

SIERRA LEONE
IVORY
COAST
GHANA

LIBERIA

TOGO
EQUATORIAL GUINEA
SAO TOME & PRINCIPE

CA

GA

BODY POLITICS

LEGAL STATUS OF ABORTION *1990*

- legal to save mother's life
- legal to protect mother's health
- legal for social and social-medical reasons
- legal on request
- no data

Sources: Henshaw; Population Crisis Committee; Tietze and Henshaw

MISSING WOMEN

DIFFERENCE BETWEEN THE NUMBER OF WOMEN IN THE POPULATION AND THE NUMBER THERE WOULD BE UNDER CONDITIONS OF EQUAL TREATMENT *1988 or most recent year* percentages

- 10
- 8
- 6
- 4
- 2

- more women than expected
- no data

Highest: UAE 57.7; Bahrain 32.7; Brunei 17.6
Lowest: USSR -6.3; Austria -5.2; Botswana -3.9
World average: 7.1

deficit of more than 1 million

Source: UN

Although more boys are born than girls, more girls would survive if they were treated equally with boys. The difference between those girls who do survive and those who would survive with equal treatment is the number of missing women.

There are 200 million fewer women than there should be. Women's bodies remain contested territory.

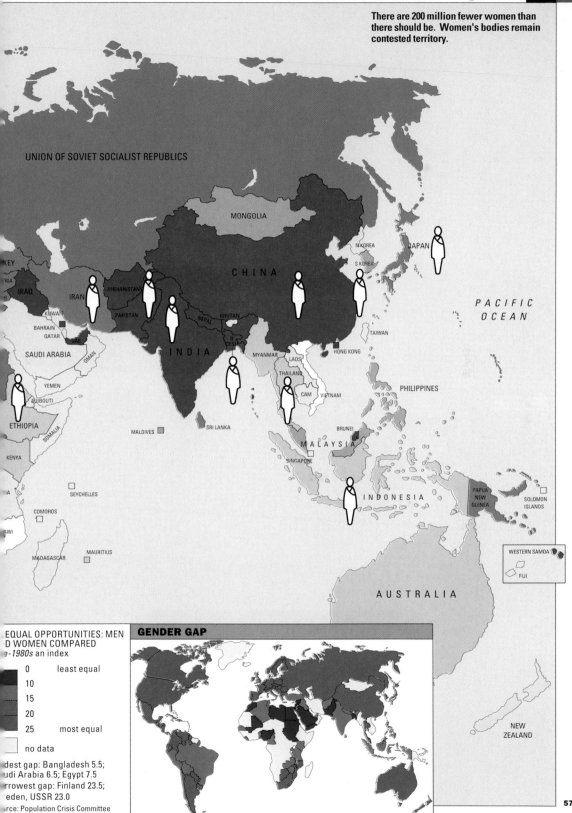

UNION OF SOVIET SOCIALIST REPUBLICS

MONGOLIA

N·KOREA

JAPAN

S KOREA

CHINA

KEY

IRAQ

IRAN

AFGHANISTAN

KUWAIT

PAKISTAN

BAHRAIN

QATAR

UAE

NEPAL   BHUTAN

SAUDI ARABIA

OMAN

B'DESH

MYANMAR

INDIA

LAOS

HONG KONG

YEMEN

DJIBOUTI

THAILAND

CAM   VIETNAM

ETHIOPIA

SOMALIA

MALDIVES

SRI LANKA

BRUNEI

KENYA

MALAYSIA

SINGAPORE

SEYCHELLES

INDONESIA

COMOROS

AWI

MADAGASCAR

MAURITIUS

TAIWAN

PACIFIC
OCEAN

PHILIPPINES

PAPUA
NEW
GUINEA

SOLOMON
ISLANDS

AUSTRALIA

WESTERN SAMOA

FIJI

NEW
ZEALAND

EQUAL OPPORTUNITIES: MEN
D WOMEN COMPARED
e-1980s an index

0	least equal
10	
15	
20	
25	most equal
	no data

GENDER GAP

dest gap: Bangladesh 5.5;
udi Arabia 6.5; Egypt 7.5
rrowest gap: Finland 23.5;
eden, USSR 23.0
rce: Population Crisis Committee

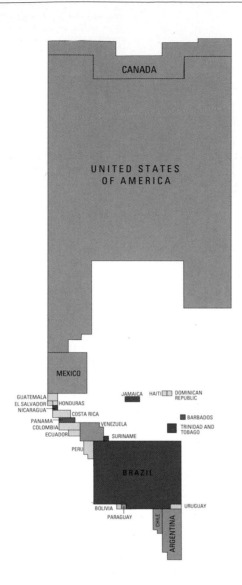

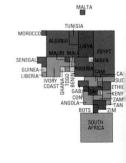

CANADA

ICELAND

IRELAND

UNITED KINGDOM

UNITED STATES
OF AMERICA

FRANCE

SPAIN

PORTUGAL

MEXICO

JAMAICA HAITI DOMINICAN REPUBLIC

GUATEMALA
EL SALVADOR HONDURAS
NICARAGUA
PANAMA COSTA RICA
COLOMBIA VENEZUELA
ECUADOR
PERU SURINAME

BARBADOS
TRINIDAD AND TOBAGO

BRAZIL

BOLIVIA URUGUAY
PARAGUAY
CHILE
ARGENTINA

MALTA

TUNISIA
MOROCCO
ALGERIA LIBYA
MAURI MALI EGYPT
SENEGAL NIGER
GUINEA NIGERIA
LIBERIA CAM CA
IVORY TOGO SUD
COAST GHANA BENIN
GAB ETHI
CON KENY
ANGOLA ZAM
BOTS TAN
ZIM
SOUTH
AFRICA

GOVERNMENT SPENDING

CENTRAL GOVERNMENT
EXPENDITURE AS A
SHARE OF WORLD TOTAL
1988 percentages

=1.0%

=0.1%

=0.01%

Highest: USA 19.8;
USSR 12.3; Japan 8.5;
Germany 8.4

Source: USACDA

CENTRAL GOVERNMENT
EXPENDITURE AS A SHARE OF
GROSS NATIONAL PRODUCT
1988 percentages

40

30

20

10

Highest: Qatar 82.5; Botswana
79.8; Jordan 65.1; Vietnam 61.4

`Those who make their living by
collecting taxes cause the people
to starve; when the people starve,
the tax collectors, having no one to
tax, starve also'.
Lao Tzu

Governments spent US $6 million million in 1988 – 30 percent of world income. In most cases they devoured the flesh and the people sucked the stone.

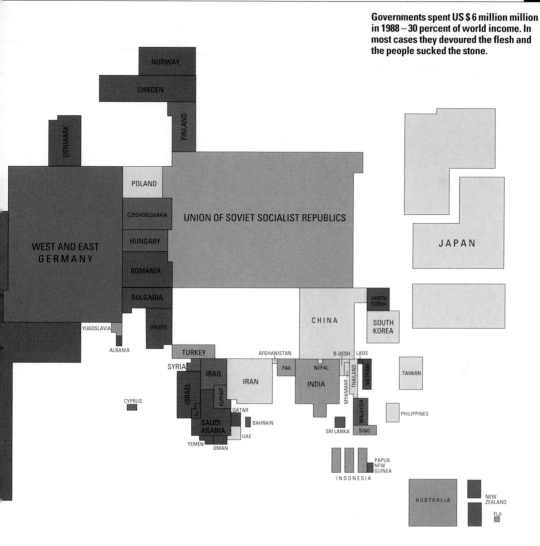

NORWAY

SWEDEN

FINLAND

DENMARK

POLAND

CZECHOSLOVAKIA

UNION OF SOVIET SOCIALIST REPUBLICS

JAPAN

WEST AND EAST GERMANY

HUNGARY

ROMANIA

BULGARIA

YUGOSLAVIA

GREECE

NORTH KOREA

CHINA

SOUTH KOREA

ALBANIA

TURKEY

AFGHANISTAN

B-DESH

LAOS

SYRIA

PAK

NEPAL

TAIWAN

IRAQ

IRAN

INDIA

MYANMAR

THAILAND

VIETNAM

ISRAEL

KUWAIT

CYPRUS

J

QATAR

BAHRAIN

SRI LANKA

MALAYSIA

SING

PHILIPPINES

SAUDI ARABIA

UAE

YEMEN

OMAN

PAPUA NEW GUINEA

INDONESIA

AUSTRALIA

NEW ZEALAND

FIJI

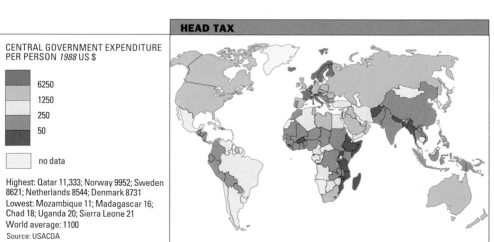

HEAD TAX

CENTRAL GOVERNMENT EXPENDITURE PER PERSON *1988* US $

- 6250
- 1250
- 250
- 50
- no data

Highest: Qatar 11,333; Norway 9952; Sweden 8621; Netherlands 8544; Denmark 8731

Lowest: Mozambique 11; Madagascar 16; Chad 18; Uganda 20; Sierra Leone 21

World average: 1100

Source: USACDA

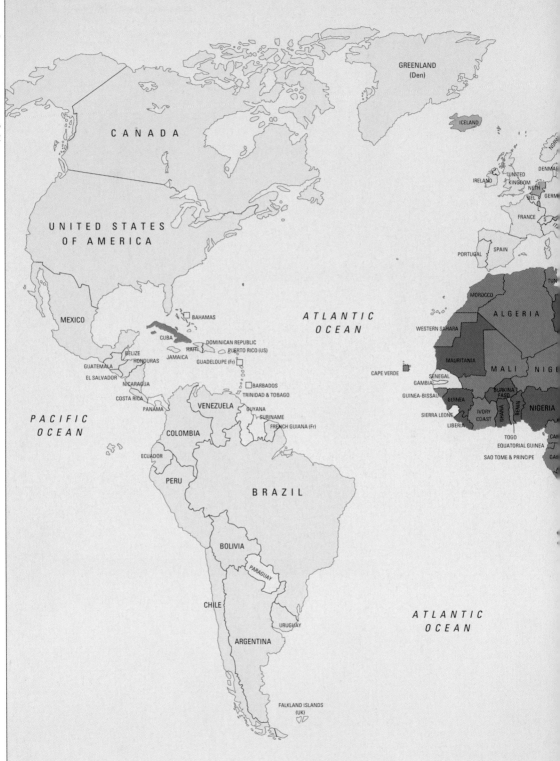

At the beginning of 1991 seven governments – out of 165 – were in power because a majority of their citizens of voting age wanted them there.

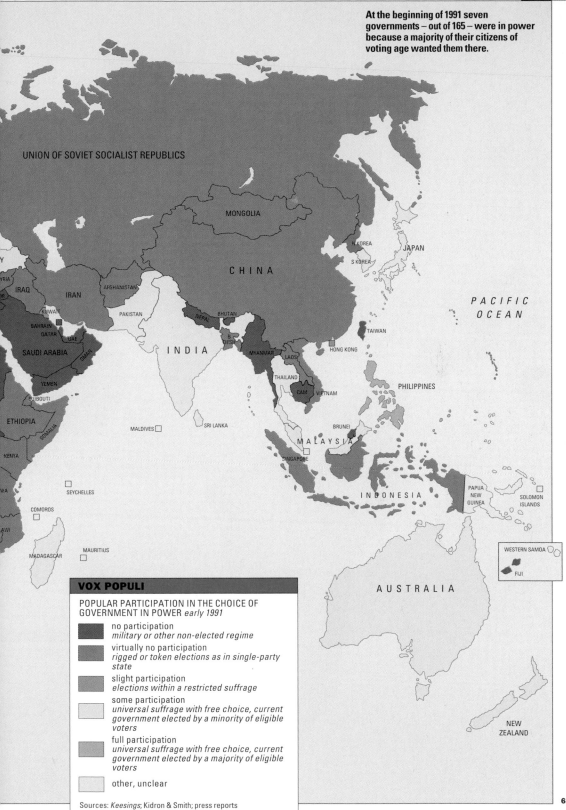

UNION OF SOVIET SOCIALIST REPUBLICS

MONGOLIA

N.KOREA

JAPAN

S KOREA

CHINA

PACIFIC OCEAN

SYRIA

IRAQ

IRAN

AFGHANISTAN

KUWAIT

PAKISTAN

NEPAL

BHUTAN

BAHRAIN

QATAR

UAE

B'DESH

TAIWAN

SAUDI ARABIA

OMAN

INDIA

MYANMAR

LAOS

HONG KONG

YEMEN

THAILAND

DJIBOUTI

CAM

VIETNAM

PHILIPPINES

ETHIOPIA

SOMALIA

MALDIVES

SRI LANKA

BRUNEI

KENYA

MALAYSIA

SINGAPORE

SEYCHELLES

INDONESIA

PAPUA NEW GUINEA

SOLOMON ISLANDS

COMOROS

MALAWI

MAURITIUS

MADAGASCAR

WESTERN SAMOA

FIJI

AUSTRALIA

NEW ZEALAND

VOX POPULI

POPULAR PARTICIPATION IN THE CHOICE OF GOVERNMENT IN POWER *early 1991*

no participation
military or other non-elected regime

virtually no participation
rigged or token elections as in single-party state

slight participation
elections within a restricted suffrage

some participation
universal suffrage with free choice, current government elected by a minority of eligible voters

full participation
universal suffrage with free choice, current government elected by a majority of eligible voters

other, unclear

Sources: *Keesings*; Kidron & Smith; press reports

Copyright: © Swanston Publishing Limited

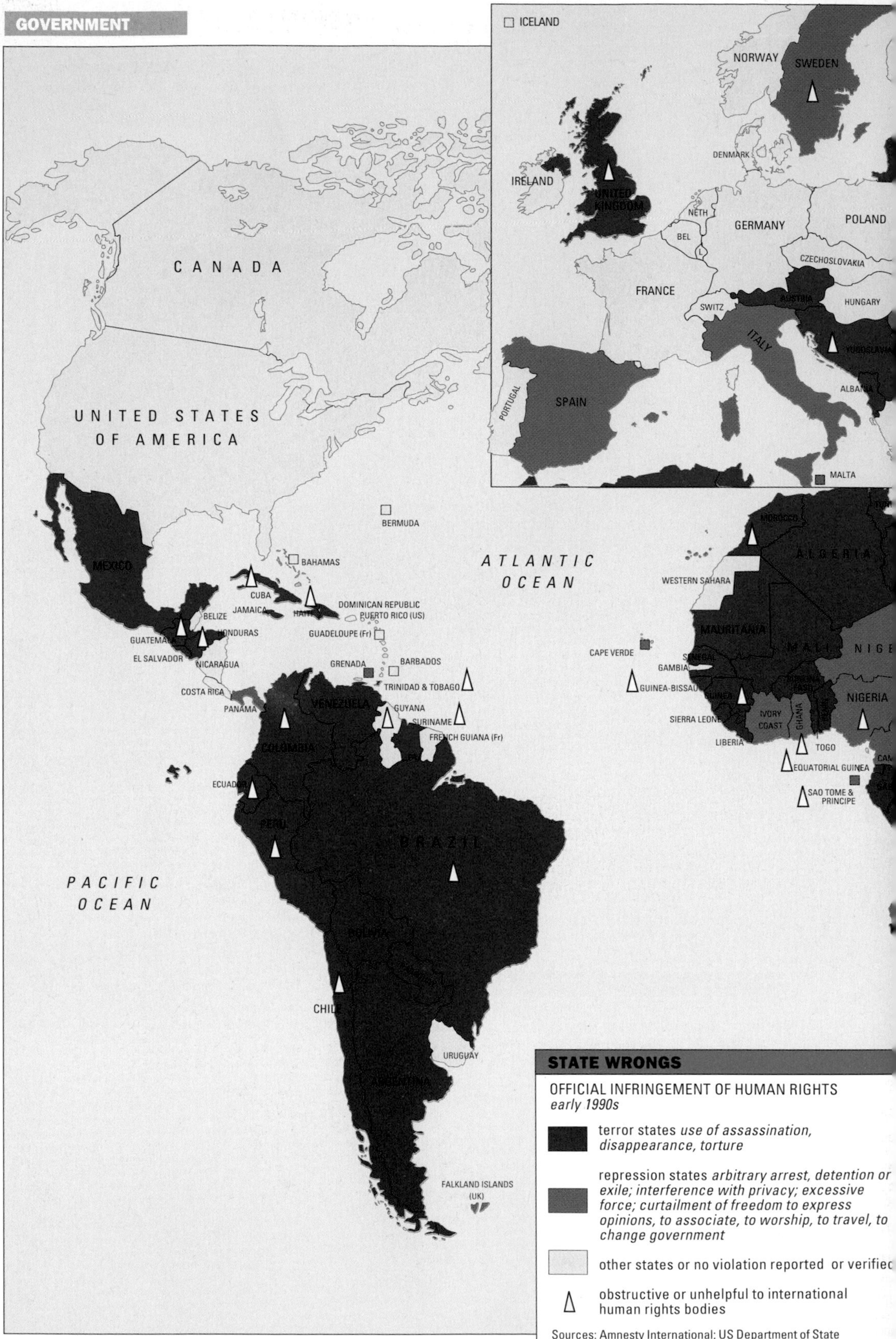

ICELAND

NORWAY

SWEDEN

DENMARK

IRELAND

UNITED KINGDOM

NETH

GERMANY

POLAND

BEL

CZECHOSLOVAKIA

FRANCE

SWITZ

AUSTRIA

HUNGARY

ITALY

YUGOSLAVIA

PORTUGAL

SPAIN

ALBANIA

MALTA

CANADA

UNITED STATES
OF AMERICA

BERMUDA

BAHAMAS

MEXICO

ATLANTIC
OCEAN

MOROCCO

ALGERIA

WESTERN SAHARA

CUBA

BELIZE

JAMAICA

HAITI

DOMINICAN REPUBLIC

PUERTO RICO (US)

GUADELOUPE (Fr)

GUATEMALA

HONDURAS

EL SALVADOR

NICARAGUA

COSTA RICA

GRENADA

BARBADOS

TRINIDAD & TOBAGO

CAPE VERDE

MAURITANIA

MALI

NIGE

SENEGAL

GAMBIA

GUINEA-BISSAU

GUINEA

BURKINA FASO

NIGERIA

PANAMA

VENEZUELA

GUYANA

SURINAME

FRENCH GUIANA (Fr)

SIERRA LEONE

IVORY COAST

GHANA

LIBERIA

TOGO

CAM

COLOMBIA

EQUATORIAL GUINEA

ECUADOR

SAO TOME &
PRINCIPE

PERU

B R A Z I L

PACIFIC
OCEAN

BOLIVIA

CHILE

URUGUAY

ARGENTINA

FALKLAND ISLANDS
(UK)

All states deal harshly with their
citizens. Many terrorize them.

BLACK SEA

USSR

TURKEY

CYPRUS

SYRIA

LEBANON

MEDITERRANEAN
SEA

ISRAEL

JORDAN

IRAQ

IRAN

UNION OF SOVIET
SOCIALIST REPUBLICS

EGYPT

RED SEA

SAUDI
ARABIA

KUWAIT

MONGOLIA

UNION OF SOVIET
SOCIALIST REPUBLICS

IRAQ

IRAN

AFGHANISTAN

KUWAIT

QATAR

UAE

SAUDI
ARABIA

YEMEN

OMAN

PAKISTAN

NEPAL

BHUTAN

INDIA

MYANMAR

LAOS

THAILAND

CAMB

VIETNAM

CHINA

KOREA

S KOREA

JAPAN

PACIFIC
OCEAN

TAIWAN

HONG KONG

PHILIPPINES

DJIBOUTI

ETHIOPIA

KENYA

SRI LANKA

MALDIVES

MALAYSIA

SINGAPORE

BRUNEI

INDONESIA

PAPUA
NEW
GUINEA

SOLOMON
ISLANDS

SEYCHELLES

COMOROS

MADAGASCAR

MAURITIUS

AUSTRALIA

WESTERN SAMOA

FIJI

RITUAL HOMICIDE

NEW
ZEALAND

ENALTY *end-January 1991*

bolished for all crimes

bolished for ordinary crimes only
xcluding crimes under military
w, or in wartime)

bolished in practice but not in law
o executions for ten years)

tained and used for ordinary crimes

data

cutions, 1989: Iran more than 1500;
Saudi Arabia 111; South Africa
60

nesty International

63

STATES RECEIVING REFUGEES FROM ABROAD
1989 numbers

one million

half a million

quarter of a million

100,000

other states

Highest: Pakistan 3.6 million; Iran 2.8 million;
Jordan 1.4 million; Ethiopia, Sudan 0.7 million

▲ major diasporas (long-term
refugee societies)

Source: USCR

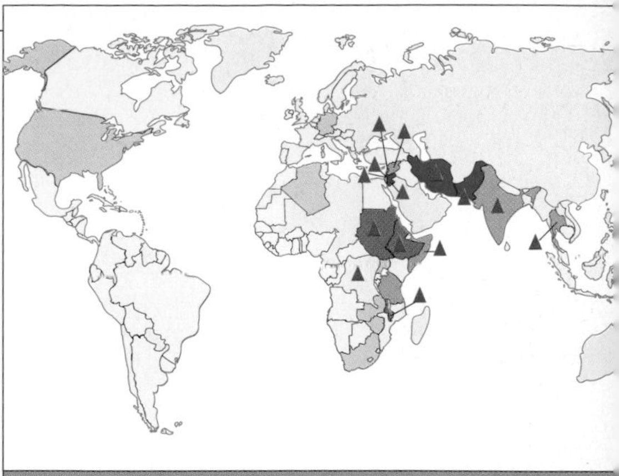

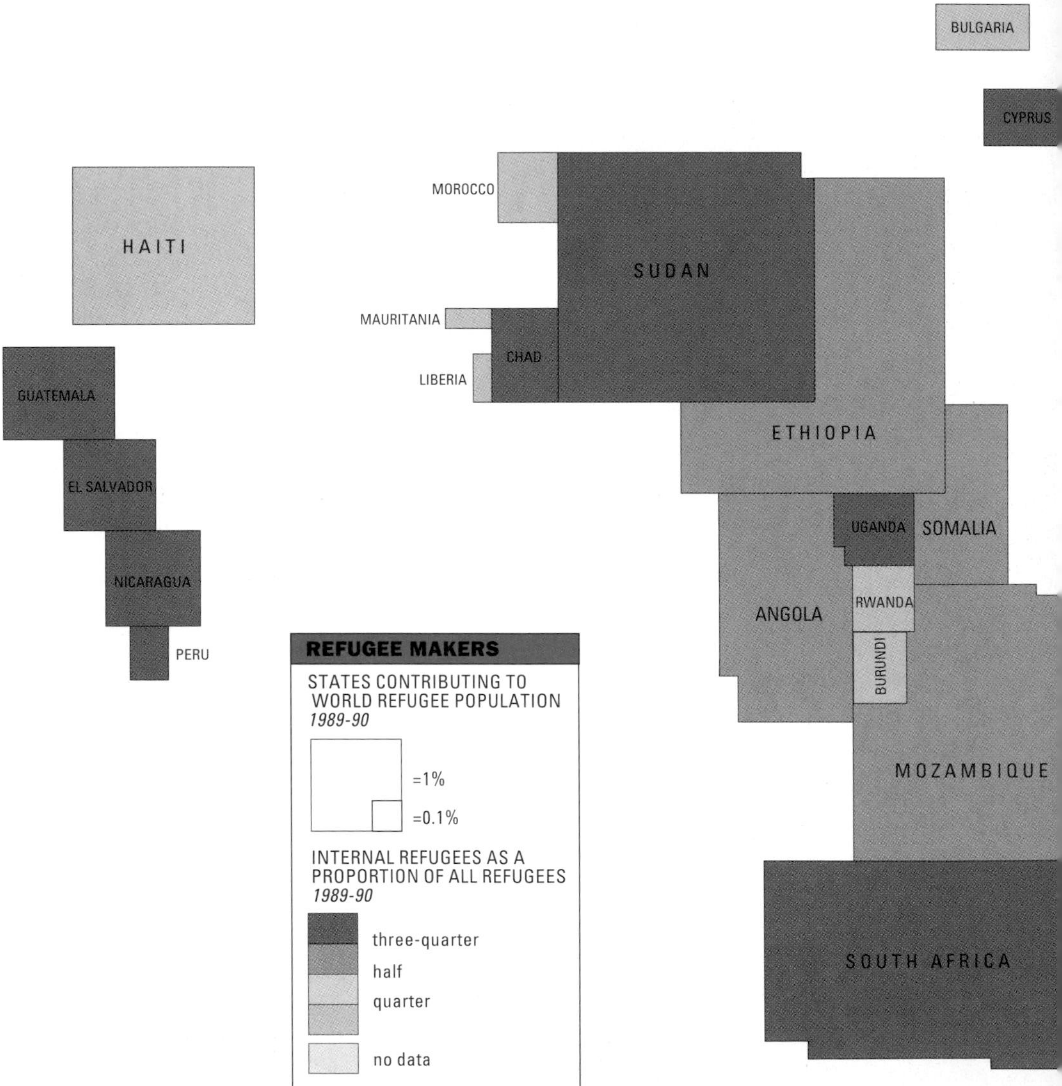

IN LIMBO

BULGARIA

CYPRUS

MOROCCO

SUDAN

HAITI

MAURITANIA

CHAD

LIBERIA

ETHIOPIA

GUATEMALA

EL SALVADOR

UGANDA   SOMALIA

NICARAGUA

RWANDA

ANGOLA

BURUNDI

PERU

REFUGEE MAKERS

STATES CONTRIBUTING TO
WORLD REFUGEE POPULATION
1989-90

=1%

=0.1%

INTERNAL REFUGEES AS A
PROPORTION OF ALL REFUGEES
1989-90

three-quarter

half

quarter

no data

Sources: USCR; press reports

MOZAMBIQUE

SOUTH AFRICA

64

At least 47 million people have been forced from their homes by war, abuse and fear. Nearly half of them are refugees in their own countries.

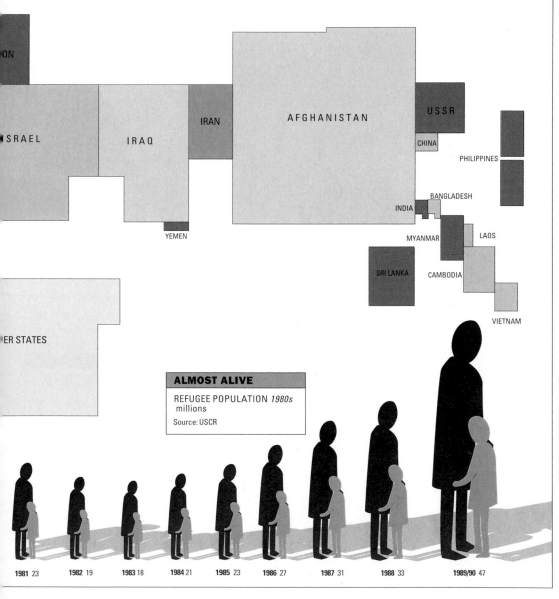

ON

ISRAEL

IRAQ

IRAN

AFGHANISTAN

USSR

CHINA

PHILIPPINES

BANGLADESH

INDIA

YEMEN

MYANMAR

LAOS

SRI LANKA

CAMBODIA

VIETNAM

ER STATES

ALMOST ALIVE

REFUGEE POPULATION *1980s*
millions

Source: USCR

| **1981** 23 | **1982** 19 | **1983** 18 | **1984** 21 | **1985** 23 | **1986** 27 | **1987** 31 | **1988** 33 | **1989/90** 47 |

GREENLAND
(Den)

ICELAND

NORWAY

DENMARK

IRELAND UNITED KINGDOM
NETH
BEL GERM

FRANCE S

CANADA

UNITED STATES
OF AMERICA

PORTUGAL SPAIN

TUN

ATLANTIC
OCEAN

MOROCCO

ALGERIA

MEXICO

WESTERN SAHARA

NIGE

BAHAMAS

CUBA

DOMINICAN REPUBLIC
HAITI PUERTO RICO (US)
BELIZE JAMAICA
GUATEMALA HONDURAS GUADELOUPE (Fr)
EL SALVADOR
NICARAGUA GRENADA BARBADOS
COSTA RICA TRINIDAD & TOBAGO
PANAMA VENEZUELA GUYANA
SURINAME
COLOMBIA FRENCH GUIANA (Fr)

ECUADOR

CAPE VERDE

SENEGAL

GAMBIA

GUINEA-BISSAU GUINEA
BURKINA
FASO
SIERRA LEONE IVORY BENIN
COAST GHANA
LIBERIA

NIGERIA

TOGO CAM
EQUATORIAL GUINEA
SAO TOME & PRINCIPE GAB

BRAZIL

PACIFIC
OCEAN

CHI

URUGUAY

ARGENTINA

FALKLAND ISLANDS
(UK)

SOCIAL ENGINEERING

STATE POLICIES AND ATTITUDES
ON DEVIATION FROM OFFICIAL
SOCIAL NORMS
early 1990s or latest year

- suppression
- criminalization / legalized discrimination
- discouragement
- neglect
- affirmative action
- unknown, unclear, inconsistent

Sources: Minority Rights Group; US
State Department; press reports;
private communications

All states know how their subjects should think and act – as one person.

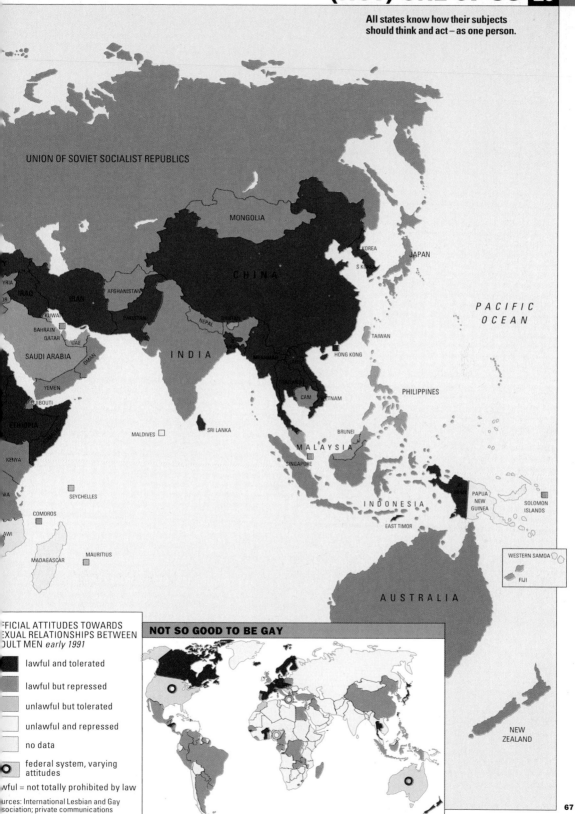

UNION OF SOVIET SOCIALIST REPUBLICS

MONGOLIA

KOREA

JAPAN

S KOREA

CHINA

PACIFIC
OCEAN

YRIA
IRAQ
IRAN
AFGHANISTAN
US
KUWAIT
BAHRAIN
QATAR
UAE
OMAN
SAUDI ARABIA
YEMEN
DJIBOUTI
ETHIOPIA
KENYA

PAKISTAN
NEPAL
BHUTAN
INDIA
MYANMAR
TAIWAN
HONG KONG

LAOS

THAILAND
CAM
VIETNAM
PHILIPPINES

MALDIVES
SRI LANKA
BRUNEI

MALAYSIA
SINGAPORE

INDONESIA
EAST TIMOR

NIA
SEYCHELLES

COMOROS
MAURITIUS
MADAGASCAR
AWI

PAPUA
NEW
GUINEA
SOLOMON
ISLANDS

WESTERN SAMOA
FIJI

AUSTRALIA

NEW
ZEALAND

OFFICIAL ATTITUDES TOWARDS SEXUAL RELATIONSHIPS BETWEEN ADULT MEN *early 1991*

- ⬛ lawful and tolerated
- ⬛ lawful but repressed
- ◻ unlawful but tolerated
- ◻ unlawful and repressed
- ◻ no data
- ◉ federal system, varying attitudes

lawful = not totally prohibited by law

Sources: International Lesbian and Gay Association; private communications

NOT SO GOOD TO BE GAY

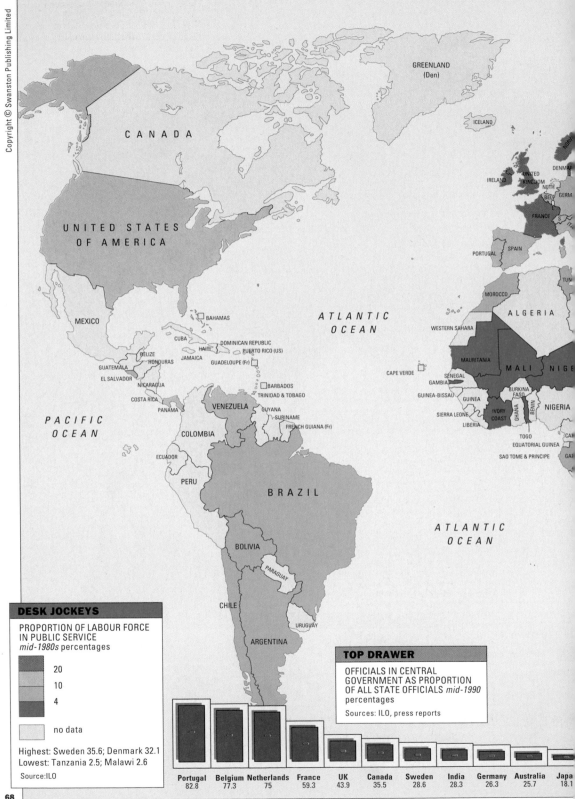

GREENLAND
(Den)

ICELAND

CANADA

NORTH

DENMARK

IRELAND   UNITED
KINGDOM   NETH
BEL
GERM

FRANCE   S

UNITED STATES
OF AMERICA

PORTUGAL   SPAIN   IT

TUN

MEXICO

BAHAMAS   ATLANTIC
OCEAN

MOROCCO

ALGERIA

CUBA

HAITI   DOMINICAN REPUBLIC   WESTERN SAHARA

BELIZE   PUERTO RICO (US)

HONDURAS   JAMAICA   GUADELOUPE (Fr)

GUATEMALA

EL SALVADOR

NICARAGUA   BARBADOS

COSTA RICA   TRINIDAD & TOBAGO

PANAMA   VENEZUELA   GUYANA

COLOMBIA   SURINAME

FRENCH GUIANA (Fr)

ECUADOR

PERU   BRAZIL

BOLIVIA

PARAGUAY

CHILE

URUGUAY

ARGENTINA

CAPE VERDE

MAURITANIA   MALI   NIGE

SENEGAL

GAMBIA

GUINEA-BISSAU   GUINEA   BURKINA
FASO
BENIN   NIGERIA

SIERRA LEONE   IVORY   GHANA
COAST

LIBERIA

TOGO
EQUATORIAL GUINEA   CA
SAO TOME & PRINCIPE   GAB

PACIFIC
OCEAN

ATLANTIC
OCEAN

DESK JOCKEYS

PROPORTION OF LABOUR FORCE
IN PUBLIC SERVICE
mid-1980s percentages

- 20
- 10
- 4

no data

Highest: Sweden 35.6; Denmark 32.1
Lowest: Tanzania 2.5; Malawi 2.6

Source: ILO

TOP DRAWER

OFFICIALS IN CENTRAL
GOVERNMENT AS PROPORTION
OF ALL STATE OFFICIALS *mid-1990*
percentages

Sources: ILO, press reports

Portugal	Belgium	Netherlands	France	UK	Canada	Sweden	India	Germany	Australia	Japa
82.8	77.3	75	59.3	43.9	35.5	28.6	28.3	26.3	25.7	18.1

There may be 80 million full-time central government officials in the world. Respectful of the rich, demanding of the poor, they serve their own ends better than others'.

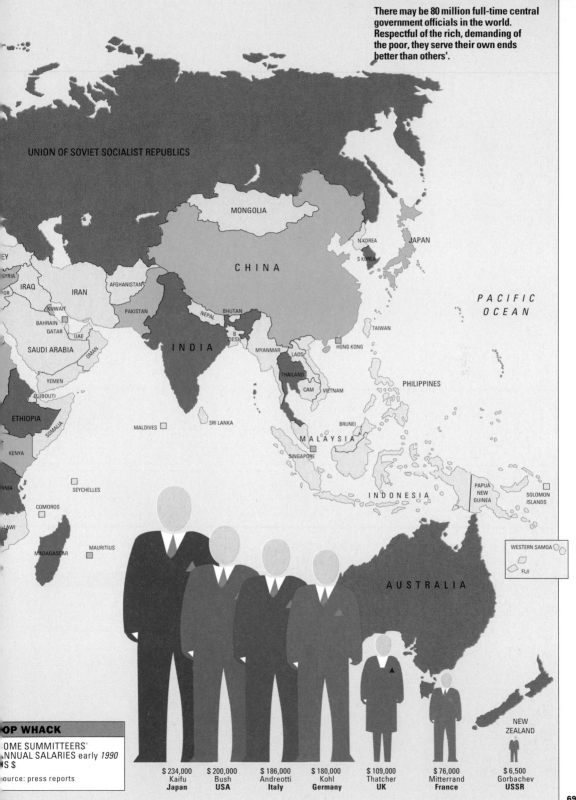

UNION OF SOVIET SOCIALIST REPUBLICS

MONGOLIA

N.KOREA
S.KOREA
JAPAN

CHINA

EY

SYRIA
IRAQ
IRAN
AFGHANISTAN
OR
KUWAIT
PAKISTAN
NEPAL
BHUTAN
BAHRAIN
QATAR
UAE
OMAN
SAUDI ARABIA
YEMEN
DJIBOUTI
ETHIOPIA
SOMALIA
KENYA
ANIA

INDIA
B
DESH
MYANMAR
LAOS
THAILAND
CAM
VIETNAM
TAIWAN
HONG KONG

PACIFIC
OCEAN

PHILIPPINES

MALDIVES
SRI LANKA
BRUNEI
MALAYSIA
SINGAPORE

SEYCHELLES

COMOROS

AWI

MADAGASCAR
MAURITIUS

INDONESIA

PAPUA
NEW
GUINEA
SOLOMON
ISLANDS

WESTERN SAMOA

FIJI

AUSTRALIA

NEW
ZEALAND

| $ 234,000 Kaifu **Japan** | $ 200,000 Bush **USA** | $ 186,000 Andreotti **Italy** | $ 180,000 Kohl **Germany** | $ 109,000 Thatcher **UK** | $ 76,000 Mitterrand **France** | $ 6,500 Gorbachev **USSR** |

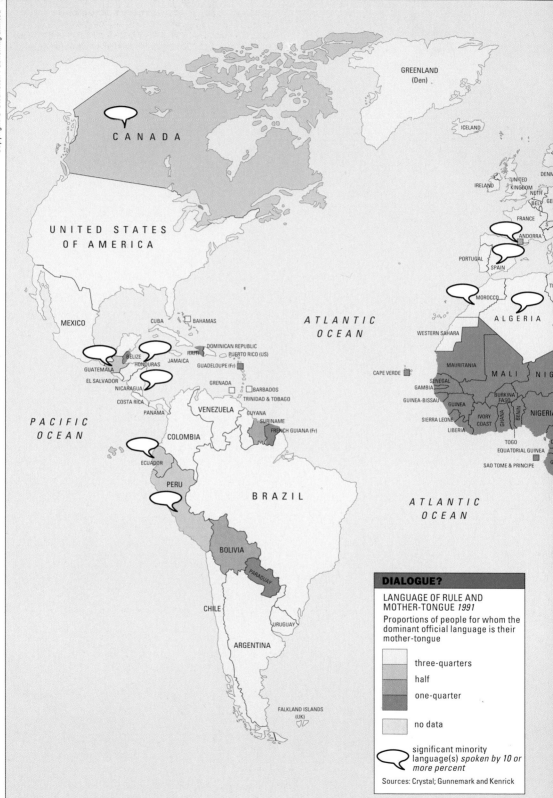

GREENLAND
(Den)

ICELAND

CANADA

NOR

DENMA

IRELAND
UNITED
KINGDOM
NETH
GERM
BEL

UNITED STATES
OF AMERICA

FRANCE

S

ANDORRA

PORTUGAL
SPAIN

TUN

MEXICO

CUBA

BAHAMAS

ATLANTIC
OCEAN

MOROCCO

ALGERIA

WESTERN SAHARA

DOMINICAN REPUBLIC
BELIZE
HAITI
PUERTO RICO (US)
GUATEMALA
HONDURAS
JAMAICA
EL SALVADOR
GUADELOUPE (Fr)
NICARAGUA
GRENADA
COSTA RICA
BARBADOS
TRINIDAD & TOBAGO
PANAMA
VENEZUELA
GUYANA

CAPE VERDE

MAURITANIA

MALI

NIG

SENEGAL
GAMBIA
GUINEA-BISSAU
GUINEA

BURKINA
FASO

NIGERIA

SURINAME
FRENCH GUIANA (Fr)

SIERRA LEONE
IVORY
COAST
GHANA
BENIN

PACIFIC
OCEAN

COLOMBIA

LIBERIA

ECUADOR

TOGO
EQUATORIAL GUINEA
SAO TOME & PRINCIPE

CAM

GAB

PERU

BRAZIL

ATLANTIC
OCEAN

BOLIVIA

PARAGUAY

CHILE

URUGUAY

ARGENTINA

DIALOGUE?

LANGUAGE OF RULE AND
MOTHER-TONGUE *1991*

Proportions of people for whom the
dominant official language is their
mother-tongue

FALKLAND ISLANDS
(UK)

three-quarters

half

one-quarter

no data

significant minority
language(s) *spoken by 10 or
more percent*

Sources: Crystal; Gunnemark and Kenrick

Most people are disenfranchized or disadvantaged linguistically – their mother-tongue is other than the dominant official language(s) or dialect(s) in their country. Only 86 of the 5000-odd existing languages are official. Of these just 5 are used in 124 states.

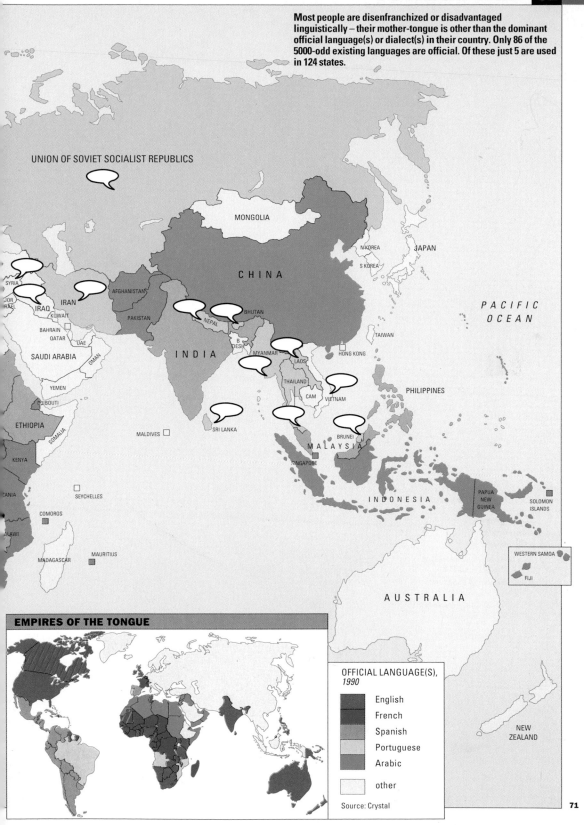

EMPIRES OF THE TONGUE

OFFICIAL LANGUAGE(S), *1990*

- English
- French
- Spanish
- Portuguese
- Arabic
- other

Source: Crystal

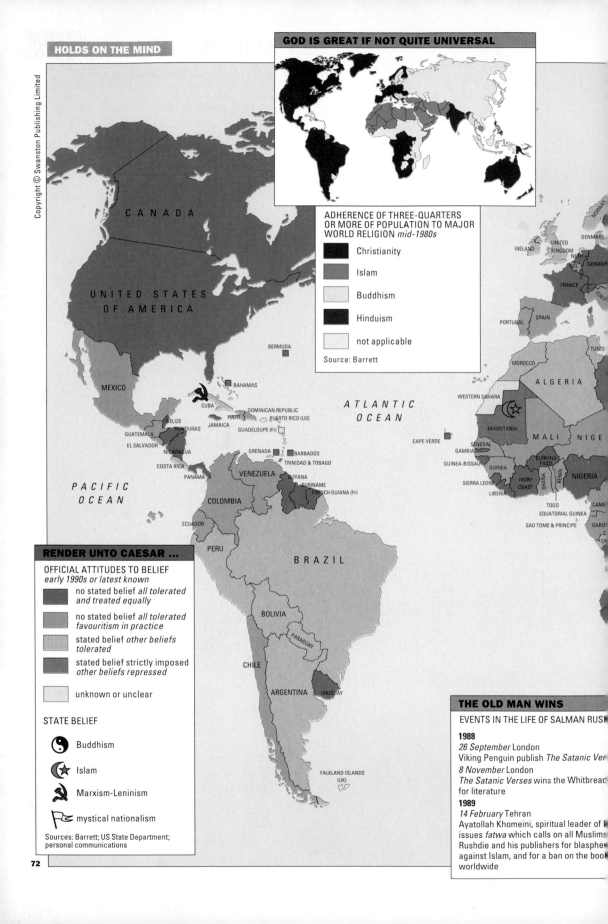

GOD IS GREAT IF NOT QUITE UNIVERSAL

ADHERENCE OF THREE-QUARTERS
OR MORE OF POPULATION TO MAJOR
WORLD RELIGION *mid-1980s*

- Christianity
- Islam
- Buddhism
- Hinduism
- not applicable

Source: Barrett

CANADA

UNITED STATES
OF AMERICA

BERMUDA

MEXICO

BAHAMAS

CUBA

BELIZE
GUATEMALA HONDURAS
EL SALVADOR
NICARAGUA
COSTA RICA
PANAMA

HAITI JAMAICA
DOMINICAN REPUBLIC
PUERTO RICO (US)
GUADELOUPE (Fr)

GRENADA
BARBADOS
TRINIDAD & TOBAGO

VENEZUELA
GUYANA
SURINAME
FRENCH GUIANA (Fr)
COLOMBIA

ECUADOR

PERU

BRAZIL

BOLIVIA

PARAGUAY

CHILE

ARGENTINA URUGUAY

FALKLAND ISLANDS
(UK)

ATLANTIC
OCEAN

PACIFIC
OCEAN

NORWAY

IRELAND UNITED
KINGDOM
NETH
BEL GERMANY
FRANCE
ITALY

PORTUGAL SPAIN

TUNIS
MOROCCO

ALGERIA

WESTERN SAHARA

MAURITANIA

MALI NIGE

SENEGAL
GAMBIA
GUINEA-BISSAU
GUINEA
SIERRA LEONE IVORY
COAST
LIBERIA

BURKINA
FASO
GHANA
BENIN
TOGO

NIGERIA

CAPE VERDE

CAME
EQUATORIAL GUINEA
SAO TOME & PRINCIPE GABO

RENDER UNTO CAESAR ...

OFFICIAL ATTITUDES TO BELIEF
early 1990s or latest known

- no stated belief *all tolerated
  and treated equally*
- no stated belief *all tolerated
  favouritism in practice*
- stated belief *other beliefs
  tolerated*
- stated belief strictly imposed
  other beliefs repressed

- unknown or unclear

STATE BELIEF

- ☯ Buddhism
- ☪ Islam
- ☭ Marxism-Leninism
- 🏴 mystical nationalism

Sources: Barrett; US State Department;
personal communications

THE OLD MAN WINS

EVENTS IN THE LIFE OF SALMAN RUS

1988
26 September London
Viking Penguin publish *The Satanic Ver*
8 November London
The Satanic Verses wins the Whitbrea
for literature

1989
14 February Tehran
Ayatollah Khomeini, spiritual leader of I
issues *fatwa* which calls on all Muslims
Rushdie and his publishers for blasphe
against Islam, and for a ban on the boo
worldwide

Belief – religious or secular, popular or sectarian – is frequently an arm of the state.

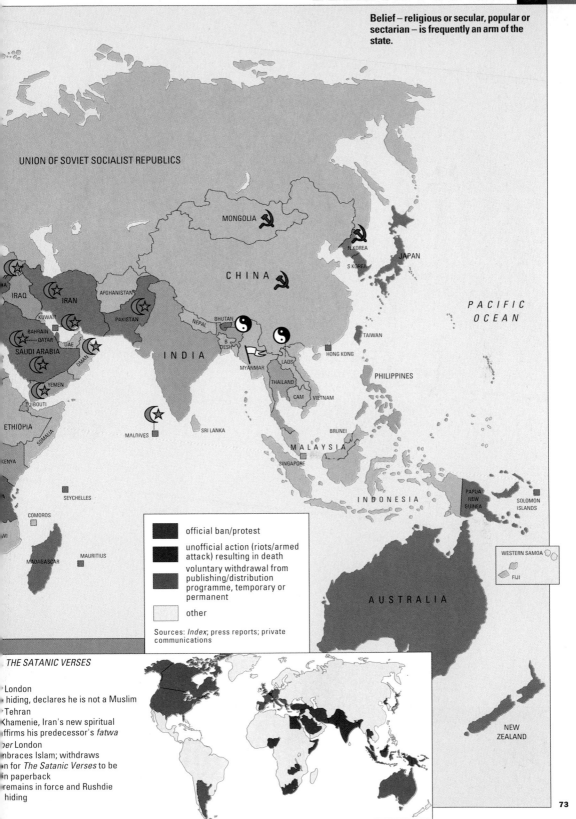

UNION OF SOVIET SOCIALIST REPUBLICS

MONGOLIA

CHINA

N.KOREA

S.KOREA

JAPAN

PACIFIC OCEAN

AFGHANISTAN

IRAQ

IRAN

KUWAIT

PAKISTAN

BAHRAIN

QATAR

UAE

SAUDI ARABIA

OMAN

YEMEN

DJIBOUTI

ETHIOPIA

SOMALIA

KENYA

NEPAL

BHUTAN

B.DESH

MYANMAR

LAOS

THAILAND

CAM

VIETNAM

HONG KONG

TAIWAN

PHILIPPINES

BRUNEI

INDIA

SRI LANKA

MALDIVES

MALAYSIA

SINGAPORE

INDONESIA

PAPUA NEW GUINEA

SOLOMON ISLANDS

SEYCHELLES

COMOROS

MADAGASCAR

MAURITIUS

AUSTRALIA

WESTERN SAMOA

FIJI

NEW ZEALAND

official ban/protest

unofficial action (riots/armed attack) resulting in death

voluntary withdrawal from publishing/distribution programme, temporary or permanent

other

Sources: *Index*; press reports; private communications

THE SATANIC VERSES

London

hiding, declares he is not a Muslim

Tehran

Khamenei, Iran's new spiritual

ffirms his predecessor's *fatwa*

er London

nbraces Islam; withdraws

n for *The Satanic Verses* to be

n paperback

remains in force and Rushdie

hiding

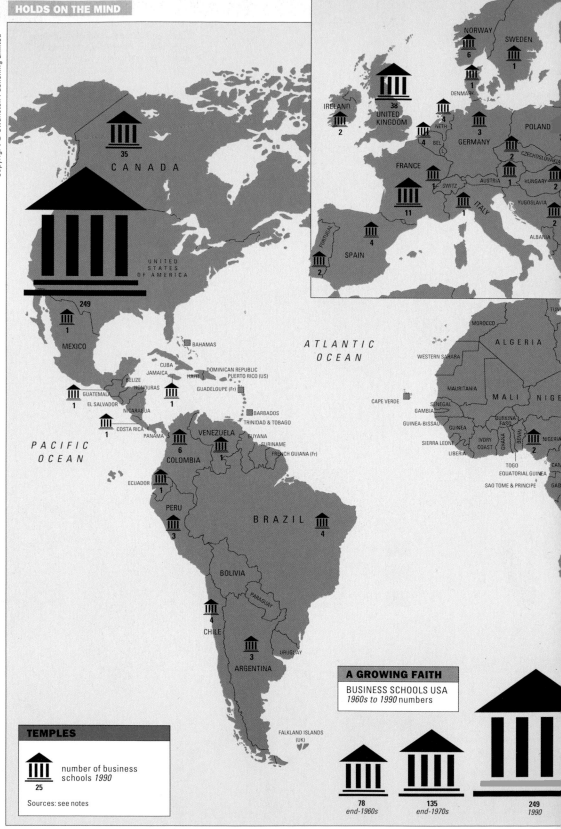

CANADA

35

UNITED
STATES
OF AMERICA

249

MEXICO

1

ATLANTIC
OCEAN

BAHAMAS

CUBA
JAMAICA
BELIZE
HONDURAS
GUATEMALA   DOMINICAN REPUBLIC
1   HAITI   PUERTO RICO (US)
EL SALVADOR   GUADELOUPE (Fr)
NICARAGUA   1

COSTA RICA   BARBADOS
1   TRINIDAD & TOBAGO
PANAMA

VENEZUELA
6   1
COLOMBIA   GUYANA
             SURINAME
             FRENCH GUIANA (Fr)

PACIFIC
OCEAN

ECUADOR
1

PERU
3

BRAZIL
4

BOLIVIA

PARAGUAY

CHILE
4

URUGUAY

ARGENTINA
3

FALKLAND ISLANDS
(UK)

NORWAY
6   SWEDEN
         1

DENMARK
1

IRELAND   UNITED
2   38 KINGDOM
             4 NETH   3 POLAND
             4 BEL   GERMANY
                              2 CZECHOSLOVAKIA
FRANCE   1 HUNGARY 2
1 SWITZ   AUSTRIA
                YUGOSLAVIA
11   1 ITALY   2
PORTUGAL
2   4   ALBANIA
    SPAIN

TUN

MOROCCO

ALGERIA

WESTERN SAHARA

MAURITANIA   MALI   NIGE

CAPE VERDE
SENEGAL
GAMBIA   BURKINA
GUINEA-BISSAU   GUINEA   FASO
SIERRA LEONE IVORY GHANA BENIN NIGERIA
         COAST   2
LIBERIA
TOGO   CAM
EQUATORIAL GUINEA
SAO TOME & PRINCIPE   GAB

A GROWING FAITH

BUSINESS SCHOOLS USA
1960s to 1990 numbers

78
end-1960s

135
end-1970s

249
1990

TEMPLES

number of business
schools *1990*
25

Sources: see notes

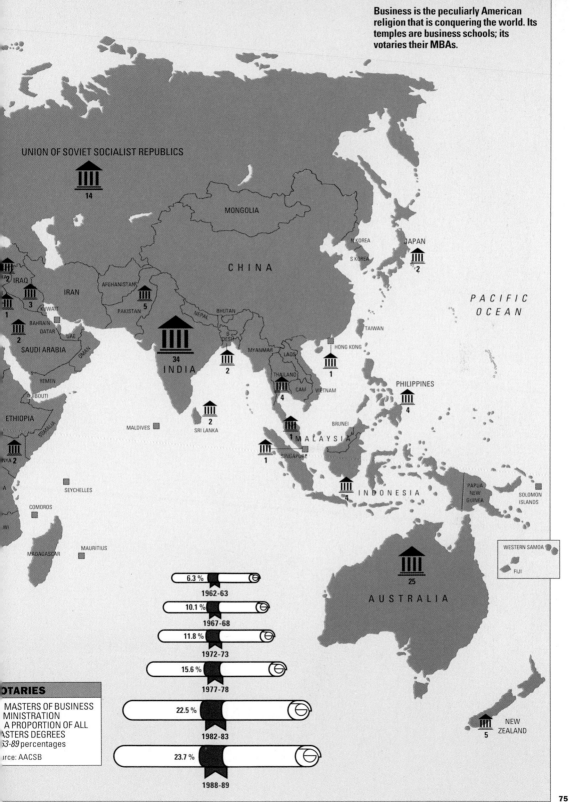

Business is the peculiarly American religion that is conquering the world. Its temples are business schools; its votaries their MBAs.

UNION OF SOVIET SOCIALIST REPUBLICS
14

MONGOLIA

N KOREA
S KOREA

JAPAN
2

CHINA

PACIFIC OCEAN

IRAQ
2

IRAN

AFGHANISTAN

1
3

KUWAIT

PAKISTAN
5

BAHRAIN
QATAR
2
UAE

SAUDI ARABIA

OMAN

YEMEN

DJIBOUTI

ETHIOPIA

SOMALIA

NYA 2

NEPAL

BHUTAN

B'DESH
2

INDIA
34

MYANMAR

LAOS

THAILAND
4

CAM

VIETNAM

TAIWAN

HONG KONG
1

PHILIPPINES
4

BRUNEI

MALAYSIA
1

SINGAPORE
1

INDONESIA
4

PAPUA NEW GUINEA

SOLOMON ISLANDS

SEYCHELLES

MALDIVES

SRI LANKA
2

COMOROS

MADAGASCAR

MAURITIUS

WESTERN SAMOA

FIJI

AUSTRALIA
25

NEW ZEALAND
5

6.3 %	1962-63
10.1 %	1967-68
11.8 %	1972-73
15.6 %	1977-78
22.5 %	1982-83
23.7 %	1988-89

OTARIES
MASTERS OF BUSINESS
MINISTRATION
A PROPORTION OF ALL
ASTERS DEGREES
63-89 percentages
urce: AACSB

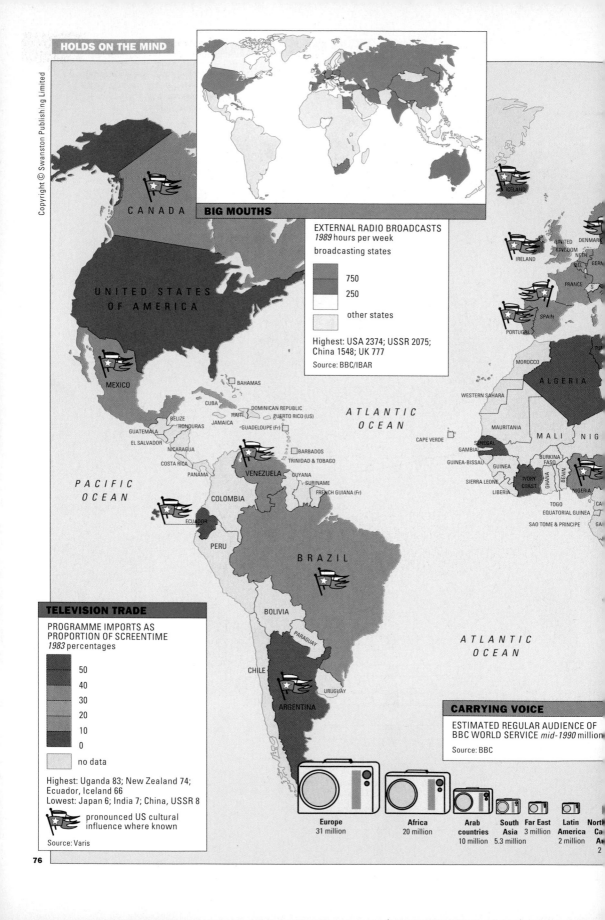

BIG MOUTHS

EXTERNAL RADIO BROADCASTS
1989 hours per week

broadcasting states

750

250

other states

Highest: USA 2374; USSR 2075;
China 1548; UK 777

Source: BBC/IBAR

CANADA

UNITED STATES
OF AMERICA

MEXICO

BAHAMAS

CUBA

BELIZE
GUATEMALA   HONDURAS
EL SALVADOR
NICARAGUA
COSTA RICA
PANAMA

DOMINICAN REPUBLIC
HAITI   PUERTO RICO (US)
JAMAICA
GUADELOUPE (Fr)

BARBADOS
TRINIDAD & TOBAGO

VENEZUELA
GUYANA
COLOMBIA   SURINAME
FRENCH GUIANA (Fr)
ECUADOR

PERU

BRAZIL

BOLIVIA

PARAGUAY

CHILE

URUGUAY

ARGENTINA

PACIFIC
OCEAN

ATLANTIC
OCEAN

ATLANTIC
OCEAN

ICELAND

IRELAND   UNITED   DENMARK
KINGDOM
NETH.
BEL.   GERM
FRANCE   S

SPAIN
PORTUGAL

MOROCCO

WESTERN SAHARA

ALGERIA   TU

MAURITANIA   MALI   NIG

CAPE VERDE
SENEGAL
GAMBIA   BURKINA
FASO
GUINEA-BISSAU   GUINEA   BENIN   NIGERIA
SIERRA LEONE   IVORY   GHANA
COAST
LIBERIA
TOGO   CA
EQUATORIAL GUINEA   GA
SAO TOME & PRINCIPE

TELEVISION TRADE

**PROGRAMME IMPORTS AS
PROPORTION OF SCREENTIME**
1983 percentages

50

40

30

20

10

0

no data

Highest: Uganda 83; New Zealand 74;
Ecuador, Iceland 66
Lowest: Japan 6; India 7; China, USSR 8

pronounced US cultural
influence where known

Source: Varis

CARRYING VOICE

**ESTIMATED REGULAR AUDIENCE OF
BBC WORLD SERVICE** *mid-1990* million

Source: BBC

Europe
31 million

Africa
20 million

Arab
countries
10 million

South
Asia
5.3 million

Far East
3 million

Latin
America
2 million

North
Ca
A
2

76

While almost all states manufacture
and broadcast their own news, most
import a large part of their views – from
a few cultural powers .

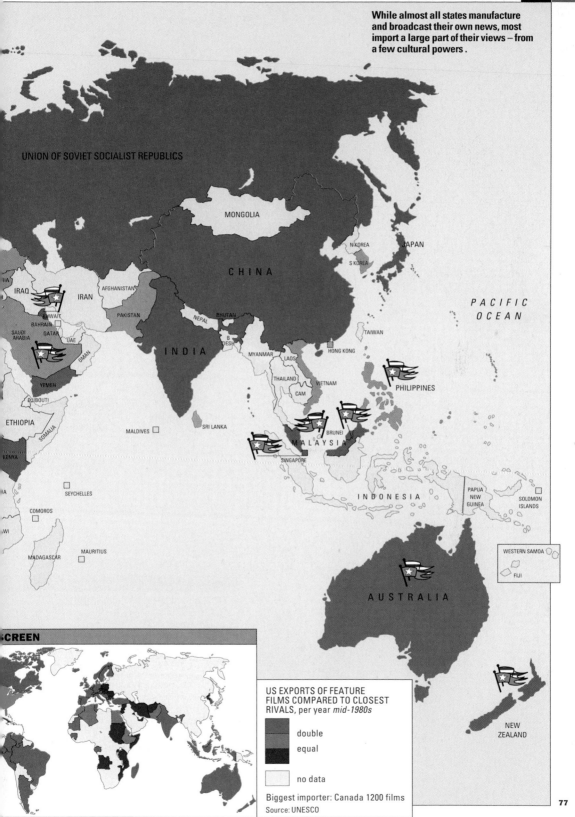

UNION OF SOVIET SOCIALIST REPUBLICS

MONGOLIA

N.KOREA

JAPAN

S KOREA

CHINA

PACIFIC
OCEAN

IRAQ

IRAN

AFGHANISTAN

KUWAIT

BAHRAIN

PAKISTAN

NEPAL

BHUTAN

TAIWAN

SAUDI
ARABIA

QATAR

UAE

B
DESH

INDIA

MYANMAR

HONG KONG

OMAN

YEMEN

LAOS

DJIBOUTI

THAILAND

VIETNAM

ETHIOPIA

CAM

PHILIPPINES

SOMALIA

SRI LANKA

KENYA

MALDIVES

BRUNEI

MALAYSIA

SINGAPORE

SEYCHELLES

COMOROS

INDONESIA

PAPUA
NEW
GUINEA

SOLOMON
ISLANDS

MADAGASCAR

MAURITIUS

WESTERN SAMOA

FIJI

AUSTRALIA

NEW
ZEALAND

SCREEN

US EXPORTS OF FEATURE FILMS COMPARED TO CLOSEST RIVALS, per year *mid-1980s*

double

equal

no data

Biggest importer: Canada 1200 films

Source: UNESCO

77

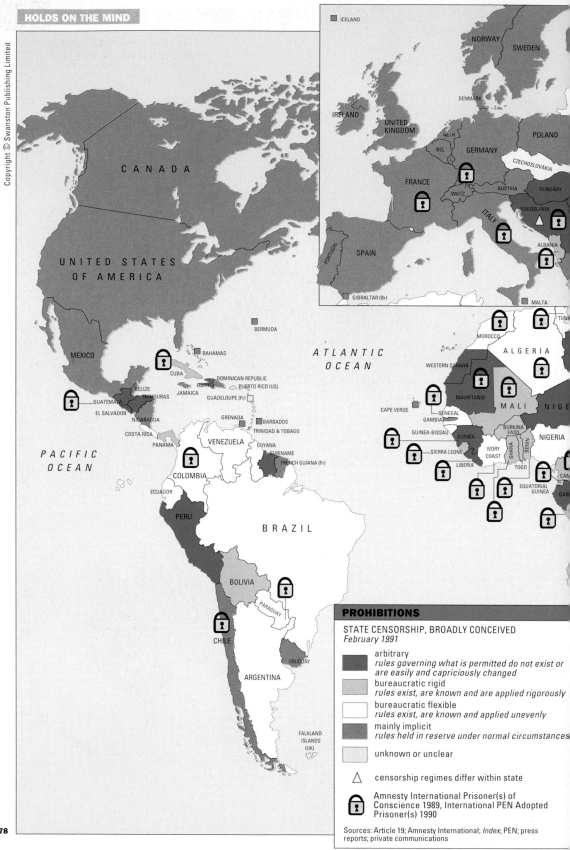

ICELAND

NORWAY
SWEDEN
DENMARK
IRELAND
UNITED
KINGDOM
NETH.
BEL.
GERMANY
POLAND
CZECHOSLOVAKIA
FRANCE
AUSTRIA
HUNGARY
SWITZ.
YUGOSLAVIA
ITALY
PORTUGAL
SPAIN
ALBANIA
GIBRALTAR (Br)
MALTA

C A N A D A

UNITED STATES
OF AMERICA

BERMUDA

ATLANTIC
OCEAN

TUN
MOROCCO
ALGERIA
WESTERN SAHARA
MAURITANIA
MALI
NIGE
CAPE VERDE
SENEGAL
GAMBIA
BURKINA
GUINEA-BISSAU
FASO
BENIN
NIGERIA
GUINEA
IVORY
SIERRA LEONE
COAST
GHANA
TOGO
LIBERIA
CAM
EQUATORIAL
GUINEA
GAB

MEXICO
BAHAMAS
CUBA
DOMINICAN REPUBLIC
HAITI
PUERTO RICO (US)
BELIZE
JAMAICA
HONDURAS
GUADELOUPE (Fr)
GUATEMALA
EL SALVADOR
GRENADA
NICARAGUA
BARBADOS
COSTA RICA
TRINIDAD & TOBAGO
VENEZUELA
PANAMA
GUYANA
SURINAME
COLOMBIA
FRENCH GUIANA (Fr)

PACIFIC
OCEAN

ECUADOR

PERU

B R A Z I L

BOLIVIA

PARAGUAY

CHILE

URUGUAY

ARGENTINA

FALKLAND
ISLANDS
(UK)

PROHIBITIONS

STATE CENSORSHIP, BROADLY CONCEIVED
February 1991

arbitrary
*rules governing what is permitted do not exist or
are easily and capriciously changed*

bureaucratic rigid
rules exist, are known and are applied rigorously

bureaucratic flexible
rules exist, are known and applied unevenly

mainly implicit
rules held in reserve under normal circumstances

unknown or unclear

△ censorship regimes differ within state

🔒 Amnesty International Prisoner(s) of
Conscience 1989, International PEN Adopted
Prisoner(s) 1990

Sources: Article 19; Amnesty International; *Index*; PEN; press
reports; private communications

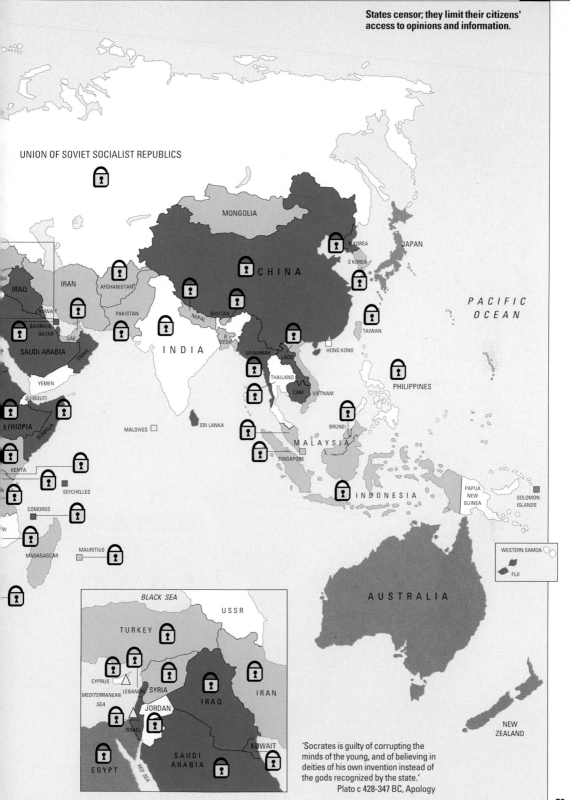

States censor; they limit their citizens' access to opinions and information.

UNION OF SOVIET SOCIALIST REPUBLICS

MONGOLIA

CHINA

N.KOREA

JAPAN

S.KOREA

PACIFIC OCEAN

IRAN

AFGHANISTAN

IRAQ

KUWAIT

BAHRAIN
QATAR

UAE

SAUDI ARABIA

OMAN

PAKISTAN

NEPAL

BHUTAN

B.
DESH

INDIA

TAIWAN

HONG KONG

MYANMAR

LAOS

THAILAND

CAM

VIETNAM

PHILIPPINES

YEMEN

DJIBOUTI

ETHIOPIA

SOMALIA

SRI LANKA

MALDIVES

BRUNEI

KENYA

SEYCHELLES

MALAYSIA

SINGAPORE

COMOROS

INDONESIA

PAPUA
NEW
GUINEA

SOLOMON
ISLANDS

MAURITIUS

MADAGASCAR

WESTERN SAMOA

FIJI

AUSTRALIA

BLACK SEA

USSR

TURKEY

CYPRUS

LEBANON

MEDITERRANEAN
SEA

SYRIA

IRAQ

IRAN

JORDAN

ISRAEL

KUWAIT

EGYPT

RED SEA

SAUDI
ARABIA

NEW
ZEALAND

'Socrates is guilty of corrupting the
minds of the young, and of believing in
deities of his own invention instead of
the gods recognized by the state.'
Plato c 428-347 BC, Apology

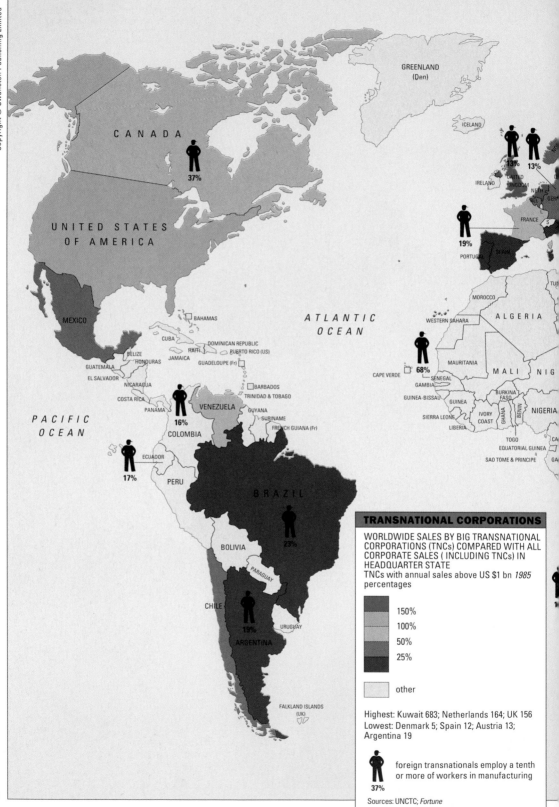

GREENLAND
(Den)

ICELAND

C A N A D A

37%

UNITED STATES
OF AMERICA

IRELAND

UNITED
KINGDOM

13% **13%**

NETH
BEL
GER

FRANCE

19%

PORTUGAL

SPAIN

MEXICO

BAHAMAS

CUBA

BELIZE
HONDURAS
JAMAICA

DOMINICAN REPUBLIC
PUERTO RICO (US)

GUADELOUPE (Fr)

A T L A N T I C
O C E A N

MOROCCO

WESTERN SAHARA

ALGERIA

TUN

GUATEMALA

EL SALVADOR

NICARAGUA

COSTA RICA

PANAMA

BARBADOS

TRINIDAD & TOBAGO

VENEZUELA

16%

COLOMBIA

GUYANA

SURINAME

FRENCH GUIANA (Fr)

CAPE VERDE

68%

SENEGAL

GAMBIA

GUINEA-BISSAU

MAURITANIA

GUINEA

SIERRA LEONE

LIBERIA

IVORY
COAST

M A L I

BURKINA
FASO

GHANA

BENIN

TOGO

N I G

NIGERIA

CA

PACIFIC
OCEAN

17%

ECUADOR

PERU

B R A Z I L

23%

BOLIVIA

PARAGUAY

EQUATORIAL GUINEA
SAO TOME & PRINCIPE

GA

CHILE

19%

ARGENTINA

URUGUAY

FALKLAND ISLANDS
(UK)

TRANSNATIONAL CORPORATIONS

WORLDWIDE SALES BY BIG TRANSNATIONAL
CORPORATIONS (TNCs) COMPARED WITH ALL
CORPORATE SALES (INCLUDING TNCs) IN
HEADQUARTER STATE
TNCs with annual sales above US $1 bn *1985*
percentages

- 150%
- 100%
- 50%
- 25%

other

Highest: Kuwait 683; Netherlands 164; UK 156
Lowest: Denmark 5; Spain 12; Austria 13;
Argentina 19

37% foreign transnationals employ a tenth
or more of workers in manufacturing

Sources: UNCTC; *Fortune*

Six hundred transnational corporations generate half the world's industrial output, a quarter of all physical goods and a fifth of all income. The smallest has an income larger than Mozambique; the largest an income greater than South Africa.

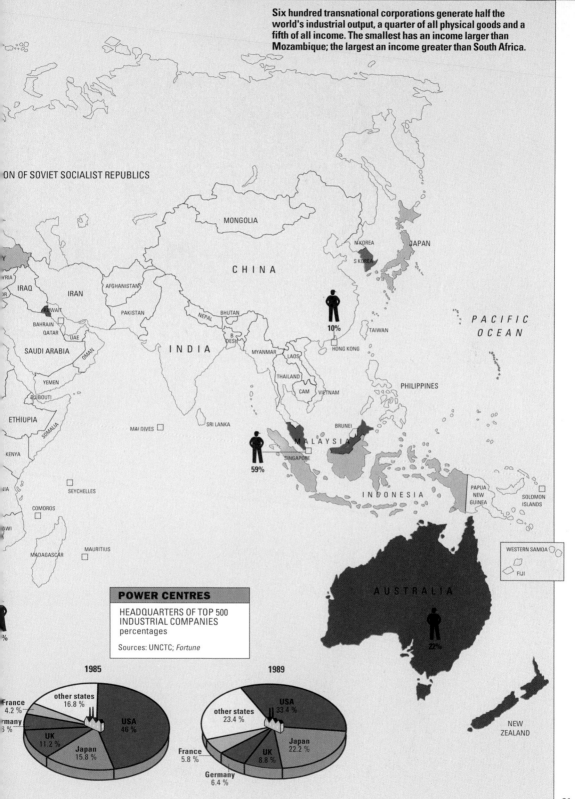

ON OF SOVIET SOCIALIST REPUBLICS

MONGOLIA

N.KOREA

JAPAN

S.KOREA

CHINA

10%

TAIWAN

HONG KONG

PACIFIC
OCEAN

SYRIA
IRAQ
IRAN
AFGHANISTAN
KUWAIT
BAHRAIN
QATAR
UAE
SAUDI ARABIA
OMAN
PAKISTAN
NEPAL
BHUTAN
B'DESH
INDIA
MYANMAR
LAOS
YEMEN
THAILAND
DJIBOUTI
CAM
VIETNAM
PHILIPPINES

ETHIUPIA
SOMALIA
SRI LANKA
MALDIVES

KENYA
MALAYSIA
SINGAPORE
59%

BRUNEI

SEYCHELLES
INDONESIA
PAPUA
NEW
GUINEA
SOLOMON
ISLANDS

COMOROS

MAURITIUS
MADAGASCAR

WESTERN SAMOA
FIJI

AUSTRALIA

POWER CENTRES

HEADQUARTERS OF TOP 500
INDUSTRIAL COMPANIES
percentages

Sources: UNCTC; *Fortune*

22%

NEW
ZEALAND

1985

France
4.2 %
Germany
6 %
other states
16.8 %
USA
46 %
UK
11.2 %
Japan
15.8 %

1989

other states
23.4 %
USA
33.4 %
France
5.8 %
Japan
22.2 %
UK
8.8 %
Germany
6.4 %

GREENLAND
(Den)

ICELAND

C A N A D A

NOR

IRELAND UNITED   DENMA
KINGDOM
NETH GERM
BEL
FRANCE
S
IT

U N I T E D   S T A T E S
O F   A M E R I C A

PORTUGAL SPAIN

MOROCCO

TUN

ATLANTIC
OCEAN

WESTERN SAHARA

ALGERIA

MEXICO

BAHAMAS

MAURITANIA

MALI NIG

CUBA
DOMINICAN REPUBLIC
BELIZE HAITI PUERTO RICO (US)
GUATEMALA HONDURAS JAMAICA
GUADELOUPE (Fr)
EL SALVADOR
NICARAGUA GRENADA BARBADOS
COSTA RICA TRINIDAD & TOBAGO
PANAMA

CAPE VERDE

SENEGAL
GAMBIA
GUINEA-BISSAU

BURKINA
GUINEA FASO

NIGERIA

VENEZUELA GUYANA
SURINAME
FRENCH GUIANA (Fr)
COLOMBIA

SIERRA LEONE IVORY GHANA BENIN
COAST
LIBERIA

TOGO
EQUATORIAL GUINEA CA
SAO TOME & PRINCIPE GA

ECUADOR

P A C I F I C
O C E A N

PERU

B R A Z I L

BOLIVIA

PARAGUAY

CHILE

URUGUAY

ARGENTINA

FALKLAND
ISLANDS
(UK)

AUCTIONED

MOTIVATIONS BEHIND PRIVATIZATION OF
STATE ASSETS *1990*

Primary

structural, *to enhance
international
competitiveness/ efficiency*

budgetary, *to limit state
subsidies/ losses*

internal political, *to broaden
a domestic political base*

external, *to raise foreign
funds/ avoid foreign pressure*

no privatization or
motivation mixed/ unclear

no data

Subsidiary

Sources: Privatization
International; Center
for Privatization; Kiker
press reports; private
communications

US $ 90 billion of state assets went private between 1988 and 1990. There is much more to come.

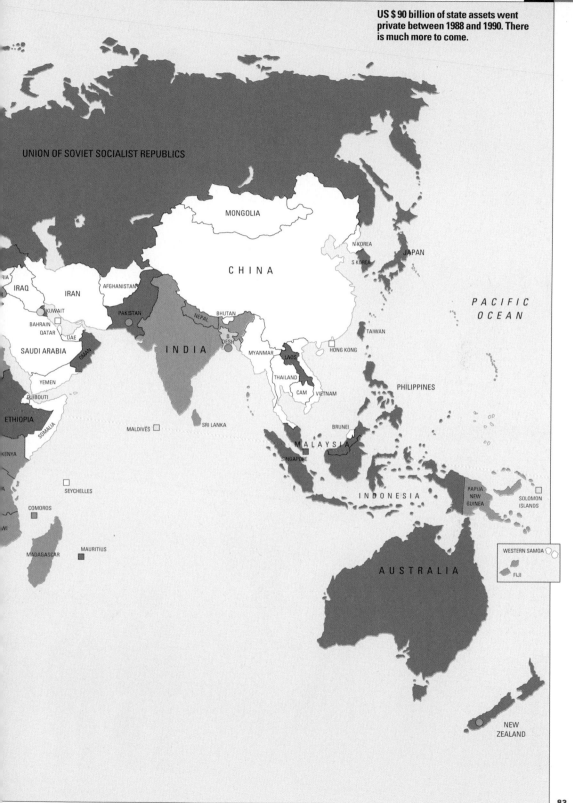

UNION OF SOVIET SOCIALIST REPUBLICS

MONGOLIA

N.KOREA

S.KOREA

JAPAN

CHINA

PACIFIC
OCEAN

RIA

IRAQ

IRAN

AFGHANISTAN

KUWAIT

BAHRAIN

QATAR

UAE

PAKISTAN

NEPAL

BHUTAN

TAIWAN

SAUDI ARABIA

OMAN

INDIA

B
DESH

MYANMAR

LAOS

HONG KONG

YEMEN

THAILAND

DJIBOUTI

CAM

VIETNAM

PHILIPPINES

ETHIOPIA

SOMALIA

MALDIVES

SRI LANKA

BRUNEI

KENYA

MALAYSIA

SINGAPORE

SEYCHELLES

INDONESIA

PAPUA
NEW
GUINEA

SOLOMON
ISLANDS

COMOROS

WESTERN SAMOA

MADAGASCAR

MAURITIUS

AUSTRALIA

FIJI

NEW
ZEALAND

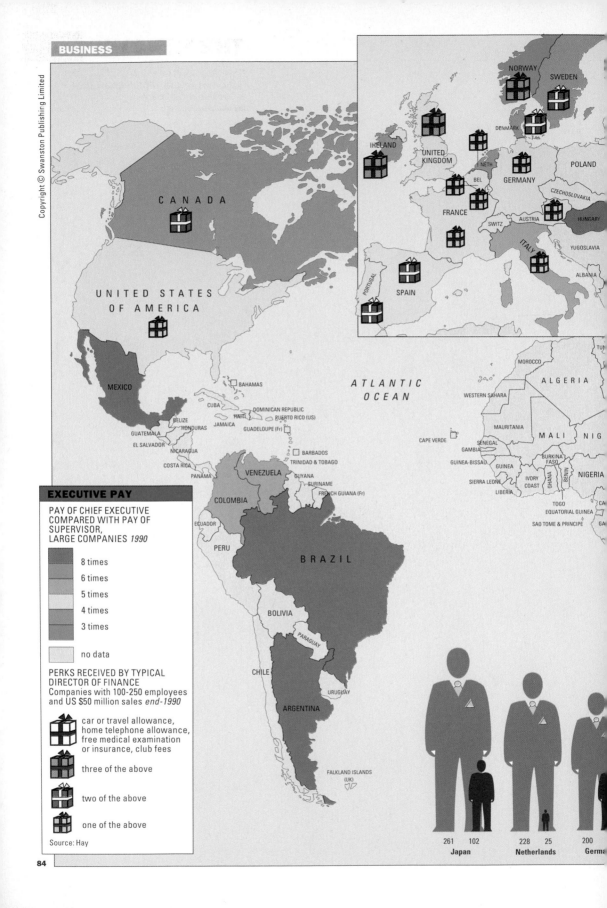

NORWAY
SWEDEN
DENMARK
IRELAND
UNITED KINGDOM
NETH
BEL
GERMANY
POLAND
CZECHOSLOVAKIA
FRANCE
AUSTRIA
HUNGARY
SWITZ
YUGOSLAVIA
ITALY
ALBANIA
PORTUGAL
SPAIN

C A N A D A

U N I T E D   S T A T E S
O F   A M E R I C A

MEXICO

BAHAMAS
CUBA
DOMINICAN REPUBLIC
HAITI
PUERTO RICO (US)
BELIZE
HONDURAS
JAMAICA
GUADELOUPE (Fr)
GUATEMALA
EL SALVADOR
NICARAGUA
COSTA RICA
PANAMA
BARBADOS
TRINIDAD & TOBAGO
VENEZUELA
GUYANA
SURINAME
FRENCH GUIANA (Fr)
COLOMBIA
ECUADOR
PERU
B R A Z I L
BOLIVIA
PARAGUAY
CHILE
URUGUAY
ARGENTINA
FALKLAND ISLANDS (UK)

A T L A N T I C
O C E A N

MOROCCO
WESTERN SAHARA
ALGERIA
MAURITANIA
M A L I
N I G
CAPE VERDE
SENEGAL
GAMBIA
GUINEA-BISSAU
GUINEA
BURKINA FASO
SIERRA LEONE
IVORY COAST
GHANA
BENIN
NIGERIA
LIBERIA
TOGO
EQUATORIAL GUINEA
SAO TOME & PRINCIPE
TUN
GA
CA

EXECUTIVE PAY

PAY OF CHIEF EXECUTIVE COMPARED WITH PAY OF SUPERVISOR, LARGE COMPANIES *1990*

- 8 times
- 6 times
- 5 times
- 4 times
- 3 times
- no data

PERKS RECEIVED BY TYPICAL DIRECTOR OF FINANCE
Companies with 100-250 employees and US $50 million sales *end-1990*

- car or travel allowance, home telephone allowance, free medical examination or insurance, club fees
- three of the above
- two of the above
- one of the above

Source: Hay

261   102
Japan

228   25
Netherlands

200
Germa

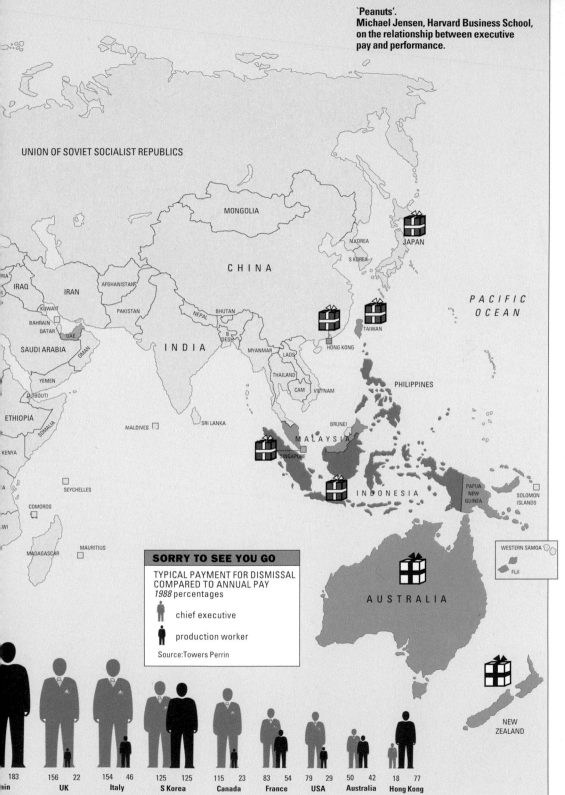

'Peanuts'.
Michael Jensen, Harvard Business School,
on the relationship between executive
pay and performance.

UNION OF SOVIET SOCIALIST REPUBLICS

MONGOLIA

N.KOREA

S KOREA

JAPAN

CHINA

PACIFIC
OCEAN

RIA

IRAQ

IRAN

AFGHANISTAN

KUWAIT

PAKISTAN

NEPAL   BHUTAN

BAHRAIN

QATAR

UAE

OMAN

SAUDI ARABIA

B
DESH

MYANMAR

TAIWAN

HONG KONG

INDIA

LAOS

YEMEN

THAILAND

DJIBOUTI

CAM   VIETNAM

PHILIPPINES

ETHIOPIA

SOMALIA

MALDIVES

SRI LANKA

KENYA

BRUNEI

MALAYSIA

SINGAPORE

SEYCHELLES

INDONESIA

PAPUA
NEW
GUINEA

SOLOMON
ISLANDS

COMOROS

WI

MAURITIUS

MADAGASCAR

WESTERN SAMOA

FIJI

AUSTRALIA

SORRY TO SEE YOU GO

TYPICAL PAYMENT FOR DISMISSAL
COMPARED TO ANNUAL PAY
1988 percentages

chief executive

production worker

Source:Towers Perrin

NEW
ZEALAND

ain	UK	Italy	S Korea	Canada	France	USA	Australia	Hong Kong
183	156 22	154 46	125 125	115 23	83 54	79 29	50 42	18 77

NORWAY

SWEDE

IRELAND UNITED KINGDOM

DENMARK

NETH

Channel Islands

BEL

GERMANY

FRANCE

SWITZ AUSTRIA

LIECH

ANDORRA

ITALY

PORTUGAL SPAIN

GIBRALTAR (Br)

Palerm

TUN

MOROCCO

ALGERIA

WESTERN SAHARA

MAURITANIA

MALI NIG

CAPE VERDE

SENEGAL

GAMBIA

GUINEA-BISSAU GUINEA

BURKINA FASO

NIGERIA

IVORY COAST

BENIN

GHANA

SIERRA LEONE

LIBERIA

TOGO

CA

EQUATORIAL GUINEA

GA

SAO TOME & PRINCIPE

CANADA

Vancouver

Montreal

Toronto

New York

UNITED STATES OF AMERICA

Los Angeles

Houston

MEXICO

Miami

BAHAMAS

Money laundering pumps $800 million a year into South Florida's local economy

ATLANTIC OCEAN

CUBA

BELIZE

CAYMAN IS

JAMAICA

HAITI

DOMINICAN REPUBLIC

PUERTO RICO (US)

GUADELOUPE (Fr)

GUATEMALA

HONDURAS

EL SALVADOR

NICARAGUA

COSTA RICA

PANAMA

Sta. Marta

Barranquilla

Cartagena

Caracas

VENEZUELA

BARBADOS

TRINIDAD & TOBAGO

Key financial and diplomatic interchange between the Sicilian and Colombian drug barons

GUYANA

SURINAME

FRENCH GUIANA (Fr)

Medellín

Bogotá

PACIFIC OCEAN

Buenaventura

Cali

COLOMBIA

ECUADOR

PERU

BRAZIL

ATLANTIC OCEAN

BOLIVIA

PARAGUAY

CHILE

URUGUAY

ARGENTINA

FALKLAND ISLANDS (UK)

Snow Belt

VENEZUELA

COLOMBIA

ECUADOR

PERU

BRAZIL

BOLIVIA

HEROIN AND COCAINE

MAJOR PRODUCERS AND MARKETS *early 1990s*

producers

major producing areas

major markets

other

All producer countries are important secondary markets

drug-money laundering centres end-1980s

cartel headquarters:

major   minor

Sources: Ardila; US Drug Enforcement Agency; Hawkes; press reports

US $500 billion is spent on prohibited drugs worldwide which generate gross profits of over $400 billion. Half of that comes from heroin and cocaine; three-quarters gets laundered.

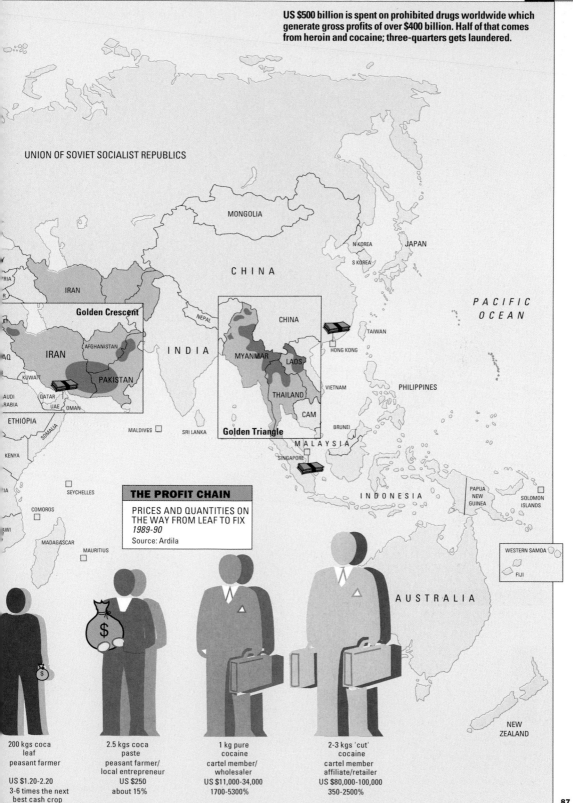

UNION OF SOVIET SOCIALIST REPUBLICS

MONGOLIA

N KOREA

S KOREA

JAPAN

CHINA

PACIFIC OCEAN

IRAN

Golden Crescent

NEPAL

CHINA

TAIWAN

AFGHANISTAN

INDIA

MYANMAR

LAOS

HONG KONG

IRAN

KUWAIT

PAKISTAN

VIETNAM

PHILIPPINES

QATAR

THAILAND

UAE OMAN

SAUDI ARABIA

CAM

BRUNEI

ETHIOPIA

MALDIVES

SRI LANKA

Golden Triangle

MALAYSIA

KENYA

SINGAPORE

INDONESIA

PAPUA NEW GUINEA

SOLOMON ISLANDS

SEYCHELLES

COMOROS

WESTERN SAMOA

FIJI

MADAGASCAR

MAURITIUS

AUSTRALIA

THE PROFIT CHAIN

PRICES AND QUANTITIES ON THE WAY FROM LEAF TO FIX
1989-90
Source: Ardila

NEW ZEALAND

200 kgs coca leaf
peasant farmer

US $1.20-2.20
3-6 times the next best cash crop

2.5 kgs coca paste
peasant farmer/ local entrepreneur
US $250
about 15%

1 kg pure cocaine
cartel member/ wholesaler
US $11,000-34,000
1700-5300%

2-3 kgs 'cut' cocaine
cartel member affiliate/retailer
US $80,000-100,000
350-2500%

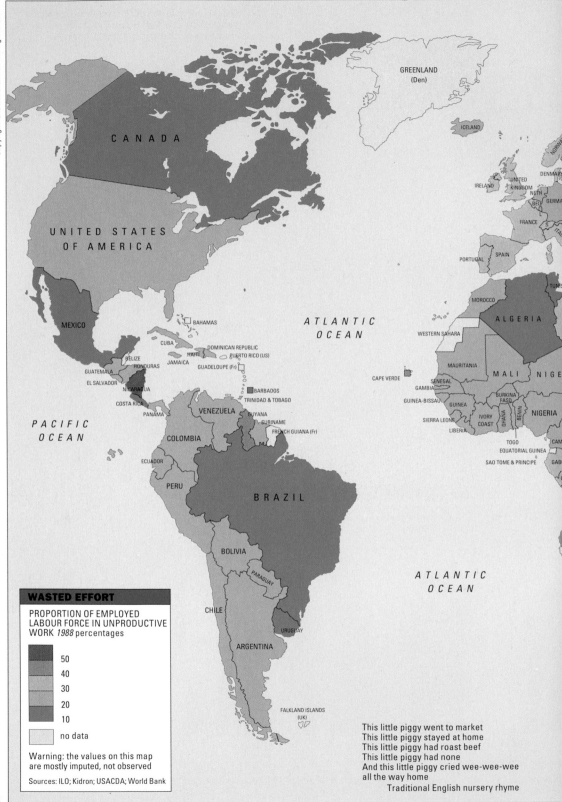

GREENLAND
(Den)

ICELAND

NORWAY

DENMARK

IRELAND
UNITED
KINGDOM
NETH
GERMA

BEL

FRANCE
S
ITAL

PORTUGAL
SPAIN

C A N A D A

U N I T E D   S T A T E S
O F   A M E R I C A

ATLANTIC
OCEAN

TUNI

MOROCCO

ALGERIA

WESTERN SAHARA

MEXICO

BAHAMAS

CUBA
DOMINICAN REPUBLIC
HAITI
PUERTO RICO (US)
JAMAICA
GUADELOUPE (Fr)

BELIZE
HONDURAS
GUATEMALA
EL SALVADOR
NICARAGUA
COSTA RICA
PANAMA

BARBADOS
TRINIDAD & TOBAGO

VENEZUELA
GUYANA
SURINAME
FRENCH GUIANA (Fr)

CAPE VERDE

MAURITANIA

MALI
NIGE

GAMBIA
SENEGAL

GUINEA-BISSAU
GUINEA

SIERRA LEONE
IVORY
COAST

LIBERIA

BURKINA
FASO

BENIN
GHANA

TOGO

NIGERIA

CAM

EQUATORIAL GUINEA
SAO TOME & PRINCIPE

GAB

P A C I F I C
O C E A N

COLOMBIA

ECUADOR

PERU

B R A Z I L

ATLANTIC
OCEAN

BOLIVIA

PARAGUAY

CHILE

URUGUAY

ARGENTINA

FALKLAND ISLANDS
(UK)

WASTED EFFORT

PROPORTION OF EMPLOYED
LABOUR FORCE IN UNPRODUCTIVE
WORK *1988* percentages

- 50
- 40
- 30
- 20
- 10

no data

Warning: the values on this map
are mostly imputed, not observed

Sources: ILO; Kidron; USACDA; World Bank

This little piggy went to market
This little piggy stayed at home
This little piggy had roast beef
This little piggy had none
And this little piggy cried wee-wee-wee
all the way home
Traditional English nursery rhyme

One in six workers – 533 million people – toil unproductively.

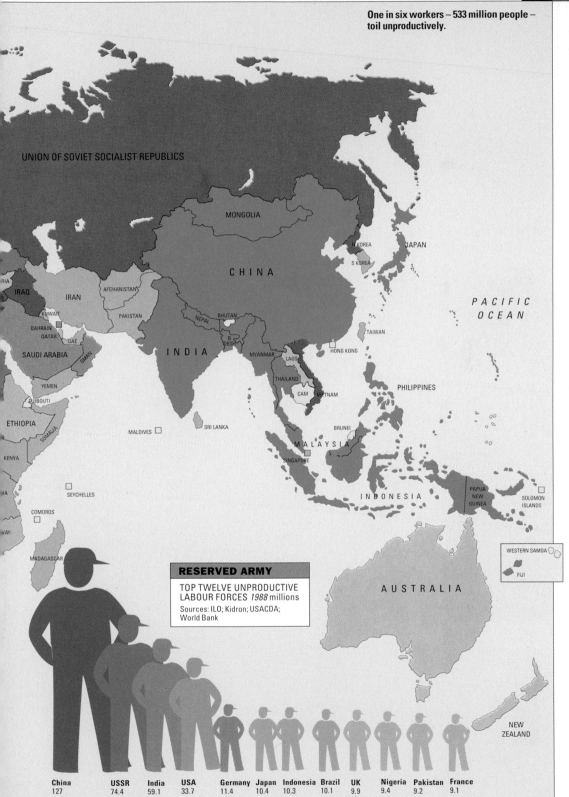

UNION OF SOVIET SOCIALIST REPUBLICS

MONGOLIA

N KOREA

JAPAN

S KOREA

CHINA

PACIFIC OCEAN

RIA

IRAQ

KUWAIT

IRAN

AFGHANISTAN

BAHRAIN

QATAR

UAE

OMAN

PAKISTAN

NEPAL

BHUTAN

B DESH

TAIWAN

SAUDI ARABIA

YEMEN

DJIBOUTI

INDIA

MYANMAR

LAOS

HONG KONG

ETHIOPIA

SOMALIA

MALDIVES

SRI LANKA

THAILAND

CAM

VIETNAM

PHILIPPINES

KENYA

BRUNEI

MA

SEYCHELLES

MALAYSIA

SINGAPORE

COMOROS

WI

INDONESIA

PAPUA NEW GUINEA

SOLOMON ISLANDS

MADAGASCAR

WESTERN SAMOA

FIJI

AUSTRALIA

RESERVED ARMY

TOP TWELVE UNPRODUCTIVE
LABOUR FORCES *1988* millions

Sources: ILO; Kidron; USACDA;
World Bank

NEW ZEALAND

China	USSR	India	USA	Germany	Japan	Indonesia	Brazil	UK	Nigeria	Pakistan	France
127	74.4	59.1	33.7	11.4	10.4	10.3	10.1	9.9	9.4	9.2	9.1

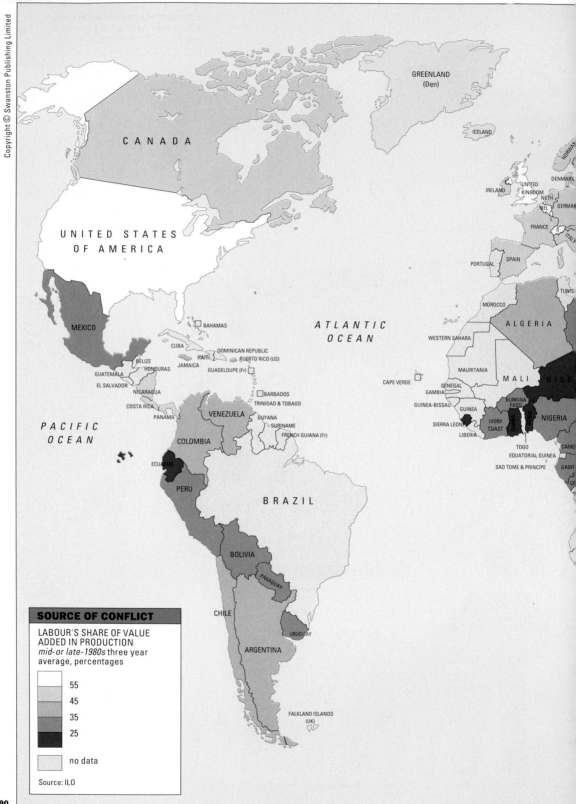

GREENLAND
(Den)

ICELAND

CANADA

UNITED STATES
OF AMERICA

ATLANTIC
OCEAN

BAHAMAS

CUBA
DOMINICAN REPUBLIC
HAITI   PUERTO RICO (US)
JAMAICA
GUADELOUPE (Fr)

MEXICO

BELIZE
HONDURAS
GUATEMALA
EL SALVADOR
NICARAGUA
COSTA RICA
PANAMA

BARBADOS
TRINIDAD & TOBAGO

VENEZUELA
GUYANA
SURINAME
FRENCH GUIANA (Fr)

COLOMBIA

PACIFIC
OCEAN

ECUADOR

PERU

BRAZIL

BOLIVIA

PARAGUAY

CHILE

URUGUAY

ARGENTINA

FALKLAND ISLANDS
(UK)

NORWAY
DENMARK
UNITED
IRELAND   KINGDOM
NETH
BEL   GERMA
FRANCE   S
ITALY

PORTUGAL   SPAIN

TUNIS

MOROCCO

ALGERIA

WESTERN SAHARA

MAURITANIA
MALI   NIGE
CAPE VERDE
SENEGAL
GAMBIA   BURKINA
GUINEA-BISSAU   FASO
GUINEA   NIGERIA
SIERRA LEONE   IVORY
COAST
LIBERIA
TOGO   CAME
EQUATORIAL GUINEA
SAO TOME & PRINCIPE   GABO
CO

SOURCE OF CONFLICT

LABOUR'S SHARE OF VALUE
ADDED IN PRODUCTION
mid- or late-1980s three year
average, percentages

	55
	45
	35
	25
	no data

Source: ILO

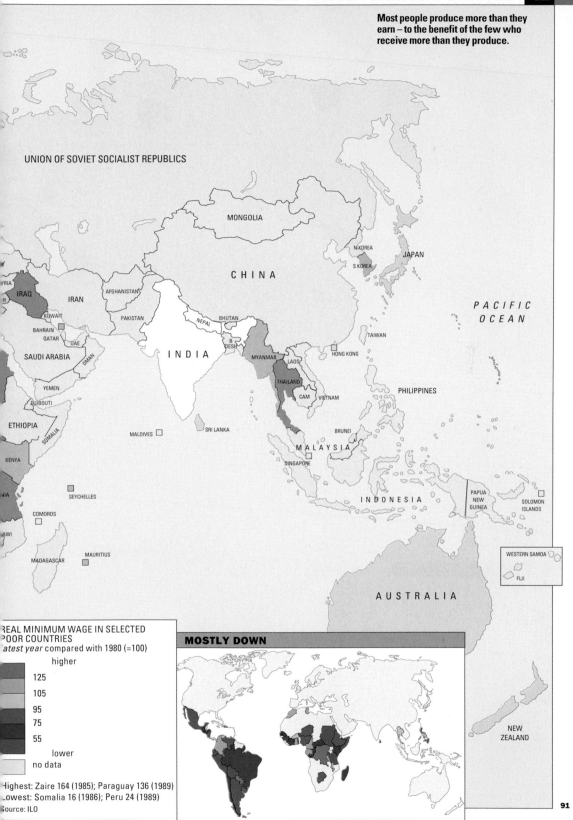

Most people produce more than they earn – to the benefit of the few who receive more than they produce.

UNION OF SOVIET SOCIALIST REPUBLICS

MONGOLIA

N.KOREA

JAPAN

S.KOREA

CHINA

PACIFIC OCEAN

SYRIA

IRAQ

IRAN

AFGHANISTAN

KUWAIT

BAHRAIN

QATAR

UAE

SAUDI ARABIA

OMAN

YEMEN

DJIBOUTI

ETHIOPIA

SOMALIA

KENYA

PAKISTAN

NEPAL

BHUTAN

B DESH

INDIA

MYANMAR

LAOS

THAILAND

CAM

VIETNAM

TAIWAN

HONG KONG

PHILIPPINES

BRUNEI

MALDIVES

SRI LANKA

MALAYSIA

SINGAPORE

INDONESIA

PAPUA NEW GUINEA

SOLOMON ISLANDS

SEYCHELLES

COMOROS

AWI

MADAGASCAR

MAURITIUS

WESTERN SAMOA

FIJI

AUSTRALIA

REAL MINIMUM WAGE IN SELECTED POOR COUNTRIES
latest year compared with 1980 (=100)

higher

125

105

95

75

55

lower

no data

MOSTLY DOWN

NEW ZEALAND

Highest: Zaire 164 (1985); Paraguay 136 (1989)
Lowest: Somalia 16 (1986); Peru 24 (1989)
Source: ILO

THE PRESENCE OF THE PRESENT

SHARE OF MINING, MANUFACTURING AND UTILITIES IN TOTAL EMPLOYMENT *late-1980s or most recent year* percentages

- 30
- 20
- 10

no data

Source: ILO

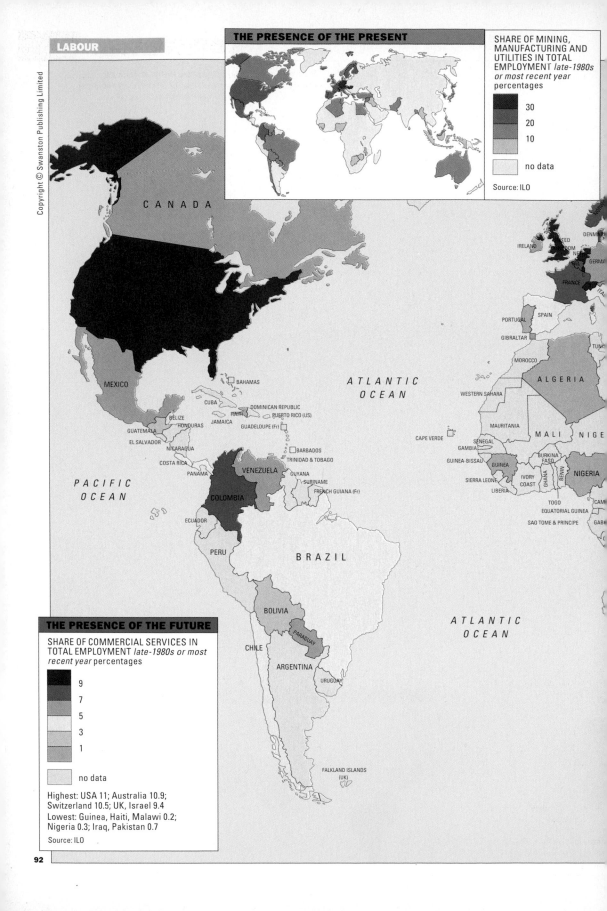

C A N A D A

DENMARK

IRELAND

UNITED KINGDOM

NETHERLANDS

GERMA

FRANCE

ITAL

PORTUGAL

SPAIN

GIBRALTAR

MEXICO

TUNI

MOROCCO

WESTERN SAHARA

ALGERIA

A T L A N T I C
O C E A N

BAHAMAS

CUBA

DOMINICAN REPUBLIC

HAITI

PUERTO RICO (US)

BELIZE

JAMAICA

GUADELOUPE (Fr)

GUATEMALA

HONDURAS

EL SALVADOR

NICARAGUA

COSTA RICA

PANAMA

BARBADOS

TRINIDAD & TOBAGO

VENEZUELA

GUYANA

CAPE VERDE

MAURITANIA

MALI

NIGE

SENEGAL

GAMBIA

GUINEA-BISSAU

GUINEA

BURKINA FASO

SIERRA LEONE

IVORY COAST

GHANA

BENIN

NIGERIA

LIBERIA

SURINAME

FRENCH GUIANA (Fr)

COLOMBIA

TOGO

EQUATORIAL GUINEA

CAM

ECUADOR

SAO TOME & PRINCIPE

GAB

P A C I F I C
O C E A N

PERU

B R A Z I L

A T L A N T I C
O C E A N

BOLIVIA

PARAGUAY

CHILE

ARGENTINA

URUGUAY

FALKLAND ISLANDS (UK)

THE PRESENCE OF THE FUTURE

SHARE OF COMMERCIAL SERVICES IN TOTAL EMPLOYMENT *late-1980s or most recent year* percentages

- 9
- 7
- 5
- 3
- 1

no data

Highest: USA 11; Australia 10.9; Switzerland 10.5; UK, Israel 9.4
Lowest: Guinea, Haiti, Malawi 0.2; Nigeria 0.3; Iraq, Pakistan 0.7

Source: ILO

Most workers still eke out a living in agriculture, many toil in industry and a few work in commercial services – the leading edge of the modern market economy.

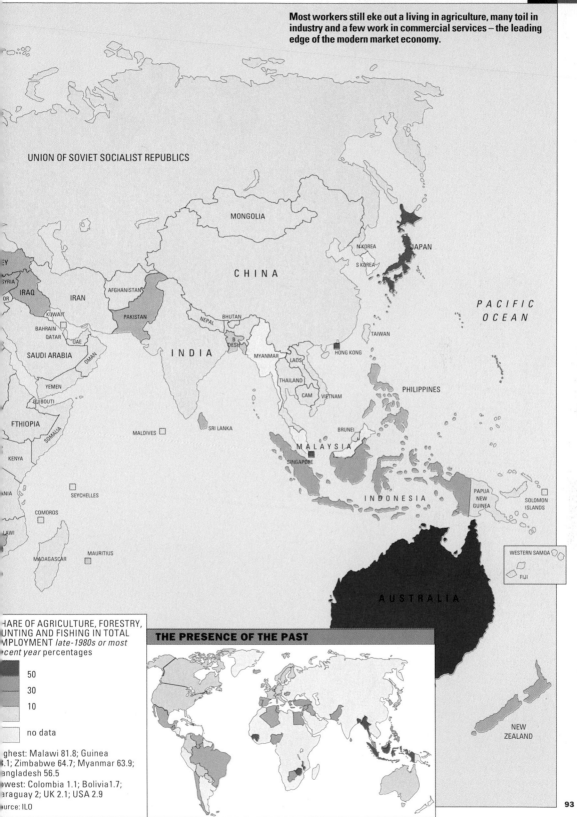

UNION OF SOVIET SOCIALIST REPUBLICS

MONGOLIA

N.KOREA
S.KOREA
JAPAN

CHINA

PACIFIC OCEAN

EY
SYRIA
IRAQ
IRAN
AFGHANISTAN
KUWAIT
BAHRAIN
QATAR
UAE
SAUDI ARABIA
OMAN
YEMEN
DJIBOUTI
PAKISTAN
NEPAL
BHUTAN
B
DESH
MYANMAR
LAOS
HONG KONG
TAIWAN

INDIA

THAILAND
CAM
VIETNAM

PHILIPPINES

FTHIOPIA
SOMALIA
KENYA

MALDIVES

SRI LANKA

BRUNEI

MALAYSIA
SINGAPORE

SEYCHELLES

INDONESIA

PAPUA
NEW
GUINEA

SOLOMON
ISLANDS

COMOROS

ANIA

WESTERN SAMOA

MADAGASCAR
MAURITIUS
LAWI

FIJI

AUSTRALIA

SHARE OF AGRICULTURE, FORESTRY, HUNTING AND FISHING IN TOTAL EMPLOYMENT *late-1980s or most recent year* percentages

50
30
10

no data

ghest: Malawi 81.8; Guinea
.1; Zimbabwe 64.7; Myanmar 63.9;
angladesh 56.5
owest: Colombia 1.1; Bolivia1.7;
araguay 2; UK 2.1; USA 2.9
urce: ILO

THE PRESENCE OF THE PAST

NEW
ZEALAND

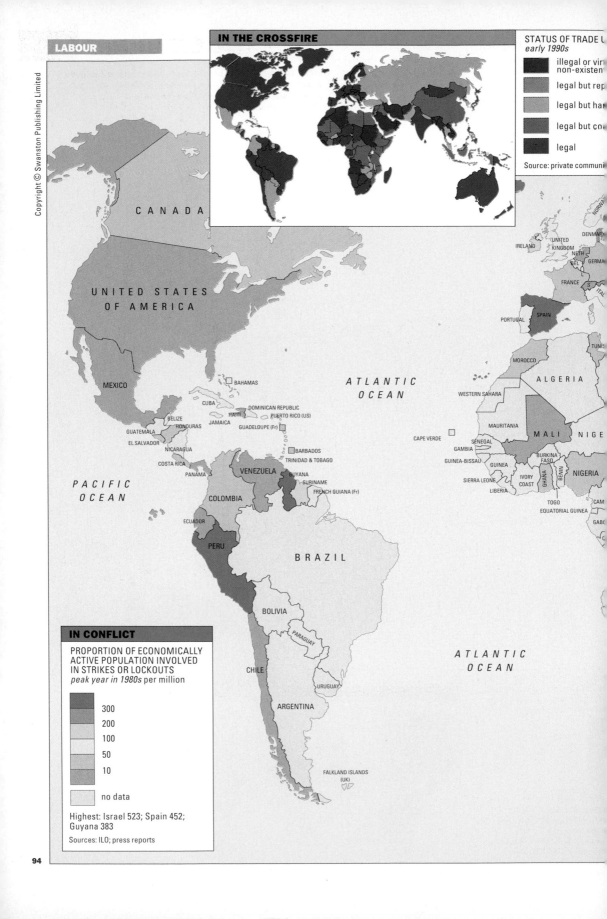

LABOUR

IN THE CROSSFIRE

STATUS OF TRADE U...
early 1990s

illegal or vir...
non-existen...

legal but rep...

legal but ha...

legal but co...

legal

Source: private communi...

CANADA

UNITED STATES
OF AMERICA

MEXICO

BAHAMAS

CUBA
DOMINICAN REPUBLIC
HAITI
PUERTO RICO (US)
BELIZE
HONDURAS
GUATEMALA
JAMAICA
GUADELOUPE (Fr)
EL SALVADOR
NICARAGUA
BARBADOS
COSTA RICA
TRINIDAD & TOBAGO
PANAMA
VENEZUELA
GUYANA
SURINAME
COLOMBIA
FRENCH GUIANA (Fr)

ECUADOR

PERU

BRAZIL

BOLIVIA

PARAGUAY

CHILE

URUGUAY

ARGENTINA

*ATLANTIC
OCEAN*

*PACIFIC
OCEAN*

*ATLANTIC
OCEAN*

FALKLAND ISLANDS
(UK)

NORWAY
DENMARK
IRELAND
UNITED
KINGDOM
NETH
BEL
GERMA
FRANCE
S
ITAL
PORTUGAL
SPAIN
TUNIS
MOROCCO
ALGERIA
WESTERN SAHARA
CAPE VERDE
MAURITANIA
MALI
NIGE
SENEGAL
GAMBIA
BURKINA
FASO
GUINEA-BISSAU
GUINEA
NIGERIA
SIERRA LEONE
IVORY
COAST
GHANA
BENIN
LIBERIA
TOGO
CAM
EQUATORIAL GUINEA
GABO

IN CONFLICT

PROPORTION OF ECONOMICALLY
ACTIVE POPULATION INVOLVED
IN STRIKES OR LOCKOUTS
peak year in 1980s per million

300
200
100
50
10

no data

Highest: Israel 523; Spain 452;
Guyana 383

Sources: ILO; press reports

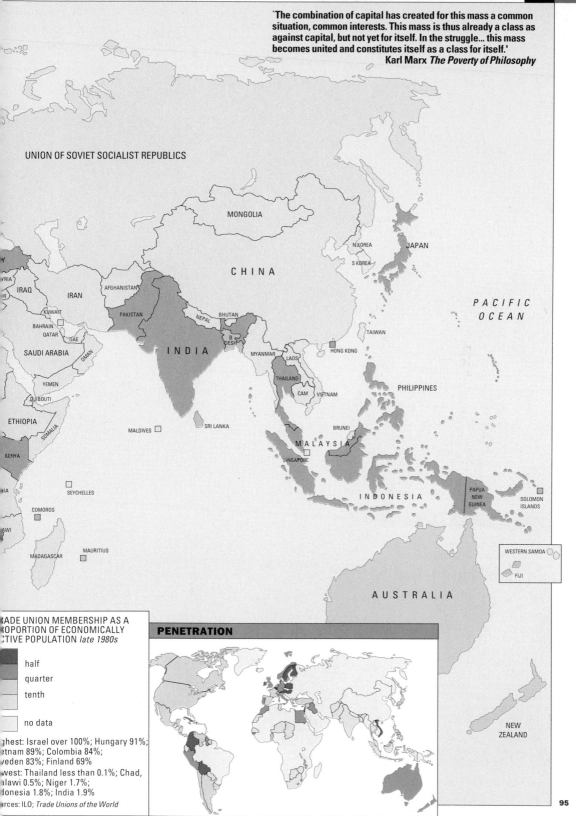

`The combination of capital has created for this mass a common situation, common interests. This mass is thus already a class as against capital, but not yet for itself. In the struggle... this mass becomes united and constitutes itself as a class for itself.'
Karl Marx *The Poverty of Philosophy*

UNION OF SOVIET SOCIALIST REPUBLICS

MONGOLIA

N.KOREA
JAPAN
S KOREA

CHINA

PACIFIC OCEAN

AFGHANISTAN

IRAQ
IRAN

KUWAIT
BAHRAIN
QATAR
UAE

PAKISTAN

NEPAL   BHUTAN

B DESH

TAIWAN

SAUDI ARABIA
OMAN

INDIA

MYANMAR

HONG KONG

LAOS

YEMEN

DJIBOUTI

THAILAND

CAM   VIETNAM

PHILIPPINES

ETHIOPIA

SOMALIA

MALDIVES

SRI LANKA

BRUNEI

KENYA

MALAYSIA

SINGAPORE

SEYCHELLES

INDONESIA

PAPUA NEW GUINEA

SOLOMON ISLANDS

COMOROS

MADAGASCAR
MAURITIUS

WESTERN SAMOA

FIJI

AUSTRALIA

PENETRATION

NEW ZEALAND

ADE UNION MEMBERSHIP AS A
ROPORTION OF ECONOMICALLY
CTIVE POPULATION *late 1980s*

half

quarter

tenth

no data

ghest: Israel over 100%; Hungary 91%;
etnam 89%; Colombia 84%;
veden 83%; Finland 69%
west: Thailand less than 0.1%; Chad,
alawi 0.5%; Niger 1.7%;
donesia 1.8%; India 1.9%
rces: ILO; *Trade Unions of the World*

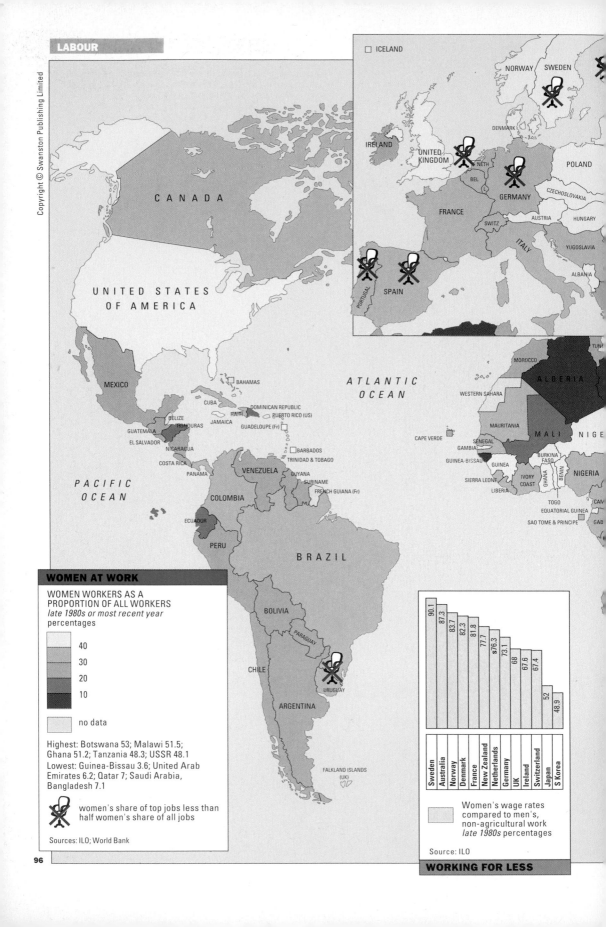

ICELAND

NORWAY   SWEDEN

DENMARK

IRELAND

UNITED
KINGDOM   NETH.   POLAND
          BEL.
                   GERMANY   CZECHOSLOVAKIA
FRANCE   AUSTRIA   HUNGARY
          SWITZ.   YUGOSLAVIA
                              ITALY
                                         ALBANIA
PORTUGAL
          SPAIN

CANADA

UNITED STATES
OF AMERICA

ATLANTIC
OCEAN

MOROCCO   TUNI

ALGERIA

BAHAMAS   WESTERN SAHARA
MEXICO
              CUBA   MAURITANIA   MALI   NIGE
                    DOMINICAN REPUBLIC
              HAITI PUERTO RICO (US)   CAPE VERDE
BELIZE JAMAICA   SENEGAL
GUATEMALA HONDURAS GUADELOUPE (Fr)   GAMBIA   BURKINA
EL SALVADOR   GUINEA-BISSAU GUINEA FASO
  NICARAGUA   BARBADOS   IVORY GHANA BENIN NIGERIA
COSTA RICA   TRINIDAD & TOBAGO   SIERRA LEONE   COAST
PACIFIC   PANAMA VENEZUELA GUYANA   LIBERIA
OCEAN   SURINAME   TOGO
        COLOMBIA   FRENCH GUIANA (Fr)   EQUATORIAL GUINEA   CAM
                                                          SAO TOME & PRINCIPE   GAB
  ECUADOR

PERU

BRAZIL

WOMEN AT WORK

WOMEN WORKERS AS A
PROPORTION OF ALL WORKERS
late 1980s or most recent year
percentages

BOLIVIA

PARAGUAY

CHILE

URUGUAY

ARGENTINA

40

30

20

10

no data

Highest: Botswana 53; Malawi 51.5;
Ghana 51.2; Tanzania 48.3; USSR 48.1
Lowest: Guinea-Bissau 3.6; United Arab
Emirates 6.2; Qatar 7; Saudi Arabia,
Bangladesh 7.1

women's share of top jobs less than
half women's share of all jobs

Sources: ILO; World Bank

FALKLAND ISLANDS
(UK)

	Sweden	Australia	Norway	Denmark	France	New Zealand	Netherlands	Germany	UK	Ireland	Switzerland	Japan	S Korea
	90.1	87.3	83.7	82.3	81.8	77.7	s76.3	73.1	68	67.6	67.4	52	48.9

Women's wage rates
compared to men's,
non-agricultural work
late 1980s percentages

Source: ILO

WORKING FOR LESS

More women than men work. They work more than men for less pay and prestige. And relatively more of them are unemployed.

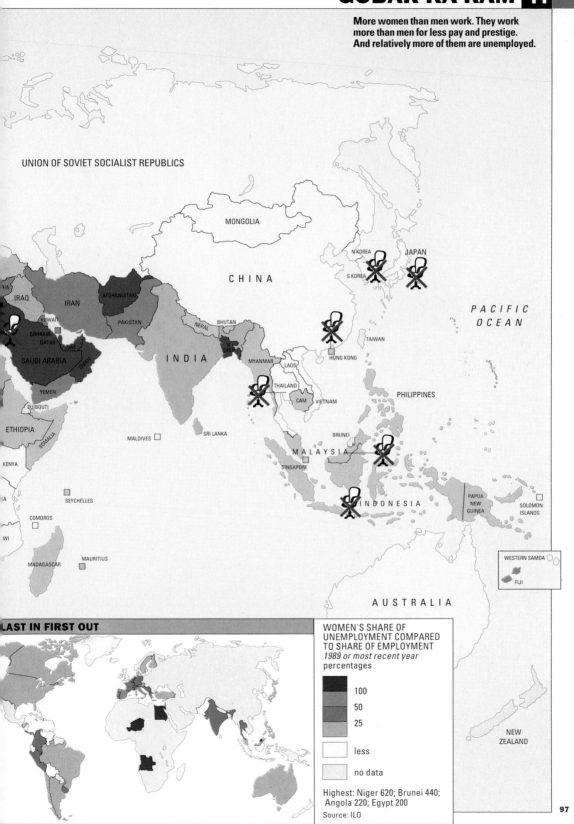

UNION OF SOVIET SOCIALIST REPUBLICS

MONGOLIA

CHINA

N KOREA

JAPAN

S KOREA

TAIWAN

HONG KONG

IRAQ

IRAN

AFGHANISTAN

KUWAIT

PAKISTAN

NEPAL

BHUTAN

BAHRAIN

QATAR

UAE

OMAN

SAUDI ARABIA

INDIA

B.
DESH

MYANMAR

LAOS

THAILAND

CAM

VIETNAM

YEMEN

DJIBOUTI

ETHIOPIA

SOMALIA

KENYA

MALDIVES

SRI LANKA

BRUNEI

PHILIPPINES

MALAYSIA

SINGAPORE

SEYCHELLES

COMOROS

INDONESIA

PAPUA
NEW
GUINEA

SOLOMON
ISLANDS

MADAGASCAR

MAURITIUS

WI

WESTERN SAMOA

FIJI

PACIFIC
OCEAN

AUSTRALIA

LAST IN FIRST OUT

**WOMEN'S SHARE OF
UNEMPLOYMENT COMPARED
TO SHARE OF EMPLOYMENT**
1989 or most recent year
percentages

- 100
- 50
- 25
- less
- no data

Highest: Niger 620; Brunei 440;
Angola 220; Egypt 200

Source: ILO

NEW
ZEALAND

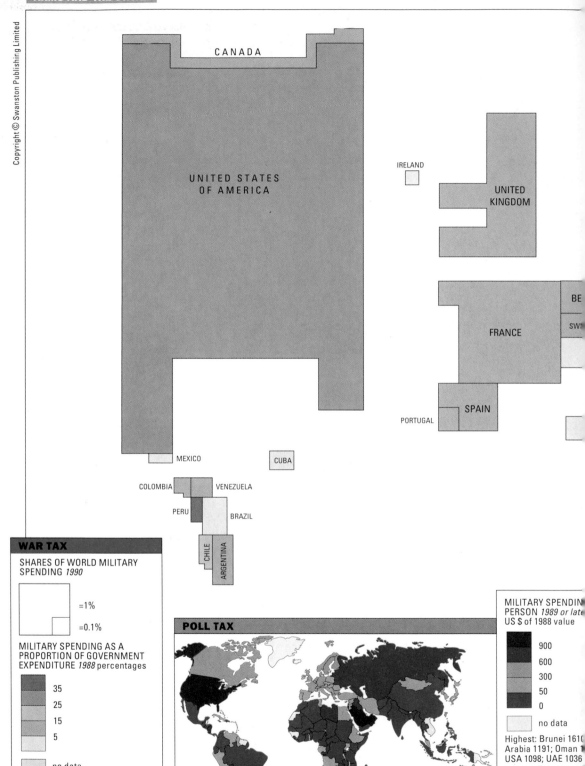

CANADA

UNITED STATES
OF AMERICA

IRELAND

UNITED
KINGDOM

BE

FRANCE

SW

SPAIN

PORTUGAL

MEXICO

CUBA

COLOMBIA

VENEZUELA

PERU

BRAZIL

CHILE

ARGENTINA

WAR TAX

SHARES OF WORLD MILITARY
SPENDING *1990*

=1%

=0.1%

MILITARY SPENDING AS A
PROPORTION OF GOVERNMENT
EXPENDITURE *1988* percentages

35

25

15

5

no data

Sources: SIPRI; USACDA

POLL TAX

MILITARY SPENDIN
PERSON *1989 or late*
US $ of 1988 value

900

600

300

50

0

no data

Highest: Brunei 1610
Arabia 1191; Oman 1
USA 1098; UAE 1036

Lowest: Zaire 0.9; M
Niger, Sierra Leone
Bangladesh 2.7

World average: 160

Source: Kidron & Smith

98

The military take US $900 billion a year –
$180 from every living being, three-
fifths as much as all expenditure on
health and education.

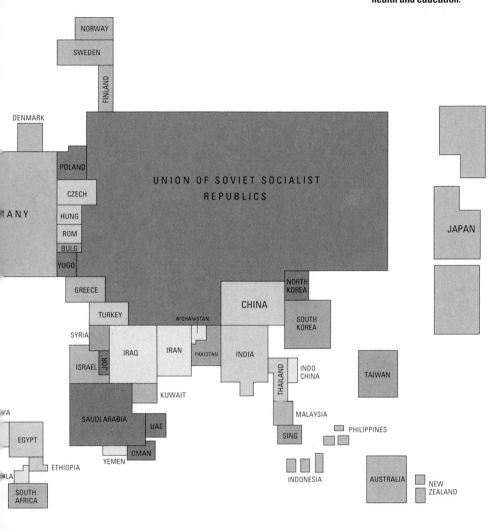

NORWAY

SWEDEN

FINLAND

DENMARK

POLAND

CZECH

HUNG

ROM

BULG

YUGO

UNION OF SOVIET SOCIALIST
REPUBLICS

ANY

GREECE

TURKEY

SYRIA

ISRAEL

JOR

IRAQ

IRAN

PAKISTAN

AFGHANISTAN

CHINA

NORTH
KOREA

SOUTH
KOREA

INDIA

JAPAN

THAILAND

INDO
CHINA

TAIWAN

KUWAIT

SAUDI ARABIA

UAE

MALAYSIA

SING

PHILIPPINES

YA

EGYPT

OMAN

YEMEN

ETHIOPIA

LA

SOUTH
AFRICA

INDONESIA

AUSTRALIA

NEW
ZEALAND

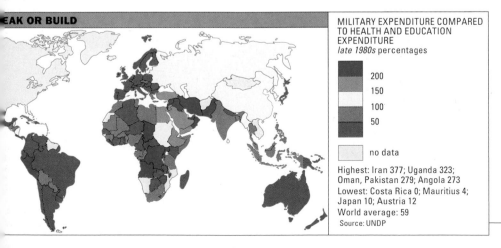

EAK OR BUILD

MILITARY EXPENDITURE COMPARED TO HEALTH AND EDUCATION EXPENDITURE
late 1980s percentages

- 200
- 150
- 100
- 50

no data

Highest: Iran 377; Uganda 323;
Oman, Pakistan 279; Angola 273
Lowest: Costa Rica 0; Mauritius 4;
Japan 10; Austria 12
World average: 59
Source: UNDP

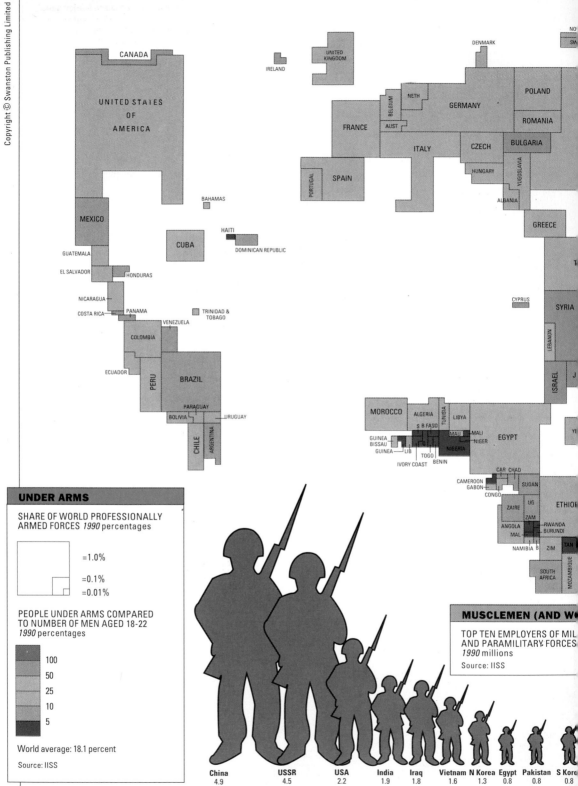

Copyright © Swanston Publishing Limited

UNDER ARMS

SHARE OF WORLD PROFESSIONALLY
ARMED FORCES *1990* percentages

=1.0%

=0.1%
=0.01%

PEOPLE UNDER ARMS COMPARED
TO NUMBER OF MEN AGED 18-22
1990 percentages

100
50
25
10
5

World average: 18.1 percent

Source: IISS

MUSCLEMEN (AND WO

TOP TEN EMPLOYERS OF MIL
AND PARAMILITARY FORCES
1990 millions

Source: IISS

China	USSR	USA	India	Iraq	Vietnam	N Korea	Egypt	Pakistan	S Kore
4.9	4.5	2.2	1.9	1.8	1.6	1.3	0.8	0.8	0.8

There are more than 46 million people under arms, at the sharp end of the killing machine – over five times the number of doctors.

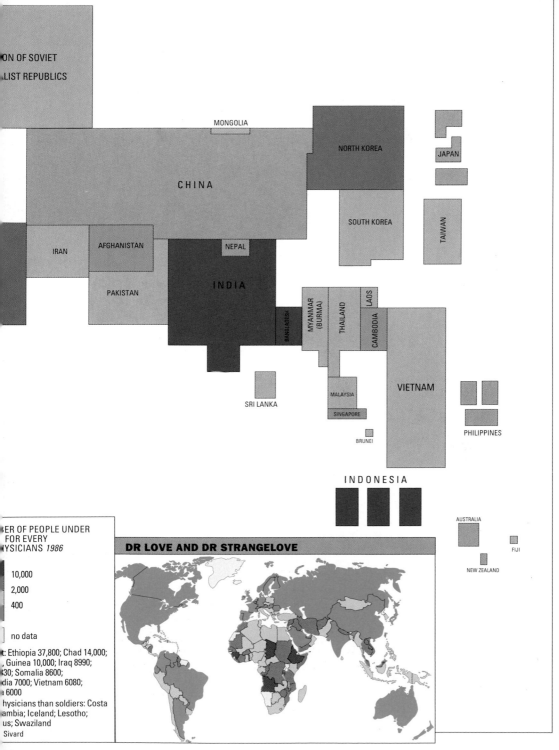

ON OF SOVIET
LIST REPUBLICS

MONGOLIA

NORTH KOREA

JAPAN

CHINA

SOUTH KOREA

TAIWAN

IRAN

AFGHANISTAN

NEPAL

PAKISTAN

INDIA

BANGLADESH

MYANMAR (BURMA)

THAILAND

LAOS

CAMBODIA

VIETNAM

SRI LANKA

MALAYSIA

SINGAPORE

BRUNEI

PHILIPPINES

INDONESIA

AUSTRALIA

FIJI

NEW ZEALAND

ER OF PEOPLE UNDER
FOR EVERY
YSICIANS *1986*

10,000

2,000

400

no data

: Ethiopia 37,800; Chad 14,000;
, Guinea 10,000; Iraq 8990;
30; Somalia 8600;
dia 7000; Vietnam 6080;
6000

hysicians than soldiers: Costa
ambia; Iceland; Lesotho;
us; Swaziland
Sivard

DR LOVE AND DR STRANGELOVE

101

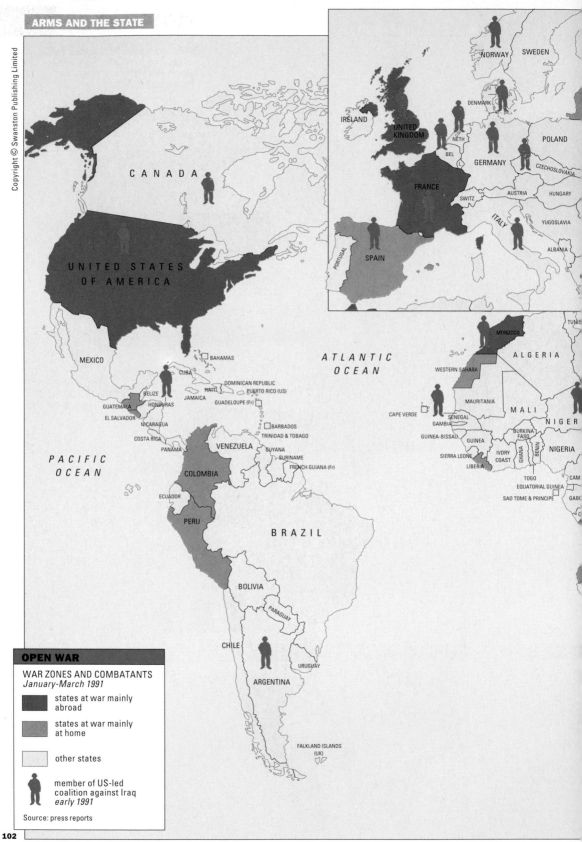

CANADA

UNITED STATES
OF AMERICA

MEXICO

BAHAMAS

CUBA
BELIZE
GUATEMALA
HONDURAS
EL SALVADOR
NICARAGUA
COSTA RICA
PANAMA

JAMAICA
HAITI
DOMINICAN REPUBLIC
PUERTO RICO (US)
GUADELOUPE (Fr)

BARBADOS
TRINIDAD & TOBAGO

VENEZUELA
GUYANA
SURINAME
FRENCH GUIANA (Fr)

COLOMBIA

ECUADOR

PERU

BRAZIL

BOLIVIA

PARAGUAY

CHILE

URUGUAY

ARGENTINA

FALKLAND ISLANDS
(UK)

ATLANTIC
OCEAN

PACIFIC
OCEAN

NORWAY   SWEDEN

IRELAND

DENMARK

UNITED
KINGDOM

NETH

BEL
(L)

GERMANY

POLAND

CZECHOSLOVAKIA

FRANCE

AUSTRIA   HUNGARY

SWITZ

ITALY

YUGOSLAVIA

ALBANIA

PORTUGAL

SPAIN

MOROCCO

WESTERN SAHARA

ALGERIA

TUNI

CAPE VERDE

MAURITANIA

MALI

NIGER

SENEGAL
GAMBIA
GUINEA-BISSAU
SIERRA LEONE
LIBERIA

GUINEA

IVORY
COAST

BURKINA
FASO

GHANA
BENIN

NIGERIA

TOGO
EQUATORIAL GUINEA
SAO TOME & PRINCIPE

CAM

GABO

OPEN WAR

WAR ZONES AND COMBATANTS
January–March 1991

states at war mainly
abroad

states at war mainly
at home

other states

member of US-led
coalition against Iraq
early 1991

Source: press reports

The (Cold) War is dead, long live war! In the early months of 1991, up to 40 wars were being fought.

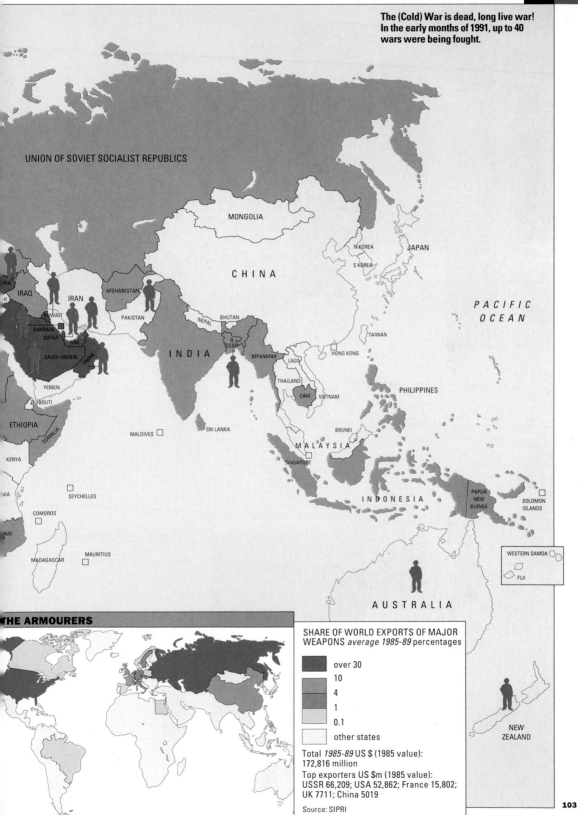

UNION OF SOVIET SOCIALIST REPUBLICS

MONGOLIA

N.KOREA

JAPAN

S.KOREA

CHINA

AFGHANISTAN

IRAQ

IRAN

PACIFIC
OCEAN

KUWAIT

PAKISTAN

NEPAL   BHUTAN

BAHRAIN
QATAR

TAIWAN

UAE

B-
DESH

HONG KONG

SAUDI ARABIA

OMAN

INDIA

MYANMAR

LAOS

YEMEN

THAILAND

DJIBOUTI

CAM   VIETNAM

PHILIPPINES

ETHIOPIA

SOMALIA

MALDIVES

SRI LANKA

BRUNEI

KENYA

MALAYSIA

SINGAPORE

SEYCHELLES

INDONESIA

PAPUA
NEW
GUINEA

SOLOMON
ISLANDS

COMOROS

MADAGASCAR

MAURITIUS

WESTERN SAMOA

FIJI

AUSTRALIA

THE ARMOURERS

SHARE OF WORLD EXPORTS OF MAJOR
WEAPONS *average 1985-89* percentages

■	over 30
■	10
■	4
■	1
■	0.1
□	other states

Total *1985-89* US $ (1985 value):
172,816 million

Top exporters US $m (1985 value):
USSR 66,209; USA 52,862; France 15,802;
UK 7711; China 5019

Source: SIPRI

NEW
ZEALAND

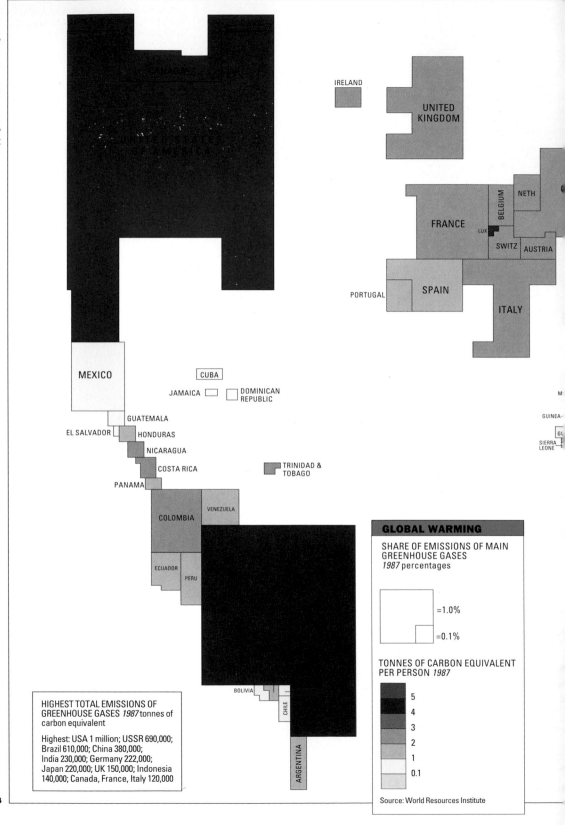

IRELAND

UNITED KINGDOM

CANADA

UNITED STATES OF AMERICA

BELGIUM
NETH

FRANCE

LUX

SWITZ
AUSTRIA

PORTUGAL
SPAIN

ITALY

MEXICO

CUBA

JAMAICA
DOMINICAN REPUBLIC

M

GUINEA-

GUATEMALA

EL SALVADOR
HONDURAS

GL
SIERRA
LEONE

NICARAGUA

COSTA RICA

PANAMA

TRINIDAD & TOBAGO

COLOMBIA
VENEZUELA

GLOBAL WARMING

SHARE OF EMISSIONS OF MAIN GREENHOUSE GASES
1987 percentages

ECUADOR

PERU

=1.0%

=0.1%

TONNES OF CARBON EQUIVALENT PER PERSON *1987*

5

4

3

BOLIVIA

2

CHILE

1

0.1

HIGHEST TOTAL EMISSIONS OF GREENHOUSE GASES *1987* tonnes of carbon equivalent

Highest: USA 1 million; USSR 690,000; Brazil 610,000; China 380,000; India 230,000; Germany 222,000; Japan 220,000; UK 150,000; Indonesia 140,000; Canada, France, Italy 120,000

ARGENTINA

Source: World Resources Institute

The 1980s was the warmest decade of the past century. It included 6 of the 10 warmest years on record.

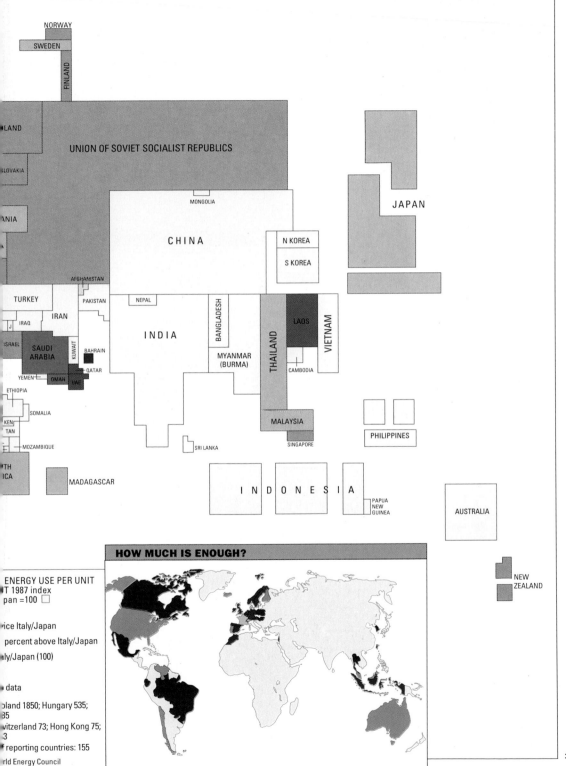

NORWAY
SWEDEN
FINLAND

UNION OF SOVIET SOCIALIST REPUBLICS

LAND

SLOVAKIA

ANIA

MONGOLIA

JAPAN

CHINA

N KOREA

S KOREA

AFGHANISTAN

TURKEY

IRAN

PAKISTAN

NEPAL

BANGLADESH

LAOS

VIETNAM

IRAQ

J

INDIA

THAILAND

ISRAEL

SAUDI
ARABIA

KUWAIT

BAHRAIN

MYANMAR
(BURMA)

CAMBODIA

QATAR

YEMEN

OMAN

UAE

ETHIOPIA

SOMALIA

MALAYSIA

PHILIPPINES

KEN
TAN

SINGAPORE

MOZAMBIQUE

SRI LANKA

TH
ICA

MADAGASCAR

I N D O N E S I A

PAPUA
NEW
GUINEA

AUSTRALIA

NEW
ZEALAND

HOW MUCH IS ENOUGH?

ENERGY USE PER UNIT
T 1987 index
pan =100 ☐

ice Italy/Japan

percent above Italy/Japan

ly/Japan (100)

data

bland 1850; Hungary 535;
85
vitzerland 73; Hong Kong 75;
3
reporting countries: 155
rld Energy Council

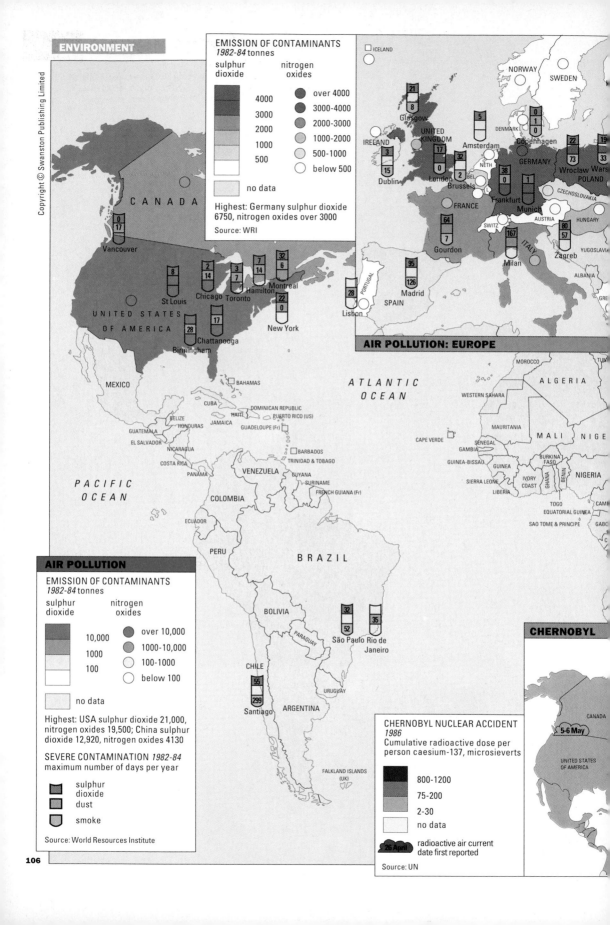

EMISSION OF CONTAMINANTS
1982-84 tonnes

sulphur dioxide	nitrogen oxides
4000	over 4000
3000	3000-4000
2000	2000-3000
1000	1000-2000
500	500-1000
	below 500

no data

Highest: Germany sulphur dioxide 6750, nitrogen oxides over 3000

Source: WRI

AIR POLLUTION: EUROPE

AIR POLLUTION

EMISSION OF CONTAMINANTS
1982-84 tonnes

sulphur dioxide	nitrogen oxides
10,000	over 10,000
1000	1000-10,000
100	100-1000
	below 100

no data

Highest: USA sulphur dioxide 21,000, nitrogen oxides 19,500; China sulphur dioxide 12,920, nitrogen oxides 4130

SEVERE CONTAMINATION *1982-84*
maximum number of days per year

sulphur dioxide
dust
smoke

Source: World Resources Institute

CHERNOBYL

CHERNOBYL NUCLEAR ACCIDENT
1986
Cumulative radioactive dose per person caesium-137, microsieverts

	800-1200
	75-200
	2-30
	no data

radioactive air current date first reported

5-6 May

26 April

Source: UN

CANADA

UNITED STATES OF AMERICA

PACIFIC OCEAN

ATLANTIC OCEAN

MEXICO
BAHAMAS
CUBA
BELIZE
GUATEMALA
HONDURAS
JAMAICA
EL SALVADOR
NICARAGUA
COSTA RICA
PANAMA
DOMINICAN REPUBLIC
HAITI
PUERTO RICO (US)
GUADELOUPE (Fr)
BARBADOS
TRINIDAD & TOBAGO
VENEZUELA
GUYANA
COLOMBIA
SURINAME
FRENCH GUIANA (Fr)
ECUADOR
PERU
BRAZIL
BOLIVIA
PARAGUAY
CHILE
URUGUAY
ARGENTINA
FALKLAND ISLANDS (UK)

Vancouver
St Louis
Chicago
Toronto
Hamilton
Montreal
New York
Chattanooga
Birmingham
São Paulo
Rio de Janeiro
Santiago

ICELAND
NORWAY
SWEDEN
IRELAND
UNITED KINGDOM
Glasgow
Dublin
London
Brussels
DENMARK
Copenhagen
Amsterdam
NETH
BEL
GERMANY
Frankfurt
Munich
FRANCE
Gourdon
SWITZ
AUSTRIA
ITALY
Milan
Madrid
SPAIN
PORTUGAL
Lisbon
CZECHOSLOVAKIA
POLAND
Wrocław
Warsaw
HUNGARY
Zagreb
YUGOSLAVIA
ALBANIA
GRE

MOROCCO
ALGERIA
TUN
WESTERN SAHARA
MAURITANIA
MALI
NIGE
CAPE VERDE
SENEGAL
GAMBIA
GUINEA-BISSAU
GUINEA
SIERRA LEONE
IVORY COAST
LIBERIA
BURKINA FASO
GHANA
BENIN
TOGO
NIGERIA
CAM
EQUATORIAL GUINEA
SAO TOME & PRINCIPE
GABO

70 percent of all city dwellers – 1530 million people – breathe unhealthy air. Another 10 percent – 220 million people – breathe air of doubtful purity.

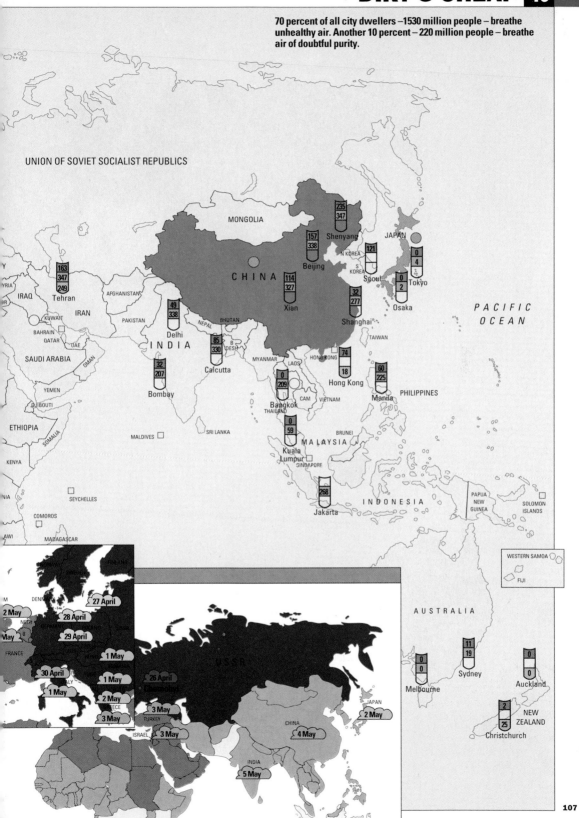

UNION OF SOVIET SOCIALIST REPUBLICS

MONGOLIA

CHINA

235	
347	Shenyang

JAPAN

157
338
Beijing

N KOREA

121
S KOREA
Seoul

0
4

114
327
Xian

0
2
Tokyo

32
277
Shanghai

Osaka

PACIFIC OCEAN

163
347
249
Tehran

SYRIA
IRAQ
IRAN

AFGHANISTAN

KUWAIT
BAHRAIN
QATAR
UAE
OMAN

SAUDI ARABIA

YEMEN

DJIBOUTI

ETHIOPIA
SOMALIA

KENYA

PAKISTAN

49
338
Delhi

INDIA

NEPAL BHUTAN
B DESH

85
330
Calcutta

32
207
Bombay

MYANMAR
LAOS

74
18
Hong Kong

HONG KONG

TAIWAN

60
225
Manila

PHILIPPINES

0
209
Bangkok
THAILAND

CAM VIETNAM

MALDIVES

SRI LANKA

0
59
Kuala Lumpur
SINGAPORE

MALAYSIA

BRUNEI

SEYCHELLES

COMOROS

MADAGASCAR

268
Jakarta

INDONESIA

PAPUA NEW GUINEA

SOLOMON ISLANDS

WESTERN SAMOA

FIJI

AUSTRALIA

0
0
Melbourne

11
19
Sydney

0
0
Auckland

2
25
NEW ZEALAND
Christchurch

NORWAY
SWEDEN
FINLAND

DENMARK

27 April

2 May
NETH

28 April

May
B

29 April

FRANCE

1 May

30 April
ITALY

1 May

26 April
Chernobyl

USSR

1 May

2 May
GREECE

3 May

TURKEY

ISRAEL

3 May

JAPAN

2 May

CHINA

4 May

INDIA

5 May

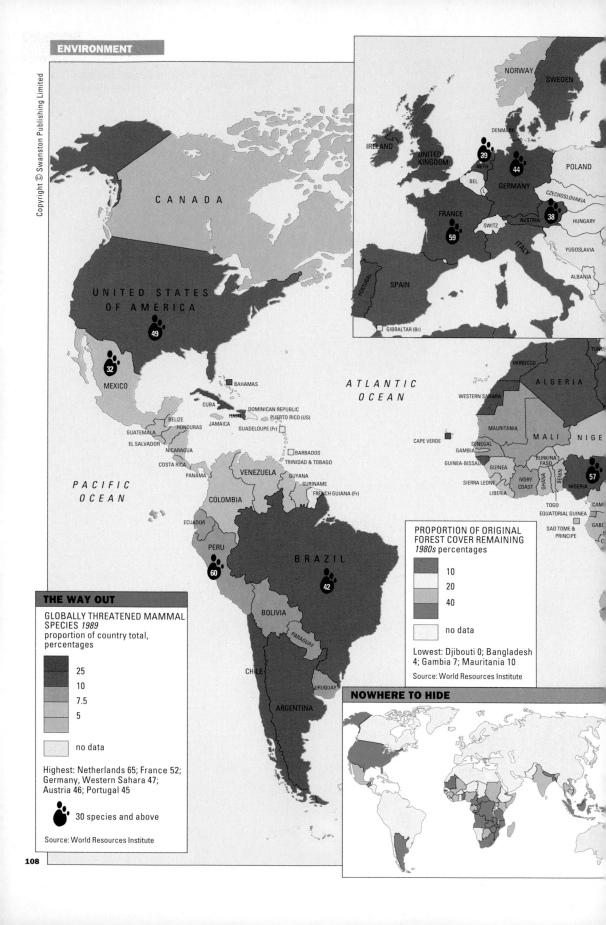

CANADA

UNITED STATES
OF AMERICA

ATLANTIC
OCEAN

MEXICO

BAHAMAS

CUBA
BELIZE   HAITI   DOMINICAN REPUBLIC
GUATEMALA   HONDURAS JAMAICA PUERTO RICO (US)
EL SALVADOR   GUADELOUPE (Fr)
        NICARAGUA
        COSTA RICA   BARBADOS
PANAMA   TRINIDAD & TOBAGO
                VENEZUELA   GUYANA
PACIFIC   COLOMBIA   SURINAME
OCEAN   FRENCH GUIANA (Fr)
        ECUADOR
        PERU   BRAZIL
        BOLIVIA
                PARAGUAY
        CHILE
                URUGUAY
        ARGENTINA

NORWAY
SWEDEN
IRELAND
DENMARK
UNITED KINGDOM   NETH
                    BEL   GERMANY   POLAND
                    L   CZECHOSLOVAKIA
        FRANCE   AUSTRIA   HUNGARY
                    SWITZ
                        ITALY   YUGOSLAVIA
PORTUGAL   ALBANIA
        SPAIN
GIBRALTAR (Br)

MOROCCO   ALGERIA   TUNIS
WESTERN SAHARA
                    MALI   NIGE
CAPE VERDE   MAURITANIA
        SENEGAL
        GAMBIA
GUINEA-BISSAU   BURKINA
        GUINEA   FASO
SIERRA LEONE   IVORY GHANA BENIN NIGERIA
        LIBERIA COAST
                TOGO   CAM
        EQUATORIAL GUINEA
        SAO TOME &   GABO
        PRINCIPE

39 44 38 59 49 32 57 60 42

PROPORTION OF ORIGINAL FOREST COVER REMAINING
1980s percentages

- 10
- 20
- 40
- no data

Lowest: Djibouti 0; Bangladesh 4; Gambia 7; Mauritania 10

Source: World Resources Institute

THE WAY OUT

GLOBALLY THREATENED MAMMAL
SPECIES *1989*
proportion of country total,
percentages

- 25
- 10
- 7.5
- 5
- no data

Highest: Netherlands 65; France 52;
Germany, Western Sahara 47;
Austria 46; Portugal 45

30 species and above

Source: World Resources Institute

NOWHERE TO HIDE

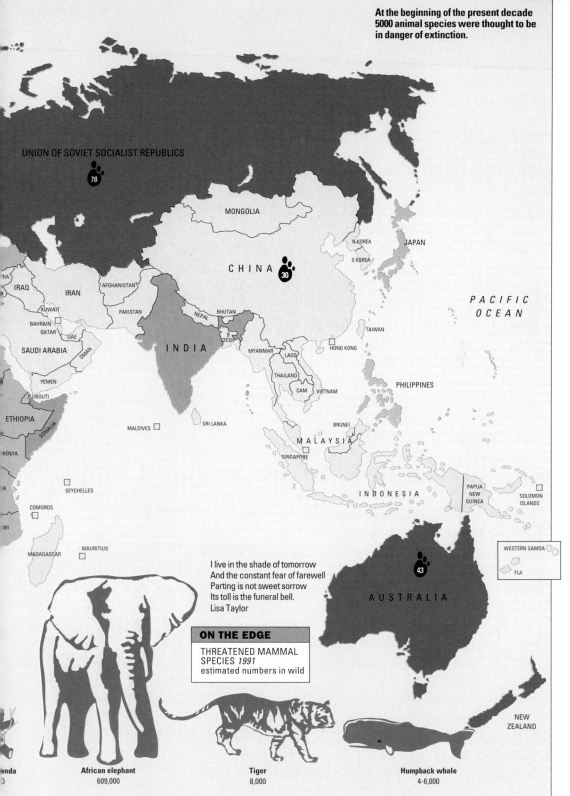

At the beginning of the present decade 5000 animal species were thought to be in danger of extinction.

UNION OF SOVIET SOCIALIST REPUBLICS

78

MONGOLIA

N.KOREA

JAPAN

S KOREA

CHINA

30

RIA

IRAQ

IRAN

AFGHANISTAN

KUWAIT

PAKISTAN

NEPAL

BHUTAN

TAIWAN

BAHRAIN

QATAR

UAE

B
DESH

SAUDI ARABIA

OMAN

I N D I A

MYANMAR

LAOS

HONG KONG

YEMEN

THAILAND

DJIBOUTI

CAM

VIETNAM

PHILIPPINES

ETHIOPIA

MALDIVES

SRI LANKA

BRUNEI

SOMALIA

KENYA

M A L A Y S I A

SINGAPORE

P A C I F I C
O C E A N

SEYCHELLES

I N D O N E S I A

PAPUA
NEW
GUINEA

SOLOMON
ISLANDS

COMOROS

WI

MADAGASCAR

MAURITIUS

WESTERN SAMOA

FIJI

I live in the shade of tomorrow
And the constant fear of farewell
Parting is not sweet sorrow
Its toll is the funeral bell.
Lisa Taylor

43

A U S T R A L I A

ON THE EDGE

THREATENED MAMMAL
SPECIES *1991*
estimated numbers in wild

NEW
ZEALAND

anda
0

African elephant
609,000

Tiger
8,000

Humpback whale
4-6,000

State	Capital	Territorial area, 000 sq kms	Privileged area, 000 sq kms	Population, mid million
Afghanistan	Kabul	647.5	–	15.9
Albania	Tirana	38.8	–	3.3
Algeria	Algiers	2,403.7	–	25.6
Angola	Luanda	1,306.0	592.0	8.5
Antigua & Barbuda	Saint John's	9.2	56.6	0.1
Argentina	Buenos Aires	1,848.6	–	32.3
Australia	Canberra	7,851.0	10,820.2	17.1
Austria	Vienna	83.9	–	7.6
Bahamas	Nassau	14.0	1,310.5	0.2
Bahrain	Manama	1.5	–	0.5
Bangladesh	Dhaka	156.8	214.6	114.8
Barbados	Bridgetown	9.2	35.9	0.3
Belgium	Brussels	30.9	23.7	9.9
Belize	Belmopan	23.1	–	0.2
Benin	Porto Novo (off.) /Cotonou	147.4	–	4.7
Bhutan	Thimphu	4.7	–	1.6
Bolivia	La Paz	1,098.7	–	7.3
Botswana	Gaborone	600.4	–	1.2
Brazil	Brasilia	11,219.7	–	150.4
Brunei	Bandar Seri Begawan	9.3	59.6	0.3
Bulgaria	Sofia	118.7	46.4	8.9
Burkina Faso	Ouagadougou	274.2	–	9.1
Burundi	Bujumbura	27.8	–	5.6
Cambodia	Phnom Penh	190.7	163.9	7.0
Cameroon	Yaoundé	512.6	–	11.1
Canada	Ottawa	15,339.5	90,202.7	26.6
Cape Verde	Praia	25.2	357.1	0.4
Central African Republic	Bangui	623.0	–	2.9
Chad	N'Djamena	1,284.0	–	5.0
Chile	Santiago	898.6	2,381.9	13.2
China	Beijing	9,916.0	319.0	1119.9
Colombia	Bogotá	1,219.4	1,187.0	31.8
Comoros	Moroni	9.7	125.8	0.5
Congo	Brazzaville	404.5	12.5	2.2
Costa Rica	San José	79.4	477.3	3.0
Cote d'Ivoire (Ivory Coast)	Abidjan	333.8	190.6	12.6
Cuba	Havana	193.1	1,382.0	10.6
Cyprus	Nicosia	23.6	14.3	0.7
Czechoslovakia	Prague	127.9	–	15.7
Denmark	Copenhagen	2,490.2	17,844.0	5.1

Note: Some independent states with small populations, such as St. Kitts-Nevis-Anguilla (pop. 20,000) and some dependencies or otherwise non-independent states such as waters. Privileged area covers 'non-territorial' sea or ocean areas claimed as Exclusive Economic (or Fishing) Zones. **Sources: Cols. 1-4:** as for maps 1 and 2: **Cols. 5 and 6**

n of age n	GNP 1989 US$ billion	Purchasing power per person 1987 US$	Central government spending % of GNP 1988	Military spending per person 1989 US$	Greenhouse gases 000 tonnes CO₂ equivalent 1987
	3.0	–	10.7	44.2	1.8
	3.8	–	44.6	51.3	1.5
	53.1	2,630	37.8	47.2	25.0
	6.0	–	25.7	128.3	3.4
	0.3	–	–	–	–
	68.8	4,650	23.8	77.1	31.0
	242.1	11,780	27.0	267.5	63.0
	131.9	12,390	41.7	147.0	17.0
	2.8	–	–	–	–
	3.0	–	32.5	477.5	2.3
	19.9	880	13.5	2.7	22.0
	1.6	–	32.6	–	0.3
	162.0	13,140	39.3	341.2	25.0
	0.3	–	–	–	–
	1.8	670	17.9	6.5	1.3
	0.3	–	–	–	0.2
	4.3	1,380	14.3	26.4	4.4
	1.1	2,500	79.8	22.7	0.9
	375.1	4,310	43.7	14.0	610.0
	3.3	–	–	1,610.0	–
	20.9	–	47.8	92.0	17.0
	2.7	–	15.6	5.5	2.4
	1.1	450	19.2	8.4	0.1
	0.9	–	–	–	5.1
	11.7	1,380	22.6	17.3	16.0
	500.3	16,380	23.6	311.4	120.0
	0.3	–	–	–	–
	1.1	590	25.7	8.9	1.8
	1.0	–	9.5	5.9	2.4
	22.9	4,860	24.3	115.8	6.4
	350.0	2,120	19.5	10.1	380.0
	38.6	3,520	12.5	28.9	69.0
	0.2	–	–	–	–
	2.0	760	41.7	37.0	1.6
	4.9	3,760	14.5	11.9	7.8
	9.3	1,120	24.8	8.4	47.0
	20.9	–	–	170.2	6.9
	4.9	–	30.9	37.1	0.5
	52.7	–	31.4	217.4	33.0
	105.3	15,120	40.8	351.0	15.0

ature on this table. Figures are rounded to the nearest 0.1 billion, million or the nearest unit. **Cols. 3 and 4:** Territorial area covers land and inland waters and territorial
Col. 8: as for map 14; **Col. 9:** as for map 25; **Col. 10:** as for map 45; **Col. 11:** as for map 48.

State	Capital	Territorial area, 000 sq kms	Privileged area, 000 sq kms	Population, mid million
Djibouti	Djibouti	28.9	116.2	0.4
Dominica	Roseau	4.0	54.8	0.1
Dominican Republic	Santo Domingo	63.0	476.6	7.2
Ecuador	Quito	1,111.3	827.7	10.7
Egypt	Cairo	1055.4	906.4	54.7
El Salvador	San Salvador	134.6	113.6	5.3
Equatorial Guinea	Malabo	34.5	109.5	0.4
Ethiopia	Addis Ababa	1,240.9	24.0	51.7
Fiji	Suva	43.1	417.7	0.8
Finland	Helsinki	345.3	24.8	5.0
France	Paris	1,722.7	4,016.2	56.4
Gabon	Libreville	287.2	246.0	1.2
Gambia	Banjul	13.1	29.6	0.9
United Germany	Bonn	385.0	883.9	79.5
Ghana	Accra	240.4	199.4	15.0
Greece	Athens	282.3	150.4	10.1
Grenada	Saint George's	3.0	44.8	0.1
Guatemala	Guatemala	117.7	148.0	9.2
Guinea	Conakry	242.9	118.4	7.3
Guinea-Bissau	Bissau	43.8	129.4	1.0
Guyana	Georgetown	225.1	169.8	0.8
Haiti	Port-au-Prince	66.8	655.3	6.5
Honduras	Tegucigalpa	130.1	303.4	5.1
Hungary	Budapest	93.0	–	10.6
Iceland	Rejkjavik	212.7	1,845.6	0.3
India	New Delhi	3,441.6	2,590.0	853.4
Indonesia	Jakarta	3,123.1	20,244.1	189.4
Iran	Tehran	1,718.0	294.5	55.6
Iraq	Baghdad	436.2	1.3	18.8
Ireland	Dublin	78.3	535.8	3.5
Israel	Jerusalem	23.8	3.0	4.6
Italy	Rome	411.1	109.9	57.7
Jamaica	Kingston	33.5	22.5	2.4
Japan	Tokyo	1,032.3	11,007.9	123.6
Jordan	Amman	92.0	0.1	4.1
Kenya	Nairobi	594.4	198.3	24.6
Korea, North	Pyong yang	351.5	923.2	21.3
Korea, South	Seoul	151.6	53.1	42.8
Kuwait	Kuwait	18.8	11.0	2.1
Laos	Vientiane	236.8	–	4.0

Note: Some independent states with small populations, such as St. Kitts-Nevis-Anguilla (pop. 20,000) and some dependencies or otherwise non-independent states such as ▌ waters. Privileged area covers 'non-territorial' sea or ocean areas claimed as Exclusive Economic (or Fishing) Zones. **Sources: Cols. 1-4:** as for maps 1 and 2; **Cols. 5 and 6▌**

...tion of ng age lion	GNP 1989 US$ billion	Purchasing power per person 1987 US$	Central government spending % of GNP 1988	Military spending per person 1989 US$	Greenhouse gases 000 tonnes CO$_2$ equivalent 1987
.2	0.3	–	–	–	–
.1	0.1	–	–	–	–
.2	5.5	–	18.6	10.5	2.4
.8	10.7	2,690	14.4	23.4	21.0
.1	32.5	1,360	36.1	97.9	17.0
.7	5.4	1,730	10.8	30.0	1.3
.2	0.1	–	21.3	–	0.1
.9	5.9	450	39.4	9.0	7.8
.5	1.2	–	26.7	5.7	0.2
.4	109.7	12,800	32.9	314.7	13.0
.2	1,000.9	13,960	44.4	522.5	120.0
.7	3.1	2,070	33.7	106.4	1.4
.5	0.2	–	–	–	0.2
.7	1,342.0	14,730	33.9	433.8	222.0
.8	5.5	480	14.8	3.3	6.3
8	53.6	–	55.9	263.2	20.0
1	0.2	–	–	–	–
7	8.2	1,960	12.5	34.8	5.1
9	2.4	–	17.5	–	4.8
6	0.2	–	–	–	1.5
5	0.2	–	–	81.3	0.4
6	2.6	780	19.3	4.6	0.3
6	4.5	1,120	19.7	49.4	5.2
0	27.1	–	39.9	81.3	13.0
2	5.4	–	28.6	–	0.4
0	287.4	1,050	22.8	11.1	230.0
5	87.9	1,660	21.9	14.1	140.0
9	97.6	–	17.3	126.8	33.0
8	35.0	–	32.9	677.1	9.3
1	30.1	8,570	53.9	107.2	9.2
7	44.1	9,180	58.7	938.6	9.3
2	872.0	10,680	53.8	265.6	120.0
4	3.0	2,510	51.5	11.3	1.2
8	2,920.3	13,140	16.8	176.5	220.0
1	5.3	3,160	65.1	191.1	1.2
8	8.8	790	25.4	9.7	3.1
2	28.0	–	49.2	83.0	20.0
1	186.5	4,830	16.9	140.1	29.0
3	33.1	13,840	37.5	722.6	7.6
2	0.7	–	49.1	–	38.0

feature on this table. Figures are rounded to the nearest 0.1 billion, million or the nearest unit. **Cols. 3 and 4:** Territorial area covers land and inland waters and territorial
6; **Col. 8:** as for map 14; **Col. 9:** as for map 25; **Col. 10:** as for map 45; **Col. 11:** as for map 48.

State	Capital	Territorial area, 000 sq kms	Privileged area, 000 sq kms	Population, mid-1 million
Lebanon	Beirut	15.4	5.0	3.3
Lesotho	Maseru	30.4	–	1.8
Liberia	Monrovia	325.2	214.2	2.6
Libya	Tripoli	1,798.4	38.9	4.2
Luxembourg	Luxembourg	2.6	–	0.4
Madagascar	Antananarivo	1,034.1	1,342.2	12.0
Malawi	Lilongwe	118.5	–	9.2
Malaysia	Kuala Lumpur	432.7	1,729.8	17.9
Maldives	Male	14.5	238.3	0.2
Mali	Bamako	1,240.0	–	8.1
Malta	Valletta	3.4	19.9	0.4
Mauritania	Nouakchott	1,131.0	279.0	2.0
Mauritius	Port Louis	5.8	65.5	1.1
Mexico	Mexico	2,177.9	3,452.1	88.6
Mongolia	Ulaanbaatar	1,565.0	–	2.2
Morocco	Rabat	487.0	679.0	25.6
Mozambique	Maputo	854.9	913.9	15.7
Myanmar (Burma)	Yangon (Rangoon)	721.0	714.1	41.3
Namibia	Windhoek	857.1	550.9	1.5
Nepal	Kathmandu	140.8	–	19.1
Netherlands	The Hague	62.0	174.9	14.9
New Zealand	Wellington	611.1	5,708.0	3.3
Nicaragua	Managua	466.2	356.7	3.9
Niger	Niamey	1,267.0	–	7.9
Nigeria	Lagos	971.2	315.6	118.8
Norway	Oslo	1,494.4	9,496.5	4.2
Oman	Muscat	258.5	774.0	1.5
Pakistan	Islamabad	826.9	387.0	114.6
Panama	Panama	999.5	921.3	2.4
Papua New Guinea	Port Moresby	575.0	1,906.2	4.0
Paraguay	Asunción	406.8	–	4.3
Peru	Lima	2,178.4	893.2	21.9
Philippines	Manila	13,726.9	–	66.1
Poland	Warsaw	323.5	181.7	37.8
Portugal	Lisbon	131.9	664.3	10.4
Qatar	Doha	14.1	–	0.5
Romania	Bucharest	242.5	83.3	23.3
Rwanda	Kigali	26.3	–	7.3
St Lucia	Castries	4.1	58.5	0.2
St Vincent & Grenadines	Kingstown	2.2	31.5	0.1

Note: Some independent states with small populations, such as St. Kitts-Nevis-Anguilla (pop. 20,000) and some dependencies or otherwise non-independent states such as Hoi waters. Privileged area covers 'non-territorial' sea or ocean areas claimed as Exclusive Economic (or Fishing) Zones. **Sources: Cols. 1-4:** as for maps 1 and 2; **Cols. 5 and 6:** a

...ion of g age on	GNP 1989 US$ billion	Purchasing power per person 1987 US$	Central Government spending % of GNP 1988	Military spending per person 1989 US$	Greenhouse gases 000 tonnes CO$_2$ equivalent 1987
8	2.3	–		–	1.0
0	0.8	1,590	–	–	–
3	1.1	700	26.6	10.4	4.0
2	23.0	–	42.5	674.6	4.5
3	9.4	–	33.9	165.0	1.6
2	2.5	630	10.1	4.6	13.0
5	1.5	480	20.0	2.3	7.3
4	37.0	3,850	31.7	118.7	26.0
1	0.0	–	–	–	–
1	2.1	540	28.2	6.1	2.1
3	2.1	–	38.3	–	0.2
1	0.9	840	36.7	24.7	0.8
7	2.1	2,620	25.6	3.0	0.2
8	170.1	4,620	27.1	7.6	78.0
2	1.7	–	–	147.0	1.9
8	22.1	1,760	33.0	34.0	3.3
3	1.2	–	16.1	18.8	3.6
4	11.0	750	13.1	5.3	77.0
8	1.5	–	–	–	–
5	3.2	720	19.4	2.9	6.8
3	237.4	12,660	55.7	368.7	43.0
1	39.4	10,540	37.2	181.8	10.0
9	2.9	2,210	54.3	824.9	8.4
0	2.2	450	19.0	2.4	1.5
0	28.3	670	30.4	7.5	53.0
7	92.1	15,940	46.1	529.3	8.7
8	7.8	–	49.7	1,186.2	4.7
6	40.1	1,590	25.5	24.8	15.0
4	4.2	4,010	32.5	45.2	3.3
3	3.4	1,840	30.3	–	1.5
4	4.3	2,580	8.2	16.9	4.1
7	23.0	3,130	10.6	70.6	23.0
3	42.8	1,880	16.5	7.2	40.0
2	67.0	–	19.8	51.8	76.0
8	44.1	5,600	36.0	98.2	17.0
4	4.1	–	82.5	–	2.9
4	42.1	–	41.2	55.4	28.0
6	2.2	570	16.4	4.7	0.3
1	0.3	–	–	–	–
1	0.1	–	–	–	–

feature on this table. Figures are rounded to the nearest 0.1 billion, million or the nearest unit. **Cols. 3 and 4:** Territorial area covers land and inland waters and territorial 6; **Col. 8:** as for map 14; **Col. 9:** as for map 25; **Col. 10:** as for map 45; **Col. 11:** as for map 48.

State	Capital	Territorial area, 000 sq kms	Privileged area, 000 sq kms	Population, mid-1 million
Sao Tome & Principe	São Tome	5.6	77.3	0.1
Saudi Arabia	Riyadh	2,204.9	55.2	15.0
Senegal	Dakar	207.9	196.5	7.4
Seychelles	Victoria	11.3	181.7	0.1
Sierra Leone	Freetown	220.4	148.7	4.2
Singapore	Singapore	1.7	4.2	2.7
Solomon Islands	Honiara	145.4	1,965.8	0.3
Somalia	Mogadishu	1,759.0	1,119.3	8.4
South Africa	Pretoria/Cape Town	1,684.4	1,066.0	39.6
Spain	Madrid	614.0	1,836.7	39.4
Sri Lanka	Colombo	95.1	494.8	17.2
Sudan	Khartoum	2,524.6	18.8	25.2
Suriname	Paramaribo	171.8	142.8	0.4
Swaziland	Mbabane/Lobqurba	17.4	–	0.8
Sweden	Stockholm	520.8	1,190.7	8.5
Switzerland	Bern	41.3	–	6.7
Syria	Damascus	197.7	14.7	12.6
Taiwan		67.9	535.8	20.2
Tanzania	Dar es Salaam	976.4	526.9	26.0
Thailand	Bangkok	574.8	1,190.0	55.7
Togo	Lomé	59.9	20.7	3.7
Trinidad & Tobago	Port of Spain	13.1	133.9	1.3
Tunisia	Tunis	188.9	25.3	8.2
Turkey	Ankara	939.0	2,664.0	56.7
Uganda	Kampala	236.0	–	18.0
USSR	Moscow	23,343.3	15,827.5	291.0
United Arab Emirates	Abu Dhabi	91.7	535.8	1.6
United Kingdom	London	351.4	5,400.8	57.4
USA	Washington, DC	10,004.8	11,258.1	251.4
Uruguay	Montevideo	420.4	244.2	3.0
Vanuatu	Port-Vila	70.3	935.4	0.2
Venezuela	Caracas	963.7	1,036.0	19.6
Vietnam	Hanoi	405.4	1,274.3	70.2
Western Sahara		–	–	0.2
Western Samoa	Apia	11.8	149.1	0.2
Yemen	Sanaa	569.9	705.2	9.8
Yugoslavia	Belgrade	342.4	86.6	23.8
Zaire	Kinshasa	2,346.2	13.7	36.6
Zambia	Lusaka	752.6	–	8.1
Zimbabwe	Harare	390.6	–	9.7

Note: Some independent states with small populations, such as St. Kitts-Nevis-Anguilla (pop. 20,000) and some dependencies or otherwise non-independent states such as Ho
waters. Privileged area covers 'non-territorial' sea or ocean areas claimed as Exclusive Economic (or Fishing) Zones. **Sources: Cols. 1-4:** as for maps 1 and 2; **Cols. 5 and 6:** a

on of age n	GNP 1989 US$ billion	Purchasing power per person 1987 US$	Central government spending % of GNP 1988	Military spending per person 1989 US$$	Greenhouse gases 000 tonnes CO_2 equivalent 1987
	0.0	–	–	–	–
	90.0	8,320	45.9	1,191.0	42.0
	4.7	1,070	33.2	12.7	3.1
	0.3	–	–	–	–
	0-.8	480	9.7	1.1	0.8
	28.1	12,790	22.0	459.6	7.1
	0.2	–	–	–	–
	1.0	–	–	3.7	2.4
	86.0	4,980	28.5	79.2	47.0
	358.3	8,990	16.1	141.1	73.0
	7.3	2,050	34.8	17.6	2.7
	10.1	750	20.4	9.7	15.0
	1.3	–	46.7	–	0.5
	0.7	–	–	10.0	0.1
	184.2	13,780	41.3	410.5	14.0
	198.0	15,400	19.3	366.2	16.0
	12.4	–	31.2	224.7	3.7
	117.9	–	16.4	333.0	–
	3.1	410	26.4	12.3	4.6
	64.4	–	16.8	38.8	67.0
	1.4	670	22.5	10.9	0.4
	4.0	3,660	52.8	107.5	2.8
	10.1	2,740	36.5	67.4	3.0
	74.8	3,780	22.0	42.3	29.0
	4.3	510	7.3	4.5	1.8
	854.1	–	27.5	631.7	690.0
	28.4	12,190	16.5	1,036.0	8.4
	834.2	12,270	34.9	458.8	150.0
	5,237.7	17,600	22.9	1,098.3	1,000.0
	8.1	5,060	18.4	48.3	2.5
	0.1	–	–	–	–
	47.2	4,310	21.9	76.5	27.0
	4.4	–	61.4	–	38.0
	–	–	–	–	–
	0.1	–	–	–	–
	8.4	–	41.2	49.5	1.3
	59.1	–	5.0	56.7	26.0
	8.8	220	52.1	0.9	16.0
	3.1	720	27.9	8.5	2.5
	6.1	1,180	42.2	36.2	5.9

eature on this table. Figures are rounded to the nearest 0.1 billion, million or the nearest unit. **Cols. 3 and 4:** Territorial area covers land and inland waters and territorial
; **Col. 8:** as for map 14; **Col. 9:** as for map 25; **Col. 10:** as for map 45; **Col. 11:** as for map 48.

NOTES

1 THE WORLD OF STATES

It is hard to grasp that the notion of the nation state, in which the political unit coincides more or less with a popular sense of national or common identity, goes no farther back than mid-nineteenth century western Europe. It is even harder to understand how such a novel idea was taken up so widely, and with such profound effect. But there it is. Over the past fifty years or so, every last rock and stream of the earth's surface, with the partial exception of Antarctica, has been attached to one or another state, held inviolate as a birthright and protected by fence or force. And over the past decade, more than a third of the earth's oceans has ended up in states' portfolios for 'the nation' to trawl in, to bore in, to lease and to patrol.

This map shows how few are the states whose territorial and maritime pretensions are unchallenged by their neighbours or inhabitants. Many have gone to war in consequence. Some have disappeared – East Germany and South Yemen in 1990 alone. (Kuwait was a near miss). Some have effectively disintegrated – the Lebanon, Liberia, Somalia, Sudan. Some are under intense internal pressure to unbundle into presumptive nation-states and, ironically, into ever-smaller nation-state components – the USSR and Yugoslavia are prime examples in Europe, but there are many more, from Myanmar or India in Asia, to Canada in North America, from Rwanda or Ethiopia in Africa, to Iran, Iraq or Turkey in the Middle East. Currently disputed claims are not necessarily the ones that led to armed clashes in the past.

A state's territory, coloured red or green on the map, is one in which it tries to enforce all its laws. A privileged area, coloured dark blue, is one in which it tries to apply only some of these laws. The privileged area of a state is its claim to an Extended Economic Zone (EEZ) or Exclusive Fishing Zone (EFZ).

Sources:
Border and Territorial Disputes, 2nd edition, Harlow: Longman, 1987; Buzan, Barry, *A Sea of Troubles? Sources of Dispute in the New Ocean Regime*, Adelphi Papers 143, London: International Institute for Strategic Studies, 1978; Central Intelligence Agency (CIA), *The World Factbook 1990*, Washington DC, 1990; Couper, Alistair, ed., *The Times Atlas of the Oceans*, London: Times Books, 1983; *Maritime Affairs – A World Handbook*, Harlow: Longman, 1985; press reports.

Acknowledgements:
The staff at the Foreign and Commonwealth Office libraries, London, including David Anderson, Susan Halls and Catherine O'Connel, were generous with time and materials.

2 THE CLAIMANT STATE

The concept of privileged areas highlights the potential value to states of tiny islands, atolls or mere rocks, as strategic platforms or sources of food or minerals.

The maritime areas included as privileged territory in the cartogram have been specially computed. They are the product of the length of a state's shoreline and the reach of its claim to an Extended Economic Zone (EEZ) or Exclusive Fishing Zone (EFZ) where these extend further than territorial waters – as they mostly do. There is an element of double counting, which increases with the convolution of a state's shoreline.

An extreme example of conflicting preoccupations with 'national' specks is provided by the Paracel and Spratly Islands, scattered across the major trade routes in the South China Sea and reputedly sitting on substantial reserves of oil and gas. The Japanese grabbed the Paracels from China during the Second World War and returned them to

Taiwan afterwards. South Vietnam occupied them until 1974 when mainland China expelled the occupiers by force. Vietnam restated its claim in 1979 on the basis of seventeenth- and eighteenth-century maps. China counter-claimed by invoking geographical work undertaken in the third century. Vietnamese and Chinese armed forces have been shadowing each other ever since.

As for the 57 or so Spratlys, they are coveted by even more states. China and Vietnam were joined by a Philippino, Mr Cloma, when he proclaimed a Free Territory of Freedomland on a Spratly in 1956. The Philippine government asserted an official claim in the 1970s by occupying seven of the islands. In 1984, Malaysia sent in 20 naval commandos to fortify a Spratly atoll that shrinks at high tide to the size of a tennis court. Vietnam and China protested. The struggle goes on.

And then there is the late Fasht al-Dibal, a minute coral reef off Bahrain and Qatar in the Persian Gulf. In 1986 Bahrain hired a Dutch dredging company to build a coastguard station on it. Qatar countered with a helicopter machine gun attack. The Gulf Cooperation Council appointed Saudi Arabia to mediate between its quarrelling neighbours. Saudi Arabia obliged and ordered the Dutch company to bulldoze the islet into the sea. A shame – expatriates in Bahrain lamented the loss of a favourite sunbathing spot.

A state's territory is one in which it tries to enforce all its laws. A privileged area is one in which it tries to apply only some of these laws. The manner in which privileged areas were computed is described in **1. The World of States**.

Sources and Acknowledgements as in **1. The World of States**

3 STATELY PRESENCE

Relations between states are nowhere near as balanced as they appear to be. Where one state's embassy is a hive of activity, its opposite number's might easily be a somnolent white elephant, kept alive for reasons of reciprocity as much as for diplomatic business. For some states, a summit amounts to a string of bilateral head to head meetings interspersed with a few obligatory plenaries. For others the plenaries are the main fare. Many states host international bodies not because these positively wish them to but because it is 'their turn'.

The diplomatic missions to which the map relates are bilateral interstate missions headed by an ambassador or official of equivalent rank (high commissioner, papal nuncio or, in the case of the Libyan diplomatic service, secretary, although here the ranking is ambiguous). It does not include consular, trade or other technical missions, nor missions to international organizations, nor full diplomatic missions without a resident, named incumbent of ambassadorial rank. The full names of the interstate organizations featured on the map are given at the end of this note. They are not all equally vibrant.

As defined for the graphic,'The Summiteers' a summit is a meeting attended in person by two or more world political leaders. It takes no account of direct telephone contact in the style of President Bush. It excludes meetings between national leaders and envoys however elevated, such as between President Gorbachev and US Secretary of State James Baker. It ignores the bilateral side-shows at set-piece multilateral summits.

The period spanned by 'The Summiteers' includes the implosion of the East European regimes and the scattering of their allies, and also the build-up of crisis in the Middle East. Both of these profoundly affected the intensity of summitry and the roster of most active political leaders. These events are not fully reflected. Some of the most energetic summiteers of the time could not be included for technical reasons. These include Presidents Gorbachev and Mitterrand in Europe, and that indefatigable Middle East cliffclimber, King Hussein of Jordan.

ADB	African Development Bank	BIS	Bank for International Settlements
ADB	Asian Development Bank	CACM	Central American Common Market
AFESD	Arab Fund for Economic and Social	CAEU	Council of Arab Economic Unity
	Development	CARICOM	Caribbean Community and Common Market
AG	Andean Group	CCASG	Cooperation Council for the Arab States of
ANZUS	Australia New Zealand United States		the Gulf
ASEAN	Association of South East Asian Nations	CE	Conseil de l'Entente
BADEA	Arab Bank for Economic Development in	CE	Council of Europe
	Africa	CEAO	Communauté Economique de l'Afrique de

	l'Ouest	NCM	Nordic Council of Ministers
CMEA	Council of Mutual Economic Assistance	NEA	Nuclear Energy Agency
	(COMECON)	OAS	Organization of American States
CP	Colombo Pact for Cooperative Economic	OAU	Organization of African Unity
	Development in Asia and the Pacific	OAPEC	Organization of the Arab Petroleum
CW	Commonwealth		Exporting Countries
EBRD	European Bank for Reconstruction and	OIC	Organization of the Islamic Conference
	Development	OPEC	Organization of the Petroleum Exporting
EC	European Commission		Countries
ECA	Economic Commission for Africa	OPEC Fund	OPEC Fund for International Development
ECE	Economic Commission for Europe	SADCC	Southern Africa Development Coordination
ECLAC	Economic Commission for Latin America		Conference
	and the Caribbean	UNCHS	United Nations Centre for Human
ECOWAS	Economic Commission of West African		Settlements
	States	UNCTAD	United Nations Conference on Trade and
EFTA	European Free Trade Association		Development
EP	European Parliament	UNDP	United Nations Development Programme
ESCAP	Economic and Social Commission for Asia	UNDRO	Office of the United Nations Disaster and
	and the Pacific		Relief Coordinator
ESCWA	Economic and Social Commission for	UNEP	United Nations Environmental Programme
	Western Asia	UNESCO	United Nations Educational, Social and
FAO	Food and Agriculture Organization		Cultural Organization
FZ	Franc Zone	UNFPA	United Nations Fund for Population Activities
GATT	General Agreement on Tariffs and Trade	UNHCR	United Nations High Commission for
IAEA	International Atomic Energy Agency		Refugees
IBEC	International Bank for Economic	UNICEF	United Nations Childrens Fund
	Cooperation	UNIDIR	United Nations Institute for Disarmament
ICAO	International Civil Aviation Organization		Research
ICJ	International Court of Justice	UNIDO	United Nations Industrial Development
IDA	International Development Agency		Organization
IDB	Islamic Development Bank	UNITAR	United Nations Institute for Training and
IDB	InterAmerican Development Bank		Research
IEA	International Energy Agency	UNOMPKF	United Nations Observer Missions and Peace
IFAD	International Fund for Agricultural		Keeping Forces
	Development	UNRISD	United Nations Research Institute for Social
IFC	International Finance Corporation		Development
IIB	International Investment Bank	UNRWA	United Nations Relief and Works Agency for
ILO	International Labour Office		Palestinian Refugees in the Near East
IMF	International Monetary Fund	UNU	United Nations University
IMO	International Maritime Organization	UP	University for Peace
INSTRAW	International Research and Training	UPU	Universal Postal Union
	Institute for the Advancement of Women	WEU	Western European Union
IOM	International Organization for Migration	WFC	World Food Council
ISBA	International Sea-Bed Authority	WFP	World Food Programme
ITU	International Telecommunications Union	WHO	World Health Organization
LAIA	Latin American Integration Association	WIPO	World Intellectual Property Organization
LAS	League of Arab States (Arab League)	WMO	World Meteorological Organization
NATO	North Atlantic Treaty Organization	WP	Warsaw Pact
NC	Nordic Council	WTO	World Tourism Organization

Sources:
The Europa World Yearbook 1990, London: Europa Publications, 1990; Reuters *Textline* database; press reports.

Acknowledgements:
Julia, Kate, Francis, David and Andrew at Reuters' helpline, and Mark and Roger in technical backup were exceptionally patient and helpful.

4 THE POPULATION OF STATES

On 1 July 1990, seven million people set out to count the population of China. The biggest census ever undertaken, it was probably also one of the most difficult. For, as well as having to contend with the normal problems of reaching the isolated, the marginal, the actively hostile, the illegal, the anti- or a-social and the many others who avoid officialdom everywhere, they had to contend with peculiarly 'Chinese' problems: how to locate the 'floating population' of 50 million or so illegals in the cities, eager for work while remaining anonymous; how to find the tens of millions of 'black babies', unregistered by parents who had violated the one-child family programme, and ignored by officials wanting to save on educational or social expenditure; how to account for the millions of 'disappeared' – victims of female infanticide, still a feature of peasant life in some areas.

In China, at least the problems were faced. In some states they are not. In states ravaged by war – there were no fewer than 40 at the beginning of this decade – wide areas are simply taken out of bounds to would-be census takers. In the Lebanon, a census would reveal such a discrepancy between the constitutional arrangements and the communal composition of the population on which they are based, that censuses have long been off limits. In other states, Nigeria is an example, political arrangements are so clearly involved with the results of the population count, that the census itself is routinely rigged. It has become as much the product of politics as its determinant. In many states, no provision is made for a specialist census administration; and population figures are supplied by officials often engaged in other, more pressing business, who have not necessarily been appointed for their numeracy or their diligence.

If it were not for international agencies, headed by the Population Division of the United Nations, we would be hard put to know how many we are, where we are, and how fast our number is growing. These agencies provide annual estimates of all states' populations and an essential critique of the often self-serving national figures.

However, even their figures should be treated with caution, particularly when used for forecasting future populations. Reproduction habits can change unexpectedly; mass migrations can swarm suddenly; wars can decimate and disperse whole populations: at the end of the 1980s, no fewer than six states – Afghanistan, Angola, Cambodia, Chad, Laos and Nicaragua – were thought to contain populations more than 10 percent below those forecast for them at the beginning of that decade.

States with under 0.05 percent of the world's population, or less than 2.65 million people, do not feature in the cartogram.

Sources:
McEvedy, Colin, & Richard Jones, *Atlas of World Population History*, London: Allen Lane, 1978; Population Reference Bureau, Inc., *1990 World Population Data Sheet*, Washington DC, 1990; press reports.

Acknowledgements:
Chris Longford at the Department of Demography, London School of Economics, pointed out some statistical traps and tracks. Fiona Bristow of Population Concern, London, signposted the way.

5 MARKET MUSCLE

Even if the trade that is admitted to were accurately recorded and if, further, every international drug dealer, arms merchant and professional smuggler, not to mention every amateur customs dodger, were to declare where they had bought their goods and where they were taking them, we still would not know much about power in the world market place – who sells how much of what. For commercial producers of goods are increasingly footloose between states. Many companies might appear to be local firms in their adoptive states, but they are essentially foreign visitors, closer to their home state than their host's and, in principle, always ready to up stakes and go in search of richer markets, cheaper facilities and better conditions.

Their existence allows a gap to open up between net exports – the difference between the amount shipped from the state and the amount shipped into it – and net foreign sales – the difference between sales by a country's firms both at home and abroad and their purchases from foreign firms at home and abroad. This is the real measure of world market power.

Where there is little or no cross-border investment in or out, as in Albania, Chad and Mongolia, the gap is notional, and net exports are a reasonable indicator of selling clout. In other cases the gap is so huge as to challenge the conventional view of a state's relative market power. The USA is such a case: measured conventionally, the USA is a cripple in world trade, with a trade *deficit* bobbing around US$150 billion a year in the mid-1980s, compared to Japan's *surplus* of $30 billion odd. But measured by net foreign sales, the USA is a true giant with a *surplus* of $60 billion, half as much again as Japan's. You could say: with a gap like that who needs to worry about the USA's payments deficit?

While some states can afford to ignore the gap, and others can derive comfort from its existence, there are others for which the difference between market power as measured by net exports and net foreign sales is alarming. At the beginning of the 1990s, the big home-grown European car manufacturers were besieging and beseeching (reports varied) the European Commission to include in the proposed quota on Japanese car imports **121** those cars manufactured in Japanese transplants inside the Community. Rightly, they and their governments saw no essential distinction between a product that rolls off a freighter and one that rolls out of a factory gate.

That the corrected vision differs significantly from the distorted ruling view is clear. The unanswered questions are to what degree and in what particulars. The scant evidence that exists suggests, reassuringly, that the major exporters are also the main generators of the foreign direct investments which create the gap in the first place. To that extent, the cartogram is a reasonable proxy for the real picture. It shows relative gross exports of states credited with 0.1 percent or more of total recorded world exports, not their relative net exports or trade balances.

The cartogram owes much to DeAnne Julius's insights and materials. The graphic 'Corrected Vision' merely transmutes her prose and figures into a different form. The caption takes enormous liberties with her work by averaging the ratio – which she gives – of net foreign sales to net exports in the USA and Japan, and applying that average to the five (European) countries that appear next on the list of top exporters.

The graphic 'Ready, Steady...' is based on 326 criteria, 200 quantitative and 126 qualitative, grouped around ten themes: economic dynamism, industrial efficiency, market orientation, financial dynamism, human resources, state's impact, natural endowment utilization, international orientation, future orientation and socio-political stability.

Sources:
International Monetary Fund (IMF), *Direction of Trade Statistics Yearbook*, Washington DC: IMF 1987 & 1990; Julius, DeAnne, *Global Companies and Public Policy, The Growing Challenge of Foreign Direct Investments*, London: Pinter Publishers for the Royal Institute of International Affairs (RIIA), 1990; Julius, DeAnne, *Foreign Direct Investments: Trojan Horse or Spur to Growth?*, preliminary draft, London: August 1990; Thomsen, Stephen, & Phedon Nicolaides, *Foreign Direct Investment: 1992 and Global Markets*, RIIA Discussion Papers, no.28, London: RIIA, 1990; *The World Competitiveness Report 1990*, Lausanne: IMD International, and Geneva: World Economic Forum, 1990; press reports.

Acknowledgements:
DeAnne Julius, Chief Economist at Shell International, London, Graham Vickery of the OECD, Paris, and Stephen Thomsen of the RIIA, London, pointed to the barely discernible tracks in the Data Desert. Stephane Garelli of the IMD, Lausanne, was generous with material and encouragement.

6 NATIONAL INCOME

Gross National Product (GNP) is the most widely-used general measure of economic power, and for that reason alone is unavoidable when making international comparisons. But it is as well to treat it cautiously.

It measures the consumption of goods and services that are bought, the savings and investments destined to produce them, and government expenditure. It does not normally count unmarketed goods produced for home consumption, and does not cover at all the untraded services, from sex to socialization, which are an essential ingredient of human life. It therefore underrates the incomes of rural and family-oriented societies and overrates industrial ones and those resting on nuclear and sub-nuclear families. It does not cover the cost, in depletion and damage, of economic activity and, therefore, understates the income of traditional and subsistence-agriculture societies where they still exist and exaggerates that of resource-based, market-oriented economies. It does not distinguish between productive and unproductive activity – between the making of butter and of guns – and therefore, at least in the short term, confuses economic with military power. In consequence whatever its virtues as a pointer to the current resources potentially available to the state, and as a standard of comparison, it is fairly hopeless as a yardstick of human welfare or of social health.

Even within its own terms, GNP accounting is flawed. It is insensitive to changes in consumption patterns, and so an imperfect guide to changes over time. Expressed in a single currency, conventionally the US dollar, it is at the mercy of exchange rates which can gyrate madly. Does the income of the world at large relative to that of the United States really rise by one percent when the dollar drops one percent on the foreign exchange markets, as happens almost daily, if not hourly, in periods of monetary excitement?

The World Bank, the best and most widely used source for GNP figures, copes with some of these flaws by not producing any for some states, including the USSR and most of Eastern Europe. Since this atlas cannot wait until 'a broadly acceptable methodology is developed', it has reluctantly made its own crude estimates of the missing numbers: for the USSR and most East European states it took the CIA estimates (for 1988) and reduced them by two-thirds – the weighted average difference between the CIA's estimates and the World Bank's 1989 figures for Bulgaria, Hungary, Poland and Yugoslavia, where both were available. As for the rest, where policy considerations can be thought to have played less havoc with the estimates, we have swallowed the CIA figures neat.

Most figures relate to 1989; some to 1988 or 1987. Only states that can claim 0.01 percent or more of the world total have been featured.

A different measure, elaborated by the International Comparison Project of the United Nations, is 'real' Gross Domestic Product (GDP), based on purchasing power. This attempts to gauge what countries could buy if they all shopped in a single world supermarket. It is better than the conventional measure in that it makes allowance for different cost structures – a haircut is a haircut is a haircut, anywhere in the world, but it is more expensive compared to a hamburger in the USA than it is compared to a chapatti in India, and the same is true generally of services in relation to manufactures.

'Real' GDP shares many of the problems of its conventional cousin: difficulties of conversion into a standard measure (in this case 'international' dollars); weaknesses in accounting for goods and services that do not come onto the market; insensitivity to the effects of economic activity on the environmental storehouse. But it does put to right some of the distortions engendered by that cousin: in broad outline, it shows that world purchasing power, although still shockingly concentrated in few states, is more evenly spread amongst them than world income.

The procedure adopted to find 'real' GDP exaggerates the difference between the two measures. The GNP figures derived as described above were multiplied by the ratio of GDP per head in purchasing power parity dollars ('international dollars') to GNP per head in US dollars as given in the UNDP's *Human Development Report 1990*. Since GNP includes, and GDP excludes, net claims on foreign income, the procedure adopted understates real interstate income disparities.

Sources:
United Nations Development Programme (UNDP), *Human Development Report 1990*, Oxford: Oxford University Press for UNDP, 1990; World Bank, *World Bank Atlas 1990*, Washington DC: World Bank, 1991; Central Intelligence Agency (CIA), *Handbook of Economic Statistics 1989*, Washington DC: CIA, 1989; CIA, *The World Factbook 1990*, Washington DC: CIA, 1990.

Acknowledgements:
Meghnad Desai of the Economics Department, London School of Economics, and Michael Ward of the International Economics Department, World Bank, Washington, have been generous with elucidation and material.

7 BANKABLES AND UNBANKABLES

For a banker like John Reed it is disappointing that the unbankables outnumber the bankables by more than five to one (see caption). From a higher standpoint, that of the financial and market systems which brought the imbalance about, it is alarming. Less than a fifth of humanity is not much of a barrier against the rages that suddenly converge and thunder through our increasingly connected and homogenized world (see **19. Critical Mass**). And even that fifth is uncertain, so painfully unequal are individuals' stakes in the current order (see **14. Rich and Poor**) and so morally shaky is the ground claimed by the more than equal (see **40. This Little Piggy**).

The financial heartland of the market system is surprisingly small. The top 25 commercial banks are based in just eight states. Just two states – the USA and Japan – house one-third of the top 1000 banks; and more than three-quarters of them reside in only 16 states.

Sources:
The Banker, London, July 1990; *Moody's Global Ratings*, vol.III, no.8, August 1990, New York: Moody's Investor Service Inc, 1990; Standard & Poor's, *Credit Review*, 26 June 1989, and press releases to 1 August 1990, New York: Standard & Poor's Corp, 1990; World Bank, *World Debt Tables 1989-90*, vols I & II, Washington, DC: World Bank, 1989.

8 FUNNY MONEY

In theory, money exists to facilitate the welfare of citizens, not the power of states. In practice, the state serves its own purposes. It forces its people to accept its currency, and then defrauds them by debasing it. Most do so directly on their own account, others, with pegged currencies, plead *force majeure*. Some, like Germany, do so modestly; others, like Brazil, flamboyantly. All do it at some time or other, and by doing it, transfer wealth from the poor and weak who are helpless victims of the process, to the rich and strong who can manipulate it to their own benefit.

Inflation is socially disruptive. It is also an expensive irritation for business that draws a growing part of its income from abroad (see **36. The Billion-Dollar Club**). Increasingly business and the state are pulling in opposite directions, the one agitating for money to be truly a part of the constitutional framework, the other fearful that its interests would suffer if money were removed from the arena of day-to-day politics.

One, parochial, outcome of the tussle is the years-long wrangling over monetary union between Britain, where the state is relatively ascendant, and the rest of the European Community, where business is. Another, very much more important example is the ever-enhancing role of the International Monetary Fund as the world's policeman and fraud catcher.

The instruments available to the IMF to restrain, if not eliminate, inflation, have increased over time. Starting with short-term Stand-by Arrangements for essentially solvent states with cash-flow problems, it added the longer-period Extended Fund Facility Arrangement for the same group of states, and then extended its stabilization measures to the poor and desperately poor, by means of its Structural Adjustment Facility and Enhanced Structural Adjustment Facility. Intent on showing the extent of the IMF's intervention, I have not drawn distinctions between these instruments on the inset map.

Sources:
Barclays Economic Review, November 1990; International Monetary Fund (IMF), *Annual Reports*, Washington DC, 1985 to 1990; IMF, *International Financial Statistics*, Washington DC: IMF, August 1990; Central Intelligence Agency (CIA), *Handbook of Economic Statistics 1989*, Washington DC: CIA, 1989.

Acknowledgements:
L.E.N. (Eustace) Fernando, Alternate Executive Director at the IMF, Washington DC, has been ultra-generous with materials and elucidation. John Caveny, of the *Financial Times*, London, and Kurt Noll of Lombard Odier & Cie, Vevey, provided materials. Steve Drake, Jonathan Franklin and Peter Kirkham of the *Financial Times*, London, Keith Edwards of the National Westminster Bank, London, Ken Horne of Hill Samuel and Co., London, and Dr Weiss of the Union de Banques Suisses, Zurich, persuaded me not to bark up the wrong tree.

9 ENERGY POWER

Unless much more energy is used, hundreds of millions more people will suffer hunger, disease, discomfort and physical and mental confinement than do at present; for energy is the feedstock of material abundance and personal choice. But if energy continues to be produced in the same way as now and from the same resources, even more people will suffer (see **48. The Scorchers**).

Controlling wasteful and frivolous uses of energy would help, but we would need to capture more of the essentially boundless radiation of the sun to escape the dilemma. But that is another story, a story in which the poor states do not frustrate a beneficial outcome by trying to follow the path mapped out by the rich ones; in which the rich in all states do not frustrate it by lavishing energy on trifles while the poor scrape for trifling amounts; in which the military do not use energy as if there were no tomorrow; in which incentives for business to produce and stay with conventional fossil fuels do not overwhelm the gestures made to encourage unconventional renewable fuels.

The main map, which shows how dependent a state is on outside supplies at current levels of energy use, also indicates how dependent many poor ones are on traditional fuels. These – wood, and animal and vegetable wastes – while doing something to alleviate scarcity in the short run, only increase and aggravate other environmental and social problems (see, for example, **19. Critical Mass**).

In some states these traditional fuels are very nearly the sole source of energy: wood alone accounts for more than nine-tenths of the fuel used in Burundi, Central African

Republic, Chad, Ivory Coast, Mali, Rwanda, Somalia and Tanzania in Africa, and also in Nepal. In other states, although these traditional fuels fall below the arbitrarily chosen 50 percent cut-off point on the map, they are still hugely important. In Brazil, India, Pakistan and Tunisia, for example, they supply more than one-third of the energy used.

International trade in energy – as depicted in 'Heat Exchange' – is primarily trade in oil and gas and their derivatives (64 percent of the total) and secondarily in coal (31 percent).

The map uses the joule as the standard general measure of energy consumption. It is equal to the amount of heat generated by an electric current of one ampere flowing for one second against a resistance of one ohm, or 0.239 calories. One gigajoule equals 1 billion (1,000,000,000) joules which is equivalent to 34.1 tonnes of coal or 23.8 tonnes of oil. One terajoule equals 1000 gigajoules.

Sources:
United Nations, *Energy Statistics Yearbook 1988*, New York: UN, 1990; World Energy Council (WEC), *Report 1989: International Energy Data*, London: WEC, 1990; Eckholm, Eric, et al, *Fuelwood: the energy crisis that won't go away*, London and Washington DC: International Institute for Environment and Development, 1984; press reports.

Acknowledgements:
Amory Lovins of the Rocky Mountain Institute, Colorado, propelled me to the World Energy Council, London, where Fred Dixon, assistant to the General Secretary, guided me through the measurements, the literature, and to Bill Clive, Chief of the Energy Statistics Unit at the UN Statistical Office, New York, who was, in turn, unstinting with advice, elucidation and materials.

10 FOOD POWER

As the example of Japan shows, you do not have to grow your own food, you do not even have to grow staple cereals, to eat well. But as the same Japan's self-serving rice lobby loudly proclaims, and the example of Iraq underlines, dependence on imports for your staple food opens up a state to external pressure. 'Food', said a combative US Agriculture Secretary in the early 1980s, 'is a weapon. It is now one of the principal weapons in our negotiating kit'.

Average agricultural yields differ wildly from state to state, depending on land, climatic, social and technical conditions. They ranged, at the end of the 1980s, from 6650 kilograms per hectare in the Netherlands down to 380 in Angola. This leaves plenty of room for improvement in the world as a whole. But no conceivable growth in productivity, even coupled with an extension of acreage, will make all states as currently configured self-sufficient (see inset map 'Carrying Capacity').

Self-sufficiency in food production does not automatically guarantee an adequate diet, or even freedom from hunger (see **15. Our Daily Bread**).

Sources:
Food and Agriculture Organization (FAO), *Land, Food and People*, Rome: FAO, 1984; Higgins, G.M., et al, *Potential Population Supporting Capacities of Lands in the Developing World*, Rome: FAO, 1982.

Acknowledgements:
Maurice Purnell, Gabriel Kouthon and their colleagues at the FAO in Rome were unfailingly helpful and resourceful. Others who propelled me along, or prevented my straying, were Bjorn Olson of the International Trade Centre, Geneva, and Karl Sauvant, Policy Research Division, UN Centre on Transnational Corporations (UNCTC), New York.

11 INDUSTRIAL POWER

Although much of what is produced and exported in the world is made by nationals for foreign owners, no one knows how much. Ownership and control are shy, self-effacing creatures. They like to merge into the background. This is particularly true in manufacturing.

Between 1950 and 1985 world output of goods increased fivefold, and exports ninefold. Manufacturing output rose seven times and exports 16 times. Exports of manufactures from 'developing' countries (primarily Hong Kong, South Korea, Singapore, Taiwan and, some way behind, Brazil and Mexico) rose from 11.16 percent of the total in 1966 to 13.83 percent in 1986, and the share of US majority-owned affiliates in these countries' exports rose from 3.9 to 7.2 percent in the same period.

The share of manufacturing exports controlled by all US firms – minority- and majority- **125** owned – must be even greater, and growing even faster, and by inference, US control over industrial production must be tending the same way. All of which reinforces the conclusion that the USA's economic might is far greater than one would expect from looking at its negative trade balance (see **5. Market Muscle**).

The little that is known about other industrial states confirms this picture. Japanese affiliates increased their share of 'developing' country exports of manufactures by more than half between 1974 and 1983, and in general, the results for Swedish firms were quite similar to those for US affiliates. Since the rest of the rich industrial pack cannot be far behind, there is little reason to doubt that industrial power on a world scale is even more concentrated than would appear from the cartogram.

The statistics on national production and exports used in this cartogram need some explanation. Most come from the World Bank and suffer from that organization's preoccupation with GDPs and from its over-cautious eschewing of estimates for some countries' production, notably that of the USSR and Eastern Europe (see notes to **6. National Income**). The statistics for the USSR were derived by converting the rouble figures for industrial production, as given by the Vienna Institute for Comparative Economic Studies, into US dollars at the rate of 1:1. This grossly exaggerates the USSR's manufacturing prowess on two counts: it includes electricity production (stripped out of other states' figures) and it overvalues the rouble to a ludicrous degree. The figures for Czechoslovakia, Poland and Iraq were derived by converting the United Nations Industrial Development Organization's estimates of manufacturing's share of national income into US dollars – using the most appropriate exchange rates recorded by the International Monetary Fund.

Sources:
Blomström, Magnus, *Transnational Corporations and Manufacturing Exports from Developing Countries*, New York: United Nations (UN), 1990; Ernst, Dieter, and David O'Connor, 'Technological Capabilities, New Technologies and Latecomer Industrialization – an Agenda for the 1990s', ch.8 of the TEP Report, Paris: OECD, 1990; International Monetary Fund (IMF), *International Financial Statistics*, Washington DC: IMF, monthly; UN, *Monthly Bulletin of Statistics*, Geneva: UN, June 1989; United Nations Industrial Development Organization (UNIDO), *Handbook of Industrial Statistics 1990*, Vienna: UNIDO, 1990; Wiener Institut für Internationale Wirtschaftsvergleiche, *Comecon Data 1988*, London: Macmillan, 1989; World Bank, *World Development Report 1990*, Oxford and New York: Oxford University Press for the World Bank, 1990.

Acknowledgements:
John Cavanagh, Institute of Policy Studies, Washington DC, pointed me towards a number of his friends. Dieter Ernst of the OECD Development Centre, Paris, persuaded me that there were no data lurking behind the virtual data, and that only time – if anything – would tell us what we need to know about ownership and control of industrial production. Karl Sauvant, Policy Analysis Research Division, UN Centre on Transnational Corporations (UNCTC), New York, helped with bibliographical advice and materials.

12 SERVICE POWER

Services are usually intangible, and their production and consumption usually take place simultaneously. As conventionally defined they include wholesale and retail trade, all transport of people and freight, communications and information-related activities, business and professional services, banking and financial services (including insurance), and personal, community and social services.

Even more than in the case of tangible goods, they are difficult to record, difficult to measure, and difficult to compare across countries and through time (see notes to **6. National Income**). But they are clearly growing as a proportion of world employment, as a share of world trade (if not of world production) and as an arena for foreign direct investment. They account for sizeable proportions of the foreign direct investments of the major trading states: 52 percent of Japan's, 47 percent of Germany's and Australia's, 44 percent of the USA's, 36 percent of Britain's, 29 percent of Canada's and 27 percent of the Netherlands'.

The map focusses on private services, that is transfers of non-merchandise real resources that are neither official nor financial – the fastest-growing sector. More about services can be gleaned from **20. Outreach** and **42. Workplaces**.

Sources:
UN Centre on Transnational Corporations (UNCTC), *Foreign Direct Investment, the Service Sector and International Banking*, UNCTC Current Studies Series A, no.7, New York: UN, May 1987; Hoekman, Bernard M., and Robert M. Stern, *Evolving Patterns of Trade and Investment in Services*, paper delivered to the Conference on Research in Income and
 Wealth, International Economic Transactions: Issues in Measurement and Empirical Research, 3-4 November 1989,

Washington DC; Hoekman, Bernard M., 'Service-Related Production, Employment, Trade and Factor Movements', in Messelin, Patrick, and Karl Sauvant, eds, *The Uruguay Round: Services in the World Economy*, Washington DC: World Bank/UNCTC, 1990; General Agreement on Tariffs and Trade (GATT) database, Geneva, 29 November 1990; Multilateral Trade Negotiations, The Uruguay Round, Group of Negotiations on Services, *Availability of Statistics on Services, Note by The Secretariat*, Geneva: GATT, 15 February 1990 (restricted); press reports.

Acknowledgements:
I have been helped in various important ways, by Robert Cassen of Queen Elizabeth House, Oxford, Bernard M. Hoekman and Lydia Silvetti of the Economic Research Division of GATT, Geneva, Henry Kierkowski, Geneva, and Gary Samson, Head of the Group of Negotiations on Services, GATT, Geneva.

13 SCIENCE POWER

Not everyone would choose to measure science output by the number of articles published in scientific journals, or gauge the influence of a scientific observation by the number of references to an article in subsequent journal articles, but the scientists themselves do and we have no option but to follow them.

Albeit reluctantly. Although the method is venerable – an article published in 1917 analysed over 6000 publications in comparative anatomy that appeared between 1543 and 1860 – it is not without problems. In its modern guise it owes much of its acceptance to the existence of a voluminous database at the Institute of Scientific Information, Philadelphia, Pa: the Scientific Citation Index (SCI) which covers some 3500 journals and a few hundred monographs, collections and so on worldwide, with an annual total close to 500,000 papers.

Many institutions use, and customize, the ISI's unique and growing archive, notably the influential CHI Research Inc, Haddon Heights, NJ; the Information Science and Scientometric Research Unit in the Library of the Hungarian Academy of Sciences, Budapest; and the Science Policy Research Unit, University of Sussex, Brighton, UK. A lot of what they do is illuminating. Essentially, though, there is a single source for the raw data. Its biases are necessarily shared.

These biases stem from the selection of journals that make up the SCI sample, from its treatment of authorship, from the choice of citation conventions and from the host of other factors, big and small, that make for local variants of the international scientific culture.

A study completed in 1980 found that the USA and the UK are favoured as against all other states – perceptibly as against Germany and France, grossly as against Japan and the USSR, and overwhelmingly as against the poor countries. The SCI sample allocated to the USA nearly twice the proportion of journals it could claim in the science serials catalogue at the British Library's Lending Division (38.8 percent as against 20.1 percent). For the UK the discrepancy was 15.3 as against 12.6 percent, for Germany 9.9 as against 8.2 percent. France came out evenly at 5.2 percent. But the USSR scored 3.5 percent with the SCI as against 8.8 percent with the British Library, Japan 3.2 and 6.1, and the rest of the world 24.0 and 39.2 percent, respectively. Other studies show different results in detail but point in the same general direction: English-language states are over-represented, the others under-represented; Latin script is favoured, as against other scripts; disciplines with a relatively dispersed literature (biology and mathematics, for example) fare worse than those with a few major journals (physics and earth space, or engineering and technology).

Nonetheless the overall conclusion is clear: the USA is the science superpower, Japan is a rapidly rising sun, and there is a very small cluster of European contenders. The future of science lies in Research and Development. Although the USA is again the big spender here, its margin is not so wide, especially if unproductive military R&D is excluded.

Sources:
Schubert, A., et al, 'Scientometric Datafiles. A Comprehensive Set of Indicators on 2649 Journals and 96 Countries in all Major Fields and Subfields 1981-1985', *Scientometrics*, vol.16, nos 1-6, Amsterdam: Elsevier and Budapest: Akademiai Kiado, 1989; Jankowski, John E., *National Patterns of R & D Resources: 1990, Final Report*, for the National Science Foundation (NSF), pp.90-316, Washington DC: NSF, 1990; Carpenter, Mark P., and Francis Narin, 'The Adequacy of the Science Citation Index (SCI) as an Indicator of International Scientific Activity', *Journal of the American Society for Informational Science*, November 1981; Frame, J.Davidson, 'National Economic Resources and the Production of Research in Lesser Developed Countries', *Social Studies of Science*, vol.IX, pp.233-46, London and Beverly Hills: SAGE, 1979; Frame, J.Davidson, and Francis Narin, 'The International **127**

Distribution of Biomedical Publications', *Federation Proceedings*, vol.XXXVI, no.6, May 1977.

Acknowledgements:
Friendly advice, ample criticism, generous directions, open reservations and sustaining material have come, in different measure and at different stages, from Jennifer Sue Bond of the National Science Foundation, Washington DC, Peter Collins of The Royal Society, London, Maurice Goldsmith of the International Science Policy Foundation, London, John Irvine of Science Policy Research Consultants, Hove, East Sussex, Francis Narin, CHI Research Inc., Haddon Heights, NJ, David Pendlebury and Henry Small of the Institute for Scientific Information, Philadelphia, Pa., Michaela Smith of the Commonwealth Secretariat, London, and Vitek Tracz, *Current Science*, London.

14 RICH AND POOR

At their last count, in 1983, the US Federal Reserve Board concluded that there were roughly eight million *affluent* families in the USA, by its own definition families with a net worth of US$250,000 and an annual income of US$75,000. The *rich* – with assets of a million US dollars and an annual income of $200,000 – numbered 600,000, 15 per thousand households; and the *truly rich* – with assets of $10 million or more – numbered 70,000, less than one per thousand. Such figures are awesome.

Not long after, in 1988, about 32 million Americans were thought to be living below the official poverty line of $6000 for a single person, nearly eight million more than in the late 1970s when dole queues were as long, 13 percent of the population compared with 11.5 percent ten years earlier. Nearly one-third of all Blacks and over one-quarter of all Hispanics were amongst the poor. Almost a fifth of all children, including 44 percent of Black children and 38 percent of Hispanic children, are poor. Such figures are equally awesome.

The USA is not the worst offender. Among the 40 states for which there are data, it comes one-third down the income-disparity list. So if it scores the highest infant mortality rate of any OECD country barring Portugal and Greece, or if parts of New York boast a life expectancy at birth lower than Bangladesh, its citizens may yet rejoice – their level of inequality is only one-third that of Brazil.

Inequality rules OK, it flourishes as the world market system deepens and spreads. One of the most obvious results of communism's collapse in Eastern Europe at the end of the last decade was the emergence of sharper public disparities in income. The uniform drabness and common oppression that prevailed under the old *nomenklatura* quickly gave way – under the new *priviligentsia*, more often than not first cousins or closer of the old rulers – to many layers of differentiation between those with a place in the world market and those without, between those who can command a rent and those who cannot. Poles have been forced further apart, as have Germans, Czechs, Hungarians, Russians and the rest. There, and throughout the world, a growing underclass of redundants, in fact if not by official admission, is forming alongside and outside the realm of 'substance'.

The gulf between states is appreciably smaller than is conventionally depicted. That is because comparisons are usually drawn on the basis of GNP per head, without taking into account the different price levels prevailing between different states and, therefore, the differing purchasing power of money (see note to **6. National Income**). More generally the population of poor states, while still desperately poor, are measurably closer to rich populations when real GDP per person is used in the comparison, than when the conventional GNP per head is used: for example, in GNP terms China's and India's income per head is only 1.6 percent of the USA's, but 12 percent and 6 percent respectively in real GDP terms.

Billionaires are different. They inhabit a single world with common prices and a single currency – the US dollar. I have assigned to them an annual income of 10 percent of their estimated net asset value.

Sources:
United Nations Development Programme (UNDP), *Human Development Report 1991*, tables 15 & 18 (draft version); 'The Billionaires', *Fortune*, 10 September 1990, New York: Time Inc. Magazines; press reports.

Acknowledgements:
Leo Goldstone, UNDP, New York, went out of his way to make material available before the appointed time.

People seldom go hungry because there is not enough food. More often it is because they cannot command an adequate share of what food exists, or the material and cultural resources to make good nutritional use of what they might find before them. That explains the not unusual spectacle of hunger amid bumper harvests, as in the Bengal famine of 1943, the Bangladeshi famine of 1974, and some of the famines in Africa in the 1990s – 'boom-famines' during which people starve because they are out of work and money-less, or because normal arrangements for the distribution of food have collapsed.

So self-sufficiency, the subject of **10. Food Power**, is only part of the food story, the part relating to the power of the state. The other part, of greater immediate relevance to the citizen, is access to what food exists, which has to do with a state's effectiveness.

The presence, or absence, of famine is the most public test of that effectiveness. But famine is not the worst that the state can inflict on the poor. Take the contrasting experience of India and China, the two population super-states. India has not undergone a major famine since independence in 1947. China has – in 1958-61 when the government's Great Leap Forward to industrialization plunged the country into the worst famine ever to have been recorded, with 23-30 million victims. Yet adjusted for population size and composition, there are some 3.9 million extra deaths a year in India as compared with China – every six to eight years more people die in India from hunger-related causes than in the gigantic Chinese disaster. Who is to say which is worse?

Food is scarce in much of Africa and getting scarcer. Famines are frequent. Its new rulers have acquired a 'global palate', a taste for expensive foreign foods, to match their taste for expensive imported consumer durables. Shortages of foreign exchange have prompted them to concentrate on non-nutritional cash crops that can be sold abroad. The consequent decline of the countryside as a provider of food has been compounded by policies to keep food cheap for the urban populace, with the result that farmers are deprived of adequate incentives and drain into the towns.

These are examples of the many states whose preoccupations and policies condemn millions to permanent undernourishment while other states do not know where to turn to offload their accumulated surplus stocks of food. The world is capable of feeding decently all its inhabitants. That it is conspicuously not doing so at present is the product not of necessity but of choice.

World hunger is not new; it is simply getting worse. The map suggests where it is most concentrated. But it does no more than suggest. It cannot be definitive since the conventional measure – calorie intake – is imperfect: it groups overeaters and undereaters in bland national averages; it does the same for the young and the old, the active and the inactive, the pregnant and the not so pregnant, the ill and the hale – all of whom have different energy and, hence, nutritional needs; and it focuses on calories rather than on a balanced diet.

Glitches in food production or distribution, a rise in unemployment, disruption caused by war, civil commotion, a change in government policy – many things can tip widespread chronic hunger into famine. Not that famine itself is so clear-cut. It is only when large numbers gathered together are *publicly* seen to be missing the barest necessities of food that the record of death is ascribed to starvation rather than a more morally neutral named disease.

Sources:
Office of US Foreign Disaster Assistance, Agency for International Development, *Disaster History. Significant Data on Major Disasters Worldwide. 1900-present*, Washington DC, August 1990; UNDP database printout 6 December 1990; Dreze, Jean, and Amartya Sen, *Hunger and Public Action*, Oxford: Clarendon Press, 1989; *Energy and Protein Requirements. Report of a Joint FAO/WHO/UNU Expert Consultation*, Geneva: World Health Organization, 1985; James, W.P.T., and E.C. Schofield, *Human Energy Requirements*, Oxford University Press for the FAO; United Nations Disaster Relief Coordinator, *Situation in Africa, an Overview*, nos 1-9, August 1984 – April 1986, Geneva: United Nations Disaster Relief Organization (UNDRO); *Disaster News in Brief (1 January-31 December 1987)*, Geneva: UNDRO, 1988; World Bank, *Social Indicators of Development 1989*, Baltimore and London: Johns Hopkins University Press, 1989; World Resources Institute, *World Resources 1990-91*, New York and Oxford: Oxford University Press, 1990; press reports.

Acknowledgements:
Djamil Benbouzid of the Nutritional Unit, World Health Organization, Geneva, put me in safe hands. Philip James of the Rowett Research Institute, Aberdeen, enlightened me greatly with a particle of his vast knowledge. Dennis King, Research Analyst at the Office of Foreign Disaster Assistance, Washington DC, undertook a special search and rushed the results. Marie-Lou Darrican of the UNDRO helped with materials.

16 LIFE SUPPORT

Living long does not necessarily mean living well, nor does living well necessarily mean living long, but the two do reinforce one another. Unfortunately the measures we have for them are crude and obscure their mutual effect.

Their primary weakness is over-aggregation: it is plain, for example, that virtually everyone in the USA can reach a local health service facility within an hour using normal means of transport, which is the conventional criterion of access to medical care. Yet it is also true that 31-37 million Americans are without any health cover and many more are underinsured and so effectively denied medical attention. It appears to be true that all Soviet citizens are covered in the same sense, but some of the medical facilities on offer are so poor, unhygienic and downright dangerous that they are often avoided (see notes to **17. Modern Plagues**).

Over-aggregation affects the map in other ways: life expectancy at birth – the basic ingredient for the main map – uses an average figure for both men and women, when in reality there are significant differences, women generally living longer than men. The same is true of access to safe drinking water – the basis for the inset map 'On Tap?' – where the typically enormous disparities between conditions in the countryside and in town are smothered under an average which flatters the first at the expense of the second.

Over-aggregation is not the only weakness of the data. Simply, they contain too many round fractions – halves, thirds, quarters – to ring true. They reek of the office and of records, not of the outside world with all its particularities. But they are the best we have and represent reality, however crudely.

Sources:
United Nations Environment Programme (UNEP), *Environmental Data Report 1989/90*, Oxford and Cambridge, Mass: Basil Blackwell, 1989; World Bank, *Social Indicators of Development 1989*, Baltimore and London: Johns Hopkins University Press, 1989; World Resources Institute, *World Resources 1990-91*, New York and Oxford: Oxford University Press, 1990; United Nations Children's Fund (UNICEF), *The State of the World's Children, 1990*, New York and Oxford: Oxford University Press for UNICEF, 1990.

Acknowledgements: as in **17. Modern Plagues**.

17 MODERN PLAGUES

HIV, the human immunodeficiency virus that causes AIDS, is probably the most sinister ever to hit humans. The virus can remain in the blood for years, perhaps decades, before any damage shows up as visible disease; the disease it causes seems always to be fatal; its victim becomes increasingly vulnerable to almost any infection – by another virus, a bacterium, a fungus or a parasite. HIV catches people at the unguarded intersection between supreme pleasure and deadly pain.

AIDS has spread fast. Within ten years of being reported as a distinct, new disease in the USA in 1981, it has turned up in 157 countries. It is now the prime cause of death amongst young adults aged 20 to 40 in major cities in the Americas, western Europe and Black Africa. In September 1990 the World Health Organization estimated that there were more than 800,000 full-blown AIDS cases among adults (three times the number reported), and that there were more than eight million people infected with HIV. By the year 2000, it estimates there will be at least 600,000 new cases of AIDS a year, and 18.3 million people will have contracted HIV.

AIDS is the most recent, most insidious and most deadly of the current social diseases – killers and debilitators that flourish because of the way we order our affairs. But it is only one of many. These range from cancers that kill 2.3 million people a year in the rich countries alone, to sick building syndrome that affects a third of all new and remodelled commercial buildings; from infectious diseases that kill one in six infants in poor countries to stomach ulcers which plague 15-20 percent of people in rich countries at some point in their lives. It is these social diseases which sustain the concept of preventable or premature deaths illustrated in the inset map 'Before Their Time'.

In addition to the usual caveats about data compiled centrally by people remote from both the scene and the topic, a caution has to be entered about the special ills which medical statistics are heir to. Chief amongst them must be the ambiguity that surrounds the proximate cause of death or disability. What will be recorded on the death certificate? The opportunist pneumonia that finally kills the AIDS victim or the underlying disease? The answer hinges on medical fashion, political pressure, bureaucratic arrangements and rearrangements and a fistful of other factors that cannot be imagined. One or more of these must lie behind the extraordinary disappearance of AIDS from the record in the Central African Republic between 1988 (230 cases reported) and 1989 (none), or in Angola (63 and none), St Kitts in the Caribbean (17 and none), or Malta in Europe (seven and none).

Sources:
Chin, James, and Jonathan M. Mann, 'HIV infections and AIDS in the 1990s', *Annual Review of Public Health*, 1990; World Health Organization (WHO), *Statistical Annual 1989*, Geneva: WHO, 1989; Uemura, Kazuo, 'Excess Mortality Ratio with Reference to the Lowest Age-Sex-Specific Death Rates Among Countries', *World Health Statistics Quarterly*, vol.42, no.1, 1989; Chin, J., et al, 'Projections of HIV infections and AIDS cases to the year 2000', *Bulletin of the World Health Organization*, vol.68, no.1, 1990; WHO, Global Programme on AIDS, *Current and Future Dimensions of the HIV/AIDS Pandemic*, a capsule survey, Geneva: WHO, 1 December 1990; WHO, *Update: AIDS cases Reported to the Surveillance, Forecasting and Impact Assessment Unit (SFI), Office of Research (RES), Global Program on AIDS*, Geneva: WHO, 1990; Panos Institute, *AIDS and the Third World*, Panos Dossier 1, London etc: Panos Institute with the Norwegian Red Cross, 1986; Panos Institute, *The Third Epidemic, Repercussions of the fear of AIDS*, London etc: Panos Institute with the Norwegian Red Cross, 1990; Panos Institute, *Triple Jeopardy, Women and AIDS*, London etc: Panos Institute, 1990; press reports.

Acknowledgements:
The World Health Organization (WHO) in Geneva is a model of what a public service institution should be and rarely is. Its officers are there to help, and that is what they do. Among the most helpful were Georgina Kainer of the Global Health Situation Assessment and Projection Division, Alan Lopez of the Statistics Division, James Chin of the Global Programme on AIDS and his secretary, Lynn Lydamore. Also generous with their time were David Thompson, Office of Publications, Mme Gastaut, Dr Kasoude and Danielle Martinez at the Office of Information and Valerie Abramov at the Press Office.
   Outside WHO, guidance, balance and orientation came from Paul Hyzler of the Department of Health and Social Security's International Department, London, Denise Corby of the Department of Health Library, London, Richard Wilshire of the Department of Employment Library, London, and the anonymous respondant at the Haemophilia Society, London.

18 O.D.

The case for legalizing all drugs is overwhelming: it would break the link between drug use and criminality, it would nudge users towards a more relaxed – and, for that reason, a generally more moderate – exercise of their habit, disrupt the slipway between drugs, flush the business into the open where it could be subject to regulation and taxation, and to anti-drug-use opinion and pressure. But legalization is not a solution in itself, as can be seen from the biggest, most pervasive and deadly of addictions – the fix on nicotine.

By official count, there are half a million Americans hooked on heroin, three million regular users of cocaine and crack, and 15 million alcoholics or alcohol-dependents. Unofficial estimates run three times higher. Taking the unofficial count and adding to it the untold addicts of all the natural and artificial mood modifiers would still not bring us anywhere near the number of nicotine addicts – perhaps 53 million, spending US$40 billion a year on their habit and costing probably as much again in health care, production bills and accidental damage. In contrast, illicit drug use of all sorts is estimated to cost some $30 billion a year.

Nicotine addiction is clearly The Big One. Consumers are locked into its sedative qualities, business into its dependable cash flow, government into its taxability. It is a public addiction and, for that reason, appears less harmful than its more private, often illegal, competitors, which it is not. It is a domesticated addiction, not generally linked to crime or violence, so appears more acceptable socially, which it is not. Like all addictions it appears to offer a sanctuary from stress and failure. And like all addictions it is strongly resistant to dissuasion, punishment or prohibition.

Sources:
United Nations Food and Agriculture Organization (FAO), *Economic Significance of Tobacco*, FAO Economic and Social Development Paper 85, Rome: FAO, 1989; Kidron, Michael, and Ronald Segal, *The Book of Business, Money and Power*, London: Pan Books and New York: Simon & Schuster, 1987; Maseroni, Robert, and Keith Rothwell, 'Tendances et effets du Tabagisme dans le monde', *World Health Statistical Quarterly*, vol.41, Geneva: WHO, 1988; US Department of Agriculture, Tobacco, Cotton & Seeds Division, data on cigarette production provided by *World Tobacco* magazine.

Acknowledgements:
Guidance and materials came in many forms from Kay Frederick, Institute for the Study of Drug Dependence, London;

George Gay, editor, *Tobacco World*, Redhill, Surrey; S.R.Lasker, Food and Agriculture Organization, Rome; Roberto Maseroni, Smoking and Health Programme, World Health Organization, Geneva.

19 CRITICAL MASS

Nearly half the world's people now live in cities of ever-increasing size and complexity. A ten-thousand-years old civilization and the peasant way of life which underpinned it are rapidly approaching their end, to be embalmed in memory and tourist brochures.

Arguably, mass urbanization is the most important feature of our times: uncontrolled and uncontrollable, it tears people from place, shears them of dignity, balance and a sense of themselves, pits them against nature and each other. It promotes outrageous, inhuman behaviour on the part of its victims, old and new. It might, just, provoke people into reordering the world to fit more comfortable contours.

What is defined as urban and rural varies from state to state. Besides, residence patterns often change faster than administrative boundaries or official definitions (which explains the 'ruralization' of some countries in western Europe); the data are sometimes quite old; and nowhere do they fully reflect the fact that economic and occupational urbanization is becoming increasingly detached from residential urbanization.

Sources:
World Resources Institute, *World Resources 1990-91*, New York and Oxford: Oxford University Press, 1990; UNEP, *Environmental Data Report 1989/90*, Oxford and Cambridge, Mass.: Basil Blackwell, 1990; press reports.

20 OUTREACH

In 1988 the world received 632 million more international letters than it sent – 631,983,000 more to be exact. Not that precision can be expected from communications statistics. They are quite simply, abysmal: those responsible for collecting them are not, and never have been, interested in purely personal contact; and only recently have they recognized the growing importance of the trade in services – which uses the communications media in much the same way as the trade in goods uses means of transport (see **12. Service Power**).

Each responsible authority seems to use its own criteria. Of those that report on mail traffic to the Universal Postal Union in Geneva, some lump postcards (almost exclusively personal) together with letters (personal, business and official) and with printed papers (mostly business); some separate them out, and some do a bit of both. Of the authorities that report to the International Telecommunication Union, also in Geneva, some measure traffic by the number of calls made, some by the number of minutes spent on the phone, some by the number of pulses sent down the wire. Some authorities do not report at all, or only fitfully. Not one segregates private from business or official calls.

Private bodies provide some of the missing pieces. The London-based International Institute of Communications has estimated telephone traffic on a comparable basis and, incidentally, showed how concentrated it is. Of the 30,000 million minutes spent on line in the world in 1988, 8480 million (28 percent) were for calls originating in the USA, 4479 (15 percent) in (West) Germany, 3543 million (12 percent) in the UK, 3260 million (11 percent) in France, 1865 million (6.2 percent) in Switzerland, 1860 million (6.2 percent) in Italy, 1283 million (4.3 percent) in the Netherlands, 1082 million (3.6 percent) in Japan, 746 million (2.5 percent) in Australia, 715 million (2.4 percent) in Mexico, 608 million (2.0 percent) in Canada, 361 million (1.2 percent) in South Korea, 278 million (0.9 percent) in Singapore, and only 1,440 million (under 5 percent) in the entire rest of the world.

Travel statistics are, if anything, less reliable than postal or telecom statistics. Not all states report to the World Tourism Organization in Madrid. Those that do, report arrivals not departures, in keeping with their greater interest in earnings from foreign visitors than in the further experience and education of their own citizens. They too do not — might indeed be unable to – segregate private from other travel.

The main map combines all domestic and foreign mail of all forms (postcards, letters and printed papers), on the grounds that even the junkiest of junk mail breaks the narrow
horizons of exclusively face-to-face contact, as does any newspaper however egregiously

uninformative. The inset map on international travel, 'Bye for Now', reverses the conventional presentation of travel statistics. It is based on a special search of the WTO's database.

Sources:
International Telecommunication Union (ITU), *Telecommunications and the National Economy*, Geneva: ITU, May 1988; ITU, *Yearbook of Public Telecommunications Statistics*, 17th edition, Geneva: 1990; Siemens, *International Telecom Statistics 1989*, Munich: Siemens AG, May 1989; Staple, Gregory C., and Mark Mullens, 'Telecom traffic statistics – MiTT matter', *Telecommunications Policy*, June 1989, London: Butterworth; Universal Postal Union (UPU), *Postal Statistics 1988*, Berne: UPU, 1989; World Bank, *Social Indicators of Development 1989*, Baltimore and London: Johns Hopkins University Press, 1989; World Tourist Office (WTO), special database search, Madrid, 2 October 1990; press reports.

Acknowledgements:
I am grateful for help that went beyond formal courtesy from Liz Jenkins, UPU duty officer, Royal Mail, London; Josh Lovegrove, Department of Employment, London; David Nicholson-Lord, *The Independent*, London; Enzo Paci, Chief, Statistics Section, WTO, Madrid; Gill Platt, BT International, London; and Mr El Zanati, Chief Librarian, ITU, Geneva.

21 THE QUALITY OF LIFE

If people were permitted to move about freely, we might learn a great deal about the quality of life as it is lived in different parts of the world at any one time. As it is, we have to make do with conjecture, and with measurements that rest on the most wobbly of assumptions, namely, that the constituents of individual happiness – or misery, as the case may be – are more or less the same everywhere; that people can increase the one, and avoid the other, through personal commitment and political will; that meaningful comparisons can be made between one person and another, and between one society and another.

These assumptions reveal more about the measurer than the measured. They reflect a view of people as social, mutually supportive creatures and a view of world society as essentially a unity occasionally marred by conflict, rather than a disparity occasionally drawn together in harmony. It is a view held by a relatively narrow circle of privileged western-educated intellectuals steeped in world affairs, a humane, optimistic view with which, broadly, this atlas agrees. But it is not a majority view and the indicators of human fulfilment or development it propounds – or of misery and suffering – are nothing if not subjective.

For what it is worth, the Human Development Index compiled by the United Nations Development Programme combines life expectancy at birth, literacy and real purchasing power. A 'minimum' value equal to the lowest observed for 1987 (42 years, 12 percent and $220 respectively) was specified as was a 'desirable' value (78 years, 100 percent and $4861). To reflect 'diminishing returns in the conversion of income into the fulfilment of human needs', logarithmic rather than absolute values were used for purchasing power. The 'minimum' and 'desirable' values were fixed as the end points, 0 and 1, and countries were located on each scale. The readings on each scale were then averaged to produce a single value – the Human Development Index (HDI).

The Human Suffering Index (HSI) compiled by the Population Crisis Committee, is more ambitious. It covers GNP per head, inflation, growth of the labour force, urbanization, infant mortality, calorie intake as a proportion of requirements, access to clean drinking water, energy consumption, adult literacy, personal freedom and governance. States were assigned a ranking from 0 to 10 in each of these categories, and the rankings summed to arrive at the final score.

Some of the indicators are weak because they rest on statistical sand; others stem from the way evidence is gathered (see for example **4. The Population of States**). A lot comes from what evidence is gathered (see **5. Market Muscle**, **6. National Income**) and even more of the weakness derives from the reduction of the evidence that is gathered to country averages as if there were, or could ever be, an average experience. What would a 'tribal' in India or an Arab in Israel make of the personal freedom category in which their states are assigned the supreme accolade, 0? For that matter, what would any of the world's underclass, marginals and redundants, who together form the majority of humanity (see **7. Bankables and Unbankables**; **40. This Little Piggy**) make of the averages assigned their country with regard to any of the indicators? We may be converging on one human type worldwide (see **19. Critical Mass**), but our experience of that world is still demonstrably diverse for reasons of class, race and gender.

These indices are particularly slow in reacting to change. The data on which they rest come from different national sources and take time to collate and harmonize. They are evaluated by committees that meet infrequently, processed, reprocessed and argued about. It is a ponderous, stately procedure. But the world is impatient. Liberianization takes Africa by storm, so that country, Chad, Somalia and Sudan move up a couple of notches in the HSI. Kuwait is almost wiped out, and loses its position in both. Recession spreads, weakening the weakest states, creating famines where there were none before, spawning new refugees, making more and bloodier conflicts. Even if the indices were on target when they were first compiled, the target is always moving. It is only in the most general terms, liberally interpreted, that they have credence.

Sources:
United Nations Development Programme (UNDP), *Human Development Report 1990*, New York and Oxford: Oxford University Press, 1990; Camp, Sharon L., and J.Joseph Spiedel, *The International Human Suffering Index*, Washington DC: Population Crisis Committee, 1987; press reports.

Acknowledgements:
Leo Goldstone, Chief of Statistics, UNDP, accommodated my deadlines when he could. John Olive, Voluntary Euthanasia Society, London, Pit Bakker, Dutch Society for Voluntary Euthanasia, and Frank Dungey, Voluntary Euthanasia Society, Wellington, and Secretary, World Federation of Right to Die Societies, were helpful within the confines of a shameful lack of resources.

22 TWO Rs

Literacy does not necessarily mean understanding. It has little to do with the content of education. It can open doors to the vast treasures of knowledge and the deep pools of wisdom that do exist, but it does not do so of itself. Arguably its greatest effect has been to bind the individual into the wider society (see **20. Outreach**; **31. Tongue-Tied**).

It should be possible to group school systems by their intention. Where the curriculum is explicitly value-loaded and designed to serve an 'ideal' society, future, past, or even present, and where all other elements of the syllabus, such as practical skills, are subordinated to that aim, we have what might be termed doctrinal education – as in the Soviet Union (still), in Iran and, perhaps, Libya. Where the curriculum is implicitly value-loaded and designed to filter out rulers and subalterns from worker-troops as in England and Wales certainly and, probably, in the rest of western Europe, we have elitist or hierarchical education. And where the curriculum is ostensibly value-free because core values are, or are assumed to be, shared throughout the society, and what is taught centres on marketable skills and attitudes, as in the USA and its imitators, we have pragmatic or market-driven education.

These are not mutually exclusive categories. In many states they overlap and intertwine so snugly that they neutralize each other and reduce the educational systems to incoherence. But there are cases, perhaps forming a majority, where the system tends towards one or other, despite internal inconsistencies and contradictions. These constitute merely one of many possible taxonomies. Would that any had been elaborated.

Sources:
United Nations Development Programme (UNDP), *Human Development Report 1990*, New York and Oxford: Oxford University Press, 1990; United Nations Educational, Scientific and Cultural Organizaton (UNESCO), *Statistical Yearbook 1989*, Paris: UNESCO, 1989; World Bank, *Social Indicators of Development 1989*, Baltimore and London: Johns Hopkins University Press, 1989; Nicholas, E.J., *Issues in Education: a comparative analysis*, London etc: Harper & Row, 1983; press reports.

Acknowledgements:
Jack Nicholas, Goldsmiths College, London, and John Sceats, retired in Sussex, persuaded me that ambition was misplaced in this case. Philip Spencer implicitly agreed with them. Madan Sarup mapped some of the way.

23 SMALL REFLECTIONS

Who among the readers of this atlas would want to be an *average* child? Not the privileged progeny of the average family in the rich states, nor the progeny of the rich in poor states, but the average child in the world, who has a one-in-ten chance of dying before reaching his or her fifth birthday, a one-in-four chance of being permanently damaged by malnutrition and preventable disease, a one-in-three chance of never learning to read properly, or of having to work – usually in the most hideous of circumstances – in fields, quarries, on building sites, in manufacturing or in prostitution.

There are thought to be 200 million child-labourers worldwide, 100 million of them in India. Most of the 200 million slaves or bonded labourers in the world are children, five million of them in Thailand. There might be 80 million more or less abandoned street children spread through the world, half of them in Latin America. In Brazil where seven million are thought to exist, hundreds are killed every year by off-duty police and vigilante businessmen eager to keep the streets free of strays. A few others have their moment of glory starring in snuff movies. There are at least 200,000 under-fifteens serving as soldiers.

Bangkok and Dhaka boast 800,000 child prostitutes each, Olangapo near an American military base in the Philippines houses 20,000, Bombay 15,000. Brazil has 500,000; Taiwan 100,000. There are 300,000 boy prostitutes in the USA.

The market for children and babies is diverse, structured, and profitable. In Bangkok the purchaser obtains a receipt as well as a child, on payment in the open street – US$160 for a plain work-child, $200 for a pretty tribal girl from the hills who can be profitable as a prostitute, up to $700 for a pretty Thai girl. In southern Sudan they come as cheap as $20. In Brazil a three-month old blond baby boy fetches $25,000 in the adoption market. In Manila, little girls go for $20,000. Guatemalan babies are less expensive – $5000 retail delivered to the USA. The 10,000 or so Thai children sold each year in neighbouring Malaysia see their price jump from $110 to $2000 as they cross the border.

It is not only in the TV compassion-spectaculars on Africa that children stand in the front-line of human cruelty, indifference, cowardice and incompetence. In Canada, one child in six goes to bed hungry; in the USA there are urban areas, including Washington DC, with infant mortality rates higher than Jamaica; in the USSR the main victims of AIDS so far have been the infant clients of the filthy, chaotic and undernourished health services.

The figures used in 'Neglected' were computed by adding the reciprocal of the net enrolment rate (average for boys and girls) to the dropout rate (as a percentage of the net enrolment rate).

For secondary, or high school enrolment, see **22. Two Rs**.

Sources:
United Nations Children's Fund (UNICEF), *The State of the World's Children 1990*, New York: Oxford University Press for UNICEF, 1990; UNICEF, *The World Summit for Children*, adapted from the above, New York: UNICEF, 1990; UNICEF, *Children and Development in the 1990s, a UNICEF sourcebook*, New York: United Nations, 19-30 September 1990; UNICEF, *Executive Board, Exploitation of Working Children and Street Children*, E/ICEF/1986/CRP.3, 13 March 1986 (mimeo); International Labour Office (ILO), *Child Labour*, Extract from the Report of the Director-General to the International Labour Conference, 69th Session, 1983, Geneva: ILO, 1985; Anti-Slavery Society, London, selected materials; private communications; press reports.

Acknowledgements:
Guidance and materials were generously extended by Marie-Louise Cardwell, Research and Documentation Officer, and Jacqueline Wetzel, UNICEF, Geneva. Guidance came from Marie-Pierre Poirrier, NGO Liaison Committee, UNICEF, Geneva, and Robert Smith, UNICEF, London. Assefa Bequele, Working Conditions and Environment Department, International Labour Office, Geneva, and Karin Valentina, Deputy Director, Anti-Slavery Society, London, explained the pitfalls and did their best to guide me round them.

24 THE LESSER EQUAL

Under ideal conditions, where women enjoy equal treatment with men, the ratio of females to males in the population (the FMR) would be somewhat higher than the 1.06 registered in Finland, arguably the state which shows the least discrimination between the sexes. For although more men are born than women, more women survive. They are tougher. But they are not so tough as to be unscathed by the despoliation that is their lot in a male-dominated world, and the FMR is everywhere lower than 1.06, sometimes considerably lower. The main map, 'Missing Women', shows in the broadest of terms how much lower. It also shows, incidentally, some rare exceptions where more women than expected have survived, usually, as in the USSR, because war and civil war have devoured the male population disproportionately.

'Missing Women' reflects as objectively as possible the consequences of male domi- **135** nance at all levels and in all parts of society. It is reinforced by the more subjective, and conventional, rankings in the inset map, 'Gender Gap', where women's status is compared to men's on a scale of one to five (from least equal to equal) in five categories (health, marriage and children, education, employment and social equality) in each state. Nowhere is the maximum score – 25 – attained.

Probably the most sensitive public indicator of unequal power is in the control of reproduction. The battle lines between the private, creative and caring realm of parenting and the public, impersonal and instrumental world of population politics and state interests run through the very centre of women's bodies. The outcome of that battle is in constant flux: sometimes when labour is seen to be scarce as in the rich states in the 1960s, women find it possible, although never easy, to extend the frontiers of control over their bodies and themselves. In times of recession and idleness such as we are now experiencing in many parts of the world women are driven back as (male) policy drives into (female) privacy. Nowhere is this more apparent than in Eastern Europe where the collapse of so-called communism, profligate with labour as with so many other things, has also meant a sharp turnabout in some of the most liberal abortion regimes in the world. In terms of freedom, the personal paid dearly for the political as the pregnant were made to carry the prelate.

Law does not necessarily reflect clinical practice. In most Muslim states, and in many Latin American and African ones, the law is more liberal than the reality, and few legal abortions are performed under the health clause; while in Israel, New Zealand and South Korea, legal abortion rates compare with those in states which permit abortion on request. Interpretations of the same law can vary widely within a state, as in Switzerland where some cantons interpret medical reasons for abortion liberally and others do not. In some ostensibly restrictive states – Bangladesh, for example – menstrual regulation, that is early abortion without a pregnancy test, is freely available, whereas in some ostensibly liberal states – Togo, for example – a legal abortion is hard to come by because the services are scarce or unavailable.

The worldwide trend towards liberalism in abortion law since the 1950s is, for these reasons, more a matter of ideology and political programme than of practice or a woman's experience. It might well be that the institutionalization of medicine and its embrace of pregnancy and childbirth, a relatively new event in the annals of history, has widened women's choices in theory while narrowing them in practice. When all is said and done it is absurd to suppose that women can choose freely while they do two-thirds of the work for one-tenth of the reward and own no more than one-hundredth of the world's wealth.

Sources:
Dreze, Jean, and Amartya Sen, *Hunger and Public Action*, Oxford: Clarendon Press, 1989; Henshaw, Stanley K., 'Induced Abortion: a world review, 1990', *Family Planning Perspectives*, vol.22, no.2, March/April, 1990; Population Crisis Committee (PCC), *Poor, Powerless and Pregnant: country rankings of the status of women*, Washington DC: PCC, 1988; press reports.

Acknowledgements:
Susan Tew, Alan Guttmacher Institute, New York, and Kathleen Mazzocco, Population Crisis Committee, Washington DC, were generous with advice and materials.

25 FIRST BITE OF THE CHERRY

Rare is the state that creates what it spends, and still rarer the state that spends wisely on behalf its subjects.

Even the most hardened cynic might be forgiven for not having plumbed the depths of state unrealism when a regime as skint as that of Myanmar (Burma) announces a plan to pay out US$15 billion that it does not possess on building by the end of the century a new city for four million people – more than the number living in Yangon (Rangoon) at present. The same might be said of the decision to restore the unrestorable in the Persian Gulf at a cost of US$50 billion to the American and allied taxpayers (and who knows how many more billions in lost revenue, environmental mayhem and other costs); or the USSR's foredoomed attempt to shore up a discredited, crumbling imperial system; or the decision of the world's biggest debtor, Brazil, to continue spending US$120 billion a year (three-quarters of all state expenditure) on the spenders themselves and much of the rest on their families and friends outside the civil service.

The point is briefer than the list is long: all states are capable, and indeed culpable, of alarming waste, according to their station, since they are all essentially beyond the reach of their citizens at the time the decisions are made (or indeed ever – see **26. Are You With Me?**). The citizens themselves might be poor or rich, taxed heavily or less heavily – the USSR state apparatus for example would have two-thirds less to spend if its citizens were taxed at the average world level. By contrast, the Japanese state would have twice as much, and the US a quarter more. The German state would come out more or less the same.

Source:
United States Arms Control and Disarmament Agency (USACDA), *World Military Expenditures and Arms Transfers 1989*, Washington DC: USACDA, October 1990.

26 ARE YOU WITH ME?

Elections are not always what they appear to be. In Albania, for example, there was a solitary spoiled ballot paper amongst the more than 1,830,000 cast in the 1987 ballot for the People's Assembly. A few years before, in the USSR, fewer than 20,000 people out of an electorate of 184 million failed to vote in the elections for the Supreme Soviet. Why they bothered – to vote if they did, or to announce officially that they did if they did not – is something of a mystery even in a one-party state. On the other hand, non-election does not necessarily mean that a regime is wholly unpopular. King Hussein of Jordan may well have won a free contest at the time of the Gulf War early in 1991.

It is also true that occasional elections, even if free, do not fully express the people's will, that ever-changing, unstructured melange of individual opinions and wishes held with varying degrees of intensity. The turnout of voters can be high or low, affected by electoral law and its enforcement: in Australia or Belgium where voting is compulsory and non-compliance fined, 95-98 percent of the electorate normally turn out; in Bolivia, Guatemala or Peru, where it is compulsory but not enforced, the tally is lower, around 60 percent. Where voting is voluntary it is affected by the mode of registration: where the state takes on the burden elections score better than where the voter has to register (70-90 percent in western Europe compared with 50-53 percent in the USA); and it is affected by the level of literacy and general education – in India and Mexico only about half of the electorate vote.

Given that those who vote voluntarily usually have some choice as between parties, it is not surprising that most governments, even freely-elected ones, represent a minority of adult opinion.

'Vox populi' is based largely on the results of elections to national assemblies as constituted on 1 January 1991. Where these results were not available, the votes for the presidential incumbent of the time were used. In the case of the Philippines, the figures are those of a referendum on the Constitution which effectively confirmed Cory Aquino in office.

Time had to stop at the start of 1991 for 'Vox populi', the map. It has not stopped in real life, notably in Thailand where a regime with a smattering of legitimacy has since given way to one without, or in Kuwait and Albania, where states with no legitimacy look to be getting a smidgeon. For states where the government's legitimacy is being challenged by force see **47. Hot Spots**.

Sources:
Derbyshire, J.Denis, and Ian Derbyshire, *Political Systems of the World*, Edinburgh: Chambers, 1989; Gorvin, Ian, general editor, *Elections Since 1945: a worldwide reference compendium*, Harlow: Longman, 1989; Kidron, Michael, and Dan Smith, *The New State of War and Peace, an international atlas*, London: Grafton Books, New York: Simon & Schuster, 1991; Leonard, Dick, and Richard Natkiel, *World Atlas of Elections, voting patterns in 39 democracies*, London: Hodder & Stoughton for *The Economist*, 1987; United States Bureau of the Census, *Statistical Abstract of the United States 1990*, Washington DC, 1990; Central Intelligence Agency (CIA), *The World Factbook 1990*, Washington DC: CIA, 1990; *Keesings Record of World Events*, Harlow, monthly; press reports.

Acknowledgements:
Terry Mayer, the Hansard Society, London, and Chris Pond, Information Office, The House of Commons, advised (but did not necessarily consent).

All states, without exception, are terrorist organizations – in the sense that they use violence to influence the behaviour of people unnamed or unknown. Even if the term is restricted to extra-legal acts of exemplary punishment, the state stands out as the archetypal terrorist, father of them all.

In 'State Wrongs', states that promote or condone or merely do not expunge the use, by their servants, of assassination, 'disappearances', torture or other cruel, inhuman or degrading treatment or punishment, and have been noticed doing so, are classed as terror states. They include the vicious, like Iran or China or El Salvador, the righteous like Israel, and the shame-faced like Australia (for its treatment, in prison, of aborigines). They include states that are shedding a gruesome past, in Eastern Europe, Paraguay, Mexico, Mozambique and those that cleave to it relentlessly, Nigeria; major offenders that use terror lavishly to uphold, in every particular, the interests and dignity of its ruling group, like Iraq or Guatemala, and minor players, like Sweden, which officially condemn it, occasionally condone it and seldom, if ever, prescribe it. Included are states in which terror is rationed, like the UK, or the USSR, and those, like India, in which it is abundantly available; and states where the central authorities are blameless in intention while the local ones are not – Western Samoa and Bulgaria.

The choice of a single category to embrace states with such a variety of intention and employing terror on such different scales reflects an unashamedly fundamentalist view: state terrorism, whatever its incidence and justification, is too corrupting of society and of essential human values to be permitted under any circumstances. It also reflects a practical difficulty: differences in scale shade into one another so subtly and secretly as to confound any attempt at ordering them.

Below the terror states, at a lower level of frightfulness, there are the repression states where arbitrary arrest, detention or exile prevail, where the legal procedures are so chaotic as to deny in practice, if not in intention, natural justice (Italy); where the state intrudes in the private spheres of home, the family, and correspondence; where it suppresses freedom of speech and of the press, freedom of peaceful assembly and association, freedom of worship, of movement; where it prevents the free choice of government; and where it polices heavily.

And then there are a few states with an apparently clean human rights record. Here all is not what it seems. It strains credulity to find the USA, for example, amongst them even in the reckoning of the impartial Amnesty International. That can only be because Amnesty, like all human rights organizations, considers human rights to be a purely domestic issue. It ignores therefore the USA's record as the great exporter of state terror – in its support of terror states such as Peru, El Salvador, Indonesia or Israel; and in its consistent support of the authority, the inviolability and integrity of the state everywhere.

Judgement naturally differs about the state's behaviour towards its citizens. In keeping with its fundamentalist stance this atlas has adopted the most damning judgement issuing from its sources, the US State Department which has more than a few axes to grind, and Amnesty International, which has none.

More detailed aspects of the state's abuse of human rights are taken up by **26. Are You With Me?**, **29. (Not) One of Us** and **35. See, Hear, Speak No Evil**.

Sources:
Amnesty International (AI), *Report 1990*, London: AI, 1990; AI, *The Death Penalty: AI Index: ACT 50/01/91*, 30 January 1991; AI, private communications; Kidron, Michael, and Dan Smith, *The New State of War and Peace, an international atlas*, London: Grafton Books, New York: Simon & Schuster, 1991; US Department of State, *Country Reports on Human Rights for 1989*, Report submitted to the Committee on Foreign Affairs, House of Representatives and the Committee on Foreign Relations, Washington DC: US Senate, February 1990; press reports.

Acknowledgements:
Kathleen Maloney, Hugh Polton, Eric Prokosch, Ignatio Saiz at Amnesty International shared their latest information and perceptions, in the fast-changing areas they monitor.

28 REFUGEE MAKERS

Nobody knows how many people there are who have been compelled to leave their homes for fear of persecution, injury or death, and would return if they could, or dared to. They must number hundreds of millions newly huddled in the world's urban slums (see **19. Critical Mass**), swarming across frontiers and oceans, segregated in special camps. Although they are fugitives from violence of one sort or another, from discrimination and deprivation, most of these people are not considered refugees in the strict sense employed by the relevant agencies.

To qualify as a refugee in that sense, a person must have crossed a recognized international boundary in his or her flight *and also* be in need of assistance and protection. Relatively few people satisfy both of these criteria.

Those that qualify do not normally include the 'internally displaced', that is refugees within their state's own frontiers. They do not include the vast mass of 'economic refugees' in flight from destitution and debilitation; the growing army of 'asylum seekers' waiting for registration as 'real' refugees; the people in 'refugee-like circumstances', that is people who are undocumented, unregistered or who, for some reason, fall outside the legal protection mechanisms of receiving countries and international agencies; the forcibly relocated by government resettlement programmes; the small minority of 'real' refugees who, welcome or not, miserable or happy, have 'entered and resettled'; and a host of the other categories and sub-categories.

The cartogram rests on a broader, though still restrictive definition which includes amongst refugees 'asylum-seekers in need of assistance and/or protection' (that is, people 'unable or unwilling to repatriate due to fear of persecution and violence in their homelands or to be permanently settled in other countries') plus selected 'populations in refugee-like circumstances' (using the top estimate of the numbers involved given by the United States Committee for Refugees – USCR) plus the 'internally-displaced' and the 'forcibly located' (also given by the USCR).

Still not included are the vast array of fugitives on whom the world's political and media spotlights have not fallen, and the ones who have stolen away from trouble rather than stampeded away. Amongst them are the archetypal refugees, the people who would not have left their homes in the first place, or would go back to them, if there were any hope there of elementary material security – the 'economic refugee'. These are the people forcibly returned in their thousands by the USA to Haiti and Mexico, by the British (in Hong Kong) to Vietnam, by the Saudis to Ethiopia; they are the people forcibly blocked by Austria on its borders with the former Communist states of Eastern Europe, by Finland at its frontier with the USSR, by western Europe as a whole on its southern and eastern reaches, by Turkey on its border with Iraq.

Also excluded from our working definition of refugee are the 'returnees': Russian Jews (and pretend Jews) to Israel (two million of whom are in prospect at the time of going to press), the 1.5 million ethnic (and not-so-ethnic) Germans who trailed into the then West Germany in 1989 and 1990; and the vast numbers who manage, against all odds, to get to their chosen destinations without attracting attention – the 500,000-or-so illegals in France, the million in Italy, the hundreds of thousands living in or passing through Spain, the millions in the USA. And then there are the officially 'entered and resettled'. Included only exceptionally are the internally-displaced by accident or design, like the victims of the Chernobyl nuclear reactor disaster in the Ukraine (see **49. Dirt's Cheap**), or the objects of 'economic development' programmes in Brazil or Indonesia; and many, many more.

However defined, refugees are created, and in a world of states, it is the state that creates them, primarily through war and the incidental effects of war (see **47. Hot Spots**), but also through discrimination short of systematic violence (see **27. Human Rights, 29. (Not) One of Us**), or through bad husbandry (see **8. Funny Money**). It is for this reason that the cartogram reverses the conventional presentation, by concentrating on the source of the problem rather than on the asylums. This can be misleading, as, for example, in the case of South Africa which, according to the UN Secretary General speaking in Oslo, late in 1988, can be held responsible for turning six million people in the states on its borders into refugees.

States are not rushing to outdo each other as havens for refugees, even 'real' refugees narrowly defined. As they multiply, refugees find it progressively difficult to go forth legally, not to say with a semblance of dignity. In the 1970s, Switzerland accepted about 70 percent of applicants for refugee status; by the end of the 1980s it was accepting seven percent. France dropped from 60 percent in 1983 to 30 percent in 1987; and the UK from 41 to 8 percent between 1982 and 1987. According to the UN High Commissioner for Refugees, acceptance rates in general were down to 7-14 percent by the **139** end of the decade. And more and more of the traditional states of asylum were adopting temporary expedients short of full acceptance: 'tolerance' in Germany, 'exceptional leave to remain' (ELR) in the UK.

Clogging the channels for refugees is a short-term expedient for governments under domestic pressure. In western Europe early in the 1990s this pressure was expressed in Jean-Marie Le Pen's significant share of the popular vote in France (10 -15 percent); in the strong resistance in Britain to the granting of 250,000 residence permits to Crown subjects in Hong Kong; in the electoral successes of the extreme right in Norway and Austria; in the shortlived but significant electoral gains of the Republikaner in Germany; in the political breakthrough of the regional 'leagues' in northern Italy. It also reflects a last-ditch stand by old-world autocracies, such as those in the Gulf, and by conservative gerontocracies, such as the one that runs Japan, who fear the cultural diversity and potential liberalism associated with substantial immigrant populations.

Whatever the reasons for the silting up of refugee channels, the results are there for all to see: complete refugee societies – in the Middle East, in Southeast Asia, in Africa - in which a generation has been born in camps. These societies have existed in sufficient size and for long enough to have developed a noticeably different culture from their original or receiving cultures, and which occasionally, and tragically, as in the Lebanon, have been forced to flee their makeshift homes – as refugees within their diaspora.

The data used relate to 1989, the last available from a single respectable source, with a few exceptions: Iraq's record was updated to the end of 1990 on the basis of current press reports, as was Albania's. Regrettably, the USSR's was not, nor those of the Gulf states other than Iraq. Nor was Iraq's subsequent record, which resulted in 2-3 million people (Kurds mainly) in flight in March/April 1991.

Sources:
United States Committee for Refugees (USCR), *World Refugee Survey - 1989 in Review*, Washington DC: 1990; Kidron, Michael, and Dan Smith, *The New State of War and Peace, an international atlas*, London: Grafton Books, New York: Simon & Schuster, 1991; press reports.

Acknowledgements:
Ginny Hamilton at the USCR, Washington DC, was exceptionally generous with her time.

29 (NOT) ONE OF US

The governing classes are distinguished from most other minorities in the belief that their own behaviour and underlying attitudes are normal, inherently superior to all others and should be generally adopted. It is an evangelical belief which contrasts strongly with the modest desire of most other minorities to indulge in their habits, beliefs and preoccupations without molestation or harassment. It is also a powerful belief in that the governing classes dispose of means to bend their subjects to their view of what constitutes acceptable, desirable or normal behaviour.

As policy that view comes in many guises. There is *outright suppression* of differences, by way of forced assimilation, genocide, expulsion, cultural and linguistic infibulation, or dilution as practised in China against the Tibetans, or in Turkey and its neighbours against the Kurds, or in Laos against the hill people, in India against the tribals. There is *legalized discrimination* against adherents of certain faiths (Jehovah's Witnesses in large parts of Africa, non-Muslims in the Middle East and beyond, Marxists in many non-Marxist despotisms), against women (in most Muslim states and large parts of Latin America), against ethnic groups (from the Gypsies in Eastern Europe to the Arabs in Israel and the Occupied Territories), and the *criminalization* of particular behaviour patterns such as homosexuality (in most of Asia, the USSR, large parts of Latin America and parts of the USA and Australia). There is active *discouragement* of the unwanted and the promotion of the favoured by way of skewed employment or educational opportunities (as in the Americas and Australasia towards the indigenous peoples, or most of Europe towards new immigrants of non-European stock). There is *neglect*, benign or otherwise, when the state stands aside while popular prejudice narrows the scope, or saps the vitality of minority groups and deviant cultures. And there is *affirmative action* or positive discrimination, the reciprocal of discouragement, to produce the suitable subject – as in large parts of Africa where policies for the advancement of women have more to do with a desire to weaken the pre-independence governing classes than with advancement for its own sake.

It is often the case that the governing class adopts one policy for one set of problems and another for a different set, as in Indonesia, where the East Timorians or West Irianians face suppression, and other non-Javanese ethnic groups and cultures are merely discriminated against and discouraged. In some large states local policy differs palpably from central or federal government policy, as in Nigeria, the USSR or the USA, where the subalterns resort to discouragement while the elevated favour neglect or affirmative action.

The distinctions drawn in 'Social Engineering' are not of severity, but of approach. They tell us more about the governing class's relative power and their political environment than about their ideological commitment. For example, it might happen that they are too divided and evenly-balanced to contemplate regimentation of any sort, and find a compromise by eschewing it altogether (as in Chad, Guinea-Bissau and Papua New Guinea) or by encouraging the differences that underpin their coalition (as in Belgium, Canada, Finland, Uganda and Zaire). Or they may constitute a more cohesive body daring to embark on 'nation-building', in which case suppression is their policy (as in Ethiopia, Fiji and Iraq). Or they might be anchored to a relatively stable, relatively homogeneous society where discouragement or neglect are sufficient for their purposes.

Whatever the instruments chosen, the common, hidden aspiration of state policy is to homogenize the population's attitudes and behaviour. In this the governing class behaves no differently to any other bureaucratic leadership, only more arrogantly, as befits those who head the largest bureaucratic machine in the state.

'Social Engineering' maps the state's general intolerance of diversity, difference, deviation and discordance. It should be read in conjunction with others that detail some of its effects in particular sectors: censorship (**35. See, Hear, Speak No Evil**), open civil conflict (**47. Hot Spots**; **28. Refugee Makers**), human rights (**27. Human Rights**), women (**24. The Lesser Equal**), and religion (**32. Believe You Me**).

The sources used for 'Social Engineering' are biased, each in its own fashion. The US State Department's informants seem to be acutely, and uniformly, sensitive to women's issues. Some of them recognize religious or racial oppression and discrimination, and a handful notice slights against members of given cultures and communities. But they appear to be utterly and uniformly oblivious to official intolerance of minority sexual, or of class, behaviour. By contrast the Minority Rights Group, London, have much of value to say about official racial, community or linguistic policies, but little on women and nothing on policies for sexual or class behaviour. Since personal informants were selected for the narrowness of their focus, it would be churlish to decry them for it.

Although these biases have been moderated by passing them through a rudimentary Delphi process, even more rudimentary than that described in the notes to **35. See, Hear, Speak No Evil**, the product is by far the most arbitrary and subjective in the atlas.

Where the rules differ in the different constituents of a federal state, the situation is marked by two concentric circles in the colours appropriate to the extremes obtaining there. This is the case in the inset 'Not So Good to be Gay' for the USA ('lawful and tolerated' to 'unlawful and repressed'), Australia ('lawful and tolerated' to 'unlawful and tolerated') and Yugoslavia ('lawful and repressed' to 'unlawful and repressed').

Sources:
Chaliand, Gerard, ed., *Minority Peoples in the Age of Nation States*, London: Pluto Press, 1989; International Lesbian and Gay Association (ILGA), *The ILGA Pink Book*, Utrecht: Rijksuniversiteit, Interfacultaire Werkgroep Homostudies, 1988; ILGA, bulletin and conference papers, 1989 and 1990; Minority Rights Group (MRG), *World Directory of Minorities*, Harlow: Longmans, 1989; Thornberry, Patrick, *Minority Rights and Human Law*, London: MRG, 1987; US State Department, *Country Reports on Human Rights Practices for 1989*, Report submitted to the Committee on Foreign Affairs, House of Representatives, and the Committee on Foreign Relations, US Senate, February 1990, Washington DC; private communications; press reports.

Acknowledgements:
Richard Carver, Africa Watch, London, generously contributed from his knowledge and judgement, while suffering grievous spiritual harm; Graham McKerrow, London, organized a last-minute rescue operation with Nigel Warner, International Lesbian and Gay Association, London, quickly, efficiently and quietly; Kaye Stearman, MRG, London, extended cautionary advice, precious time and understanding to great effect; David Wildman, Librarian, Royal Geographical Society, gave generous support during a false start.

30 THE BUREAUPOLISTS

Rarely docs a state bureaucracy, even a civilian one operating in a parliamentary democracy, invite inspection of its day-to-day workings. Exceptionally, it might reveal a little – to the World Bank, the International Monetary Fund or other creditors as part payment for support; or to themselves when the stench of financial corruption or policy failure threatens to overwhelm their people. Generally they sit tight with blinds drawn.

A small number of states – 20 out of the 160-odd – declare how much they spend on paying their officials. A mote of information in truth, but enough to support a mighty beam of inference. These few include the USA, Japan, Germany, France, Sweden, the Netherlands and Finland amongst the rich, and India, Pakistan, Bangladesh, South Korea, Colombia, Sudan and Zimbabwe among the poor. Together they account for a third of world population and 63 percent of world output as measured conventionally (by Gross Domestic Product).

In these countries the state absorbed 16.3 percent of the combined gross output, and civil service pay accounted for 59 percent of that, which translates into 9.6 percent of their combined gross output. This was in the mid-to-late 1980s for which the data exist.

So far so good. The next stage – converting money into heads – is trickier. In poor countries, where bureaucratic skills are in short supply (especially as compared to bureaucratic attitudes) and the mildly-privileged have few other avenues of advancement into the ranks of the truly-privileged, civil service pay is roughly 4.4 times the average income per head. In rich countries, where the skills are abundant and career opportunities more available, it is 1.7 times.

Adjusting for these sharp differences and extrapolating from the group of 20 countries to the rest of the world allows us to estimate a central government bureaucracy of 43.5 million, 5.4 percent of the labour force, in the rich states (Europe, North America, Australasia and Japan), and 34.9 million, 1.4 percent of the labour force, in the poor (all the rest) – a grand total of 78 million, or 2.4 percent of the world labour force.

The 'public service' of the main map includes local as well as central government administrative employment.

Sources:
International Labour Office (ILO), Commission paritaire de la fonction publique, Quatrième Session, *Rapport I: Rapport Generale*, Geneva: ILO, 1988; ILO, *World Labour Report*, vol.IV, Geneva: ILO, 1989; United Nations (UN), *National Accounts Statistics*, New York: UN, 1987; World Bank, *Social Indicators of Development 1989*, Baltimore and London: Johns Hopkins University Press, 1989; World Bank, *Statistics for 185 economies*, private communication, 18 December 1990; press reports.

Acknowledgements:
A number of people provided guidance. They are: Portia Eltvedt, Mark Keese and Eileen Minihane at the Organization for Economic Cooperation and Development (OECD), Paris; Jane Henderson and Helen Thompson at the Royal Institute of Public Administration, London; Catherine Bourtembourg at the International Institute of Administrative Sciences, Brussels; and David Beetham and Kevin Theakston at the University of Leeds.

31 TONGUE-TIED

The queen of imperial languages is English, the nearest the world has come to a common tongue. By the mid-1980s English was the mother-tongue of 300 million people, conservatively estimated. Another 300 million or so used it as a second language, and a further 100 million used it fluently as a foreign language. This is an increase of 40 percent since the 1950s. Other estimates put the total, including people with a lower level of fluency, at more than 1000 million, well over a quarter of the world's teenage and adult population.

English is used as an official or semi-official language in over 70 states and has a prominent place in another 20. It is the premier language of books, newspapers, aviation and air traffic control, international business and academic conferences, science, technology, medicine, diplomacy, war, sports, international competitions, pop music and advertising. Over two-thirds of the world's scientists write in English. Three-quarters of the world's mail is written in English. Of all the information stored in electronic retrieval sytsems, 80 percent is stored in English. English radio programmes are received by over 150 million people in 120 states (see **34. Programmed Views**). Over

50 million children study English as an additional language at primary school; over 80 million study it at secondary level (these figures exclude China where over 100 million people are thought to have tuned into the BBC television English series 'Follow Me' at some time). In any one year, the British Council helps a quarter of a million foreign students to learn English, in various parts of the world. In the USA, 337,000 foreign students of English were registered in 1983.

The main map greatly exaggerates the linguistic power of the world's population. Although there are many people for whom the dominant language is not a mother tongue (or home language) yet who can use it effectively and fluently and so participate fully in public affairs, there are very many more who claim the dominant language as their mother tongue and yet, by reason of poor education, narrow experience or inadequate nurturing, use it so uncomfortably or in such a distinctive form as to be excluded from effective participation in the advantages it confers. For language is as much a barrier as a bridge.

In the case of some ex-colonial states it is not always easy to know what the real status of an indigenous second official language is. Whether its speakers have access to 'rule' depends partly on the extent to which the language is taught at school, on the prevalence of literacy, or some such shoehorn factor. In all cases the indigenous language has been given the benefit of the doubt.

In this map China appears as it does on grounds that Mandarin, the Beijing variant of the northern Chinese dialect, is unintelligible as a spoken language to a majority of Chinese (although the Chinese written script is common currency for them all). India is treated in the same way on different grounds: that Hindi and English, the All-India official languages, serve as mother tongues to a minority and, in a relatively small group, respectively, of the population, and that they so dominate the central administration, the military, business, higher education in general and the sciences in particular, as to overshadow completely the 14 official regional languages. On the other hand, the USSR is classed as a state in which the majority use the official language, Russian, as their mother tongue, even though the overall majority is slight (perhaps two percent) across the USSR as a whole, and, increasingly, in many of the constituent republics, the languages of rule are non-Russian.

Sources:
Crystal, David, *The Cambridge Encyclopedia of Language*, Cambridge etc: Cambridge University Press, 1987; Gunnemark, Erik, and Donald Kenrick, *A Geolinguistic Handbook*, 1985 edition, Gothenberg: Gunnemark, 1986; McCallen, Brian, *English: A World Commodity; the international market for training in English as a foreign language*, Special Report no.1166, London: Economist Intelligence Unit, January 1989.

Acknowledgements:
One trail led from Judith Stanley-Smith, London, to Ned Thomas, then of the University College of North Wales, Aberystwyth, and now of the University of Wales Press, and finally to Donall O'Riagain, Secretary General, European Bureau of Lesser Used Languages, Dublin, all of whom were helpful. Another trail led from Michael Coyne, English Language Information Unit, British Council, London, who was kindness itself, to David Crystal, University College of North Wales, Bangor, generous in spirit and in deed, to Louis Greenstock, Librarian at the Centre for Information and Language Teaching, London, and finally, and most productively, to Donald Kenrick, who helped with guidance and a blue pencil more than can be expected from an inner-city neighbour. A third trail started in Brighton with Gordon White, went on to Oxford where Glen Dudbridge gave much time and illumination,and ended pleasantly and informatively in York with Steve Harlow. Sun Shuyan, Oxford, allayed some doubts, mine and hers.

32 BELIEVE YOU ME

Even unimpeachably secular states in which orthodox faiths or ideologies are treated evenhandedly in practice, believe in something: in the rule of law, in belief as a matter for the individual and in the individual as the ultimate repository of sovereignty. Like all others they adhere, if only implicitly, to a set of values which shape their activities. Most states are less reserved. They range from the secular in theory but partisan in practice, through the committed but tolerant, to the fundamentalist (committed and repressive).

Some of them, such as the ones that profess Marxism-Leninism, like China, or extreme, mystical nationalism, like Myanmar (Burma), uphold beliefs which are not those of their people. Others which seem to uphold the prevailing popular beliefs do so only in the most general sense. In practice the governing classes profess a distinct variant of the prevailing belief, as in large parts of Latin America or the Middle East. For **143** if one thing is certain, it is that the progressive emergence of a few world cults has resulted in a doctrinal tapestry within each which is rich enough to cover the most varied and incompatible social and political purposes.

State beliefs have not been unaffected by recent shifts in world power. Marxism-Leninism as an official doctrine, with its prophets, holy texts, licensed interpreters, sacred shrines, ritual practices and sacraments, is in steep decline. Mystical nationalism, with a similar spiritual armoury, is on the rise. At a popular level, the volatility of social change, experienced as personal insecurity, has resulted in an unprecedented and continuing surge of fundamentalism which is putting the established religions under ever-greater strain. Only the slightest glimmer of these changes could be captured.

Claims made about popular adherence to a particular belief, religious or other (as in the inset map 'God is Great if not Universal'), should be taken with a pillar of salt. Like taxes, confessions of faith respond to someone else's demands, and are paid willy-nilly. Unlike taxes non-payment is difficult to gauge, since the currency it is paid in is, at least in part, spiritual. That being the case, this atlas has reluctantly followed the religious encyclopedists who, for obvious reasons, assign to everyone – babes in arms and dodderers in bed included – a coherent system of beliefs. The result is that numbers and, by implication, the general level of commitment to conventional faiths, are grossly overstated.

Sources:
Barrett, David B., ed., *World Christian Encyclopedia, A comparative study of churches and religions in the modern world AD 1900-2000*, Oxford: Oxford University Press, 1982; *Index on Censorship*, London: Writers and Scholars International Ltd, monthly; US State Department, *Country Reports on Human Rights Practices for 1989*, Report submitted to the Committee on Foreign Affairs, House of Representatives, and the Committee on Foreign Relations, US Senate, Washington DC, February 1990; press reports.

Acknowledgements:
John Sceats, retired schoolteacher, Southwick, unwittingly sparked a line of inquiry that led to this; Geoffery Willis, Chaplain, Lee Abbey, North Devon, provided good listening very early on; Ken Leach, Runnymede Trust, London, told me whom to speak to; Peter Clark, King's College, London, and John Creasy, Dr William's Library, London, told me what to look for; Martin Palmer and Joanne O'Brien, International Consultancy on Religious Education and Culture (ICOREC), Manchester Polytechnic, put me right. Gillon Aitkin, Aitkin & Stone, London, added substance to the Rushdie file.

33 TEMPLES AND VOTARIES

The spread of business studies from their origins in the Wharton School at the University of Pennsylvania, Philadelphia, in 1881 has been and remains phenomenal. There were just 13 business schools in 1908; today, on one reckoning, there are 1200 in the USA alone. In the rest of the world the number has grown from nothing to more than 300. And they are still striding along, covering new ground in new territories such as Eastern Europe as well as in the old.

They clearly relate to a need the need a business feels to master change, to tailor its public responses and adjust its internal organization to the unpredictable and ever-mutating conditions of markets at least cost to itself. Whether business schools answer that need adequately or at all is a different matter, and a difficult one to decide, for their business is to contemplate other bodies' navels rather than their own, and therefore they remain a bit of a mystery in themselves. Academic institutions? Schools of applied arts? Ideological seminaries? Nurseries for management networks? A bit of each – and more – perhaps.

Nobody really knows how many there are. The American schools included amongst the 'Temples' are the 257 members of the American Assembly of Collegiate Schools of Business (AACSB) accredited to grant the Masters in Business Administration (MBA) degree. There are of course many more that could be considered eligible: the 890 Graduate Schools of Management or the 1200 Undergraduate Institutions that administer the Graduate Management Admission Test (GMAT), or the host of institutions that run executive or diploma courses short of an academic degree. The Canadian schools included are members of the Canadian Federation of Deans of Management and Administrative Studies (CFDMAS). The European schools are those which grant the MBA or its equivalent and which replied to a special European Foundation for Management

Development (EFMD) questionnaire by February 1991 (45 percent of those polled) augmented by those listed in the Economist Publication's *Which MBA?*, by private communications from the London Business School (LBS) and, for countries not covered by any of these, the list of schools that require the American GMAT as of April 1990. The Latin American schools are members of the Consejo Latinamericano de Escuelos de Administracion (CLADEA) that satisfy the MBA criterion. Schools in South Asia are members of the Association of Management Development Institutions in South Asia (AMDISA) that offer an MBA programme. In Southeast Asia the schools are members of the Association of Southeast Asian Deans of Graduate Schools of Management (ADSGM). In Australia they are those listed in Steve Lewis's 'Guide to MBA Courses' in the *Financial Review* published in Sydney, 18 September 1990. Schools in Africa, the Caribbean, the Far East, the Middle East and New Zealand are those that require the American GMAT as listed in the Graduate Management Admission Council's *90-91 Bulletin of Information*.

These are far from being all the institutions that offer business studies, nor all of those that call themselves business schools, nor indeed all the respectable business schools, respectable in the sense that what they do is valued by people other than their faculty. At a rough guess, we might have picked up a third of the 'respectable' total – enough to give a sense of the exponential growth and geographical spread of the genus. Impressions should be tempered, however. The presence and, especially, the absence of a business school is an imperfect indication of the strength of the modern business culture in any one country. There are, for example, only two business schools listed for Japan, but there are no less than 3000 Japanese enrolments in American business schools every year. And the major schools in the USA and Western Europe frequently draw one-third or more of their students from abroad, many of whom, especially from poor countries, are amongst the most ardent of the business culture's devotees, votaries – and missionaries. For business studies are as much a declaration of faith in what passes nowadays for modernity and civilization as they are a set of pragmatic insights or operational techniques.

Sources:
American Assembly of Collegiate Schools of Business (AACSB), *Membership Directory 1990-91*, St Louis: AACSB, 1990; Association of Management Development Institutions in South Asia (AMDISA), *Fact Book and Faculty Directory*, Hyderabad: AMDISA, 1990; Association of Southeast Asian Deans of Graduate Schools of Management, Manila private communication; Barnes, William, *Management Catalyst, The Story of the London Business School, 1964 to 1989*, London: Paul Chapman for the LBS, 1989; Byrt, William, ed., *Management Education, An International Survey*, London and New York: Routledge, 1989; Canadian Federation of Deans of Management and Administrative Studies, Toronto, private communication; Consejo Latinamericano de Escuelas de Administracion, Lima, private communications; Economist Publications, *Which MBA? A Critical Guide to Programs in Europe and the USA*, 2nd enlarged edition, Special Report no.1192, London: The Economist Publications, March 1990; European Foundation for Management Development, Brussels, private communications; Fondation Nationale pour l'Enseignement de la Gestion des Entreprises, Paris, private communication; Hobsbawm, Eric J., *The Age of Capital 1848-1975*, London: Weidenfeld & Nicolson, 1975; Krasna, Jodi Z., ed., *The Official Guide to MBA Programs*, 1988-90 edition, Princeton: Warner Books for the Graduate Management Admission Council, 1988; Lewis, Steve, 'Guide to MBA Courses', *Financial Review*, Sydney, 18 September 1990; Paliwada, Stanley J., ed., *Guide to Business Schools*, 8th edition, London: Pitman for the Association for MBAs, 1990; press reports.

Acknowledgements:
It is a rare privilege to stumble across a community as generous and helpful as the denizens of business schools and their associations. Copious thanks are owed to more people than can be listed, and the list is already long. They are: Andre in the office of the Graduate Management Admission Council, Princeton, NJ; Angelica, Secretary, Association of Management Training Institutions of Eastern and Southern Africa, Arusha; William Barnes, former Secretary of the London Business School; Bill Braddick, former Director General, EFMD, Brussels; David Chambers, London Business School; John Child, Aston Business School, Birmingham; Jean-Claude Cuzzi, Secretary General, FNEGE, Paris; Goola Dastur, Graduate School of Management, Melbourne; John Fairfax, *Financial Review*, Sydney; Gay Haskins, Director General, EFMD, Brussels; Adolf Ihde, Assistant Director, EFMD, Brussels; Bill Laidlaw, Executive Vice President, AACSB, St Louis, Mo; Roger McCormick, Director General, Association of MBAs, London; Gabina Mendoza, Director, Asian Institute of Management, Manila; Robin Murray, Brighton; Max Mwanahiba, Executive Director, AMTIESA, Arusha; Stanley Paliwada, Graduate School of Business, University of Calgary; John Palmer, European editor, *The Guardian*, London and Brussels; Martine Plompen, EFMD, Brussels; Jean-François Poncet, Coordinateur, Interman, ILO, Geneva; Derek Pugh, Open University School of Management, Milton Keynes; Jim Roxborough, Management Foundation, Oxford; Nassir al-Saigh, Director General, Arab Organization of Administrative Sciences, Amman; Maria Sheldon, Secretary's Office, London Business School; Alan Smith, Erasmus Bureau, Brussels; A.V.Srinivasan, Secretary General, AMDISA, Hyderabad; John Stopford, London Business School; Jorge Talavera, Executive Director, CLADEA, Lima; Lesley Wilson, Deputy Director, EC Tempus Programme, Brussels; Roger Wolf, Dean, Business School, Toronto; Yugi Yamada, Head, Industry Division, Asian Productivity Organization, Tokyo.

34 PROGRAMMED VIEWS

In its day, television brought the state right into the family living room at a time and in a manner of the state's choosing. There was little alternative. Where it was not a state monopoly television broadcasting was highly centralized, and tightly controlled by the state (see **35. See, Hear, Speak No Evil**). The situation has not changed fundamentally. The state is still powerful, sometimes almighty, in the world's 650 million television households, embracing one-in-eight of all people, but it is gradually losing its grip before the combined onslaught of satellite broadcasting and the video cassette recorder, the latter present in one-third of all households with television. A foretaste of what this might mean came in Eastern Europe in the winter of 1989 when the corrupt *anciens régimes* finally collapsed in the presence of the television camera eye, partly as a consequence of that very presence. The main map depicts a world in which the state's grip is still vigorous.

The inset, 'Big Mouths', separates the global radio broadcasters from the regional, local, and the plainly pretentious. Like some other maps in this atlas it is stronger in depicting quantitative relations than relative effects, and for that reason is accompanied by the graphic, 'The Carrying Voice', which highlights the British Broadcasting Corporation's World Service. Regularly heard by an estimated 120 million people in 38 languages, that unique broadcaster reaches a third more listeners than its closest rival, Voice of America, and ten times the audience of Radio Moscow.

The US flag shows where imports account for more than one-third of television screen-time, and where imports from the USA account for more than twice imports from the next biggest foreign supplier.

The USA clearly dominates world cinema as shown in the graphic, 'Big Screen'. There are considerable film moguls elsewhere, notably in India and Japan, with substantial markets abroad, but they are dwarfed by the Titans of Hollywood, even if some of these Titans now draw their funds from Tokyo.

Sources:
Varis, Tapio, *International Flow of Television Programmes*, Reports and Papers on Mass Communication, no.100, Paris: UNESCO, 1985; United Nations Educational Scientific and Cultural Organization (UNESCO), *Statistical Yearbook 1989*, Paris: UNESCO, 1989; *Screen Digest*, monthly, London; Smith, Anthony, *The Geopolitics of Information*, London: Faber & Faber, 1980; British Broadcasting Corporation (BBC), press releases and verbal communications; press reports.

Acknowledgements:
Some had views, some information, some both. All evinced patience and generosity. They are, in alphabetical order: Alan Cooper, International Broadcasting and Audience Research (IBAR), BBC, London; Gerald Fitzmaurice, International Institute of Communications, London; Carol Forrester, IBAR, BBC, London; Paul Gerhardt, National Education Officer, Thames Television, London; Anne James, The Radio Academy, London; Jan Kacparek, Librarian, Independent Television Commission (ITC, formerly Independent Broadcasting Authority), London; Henryk Kierzkowski, Graduate Institute, Geneva; Barry MacDonald, former Librarian, ITC, London; Colin Robinson, Open University Production Centre, Milton Keynes; Wilf Stevenson, Director, British Film Institute, London; Anthony Smith, Magdalen College, Oxford; Mike Svennivik, Research Department, ITC, London; Tapio Varis, then of the University of Tampere, Finland; Robert Wilson, Press Office, BBC Overseas Service, London.

35 SEE, HEAR, SPEAK NO EVIL

There is a world of difference between sifting through opinions and information to find what might be apt for given circumstances or to make them digestible, and censorship – the outlawing of views and news by people dedicated to the task. The one is inseparable from social life, the other a naked exercise of social power.

Formally, most states renounced that power when they adhered to the United Nations Universal Declaration of Human Rights which, in Article 19, holds that 'Everyone has the right to freedom of opinion and expression; this right includes freedom to hold opinions without interference and to seek, receive and impart information and ideas through any media and regardless of frontiers'.

Declarations, of course, are one thing, and state practices another. They employ an array of instruments: killings, kidnappings, disappearances (see **27. Human Rights**); arrests, detention and imprisonment; dismissals, threats, and harassment; restrictions on movement and expulsions; confiscations and closures; prevention of imports and reception; control of news agencies, setting of guidelines, favouritism, leaks, control of access, training of media staff, surveillance of press clubs, herding and corralling of journalists; disinformation; legislation, licensing, bans, expulsions; ownership; bribes; allocation of scarce resources including newsprint, frequencies, typewriters, advertising...

Among their standard targets are editors, producers, journalists and printers, writers and academics, human rights activists, political dissidents; artists of all varieties. And among the many justifications for censorship there are: the protection of innocents from unfair criticism, from defamation, from the invasion of privacy; the protection of national or state security; the control of sedition; protection of public health, public morals, public order; preservation of a linguistic, cultural or public regime; correction of media bias; enforcement of contractual obligations.

The categories featured in the main map characterize censorship regimes; they are not intended to represent a hierarchy of severity. Within each category there are the more frightful and the less frightful states, those that respond to what they deem unacceptable behaviour with ferocity and those that do so temperately.

The character of a censorship regime is heavily influenced by the relative size of the technical and general intelligentsia in a country, the related complexity of its economy, and its governing class's feeling of security. *Arbitrary* censorship regimes, in which discernible rules either do not exist or can be easily or capriciously changed, tend to thrive where the intelligentsia is tiny and can be ignored without immediately adverse economic effect, where power is narrowly, even personally, held, and felt to be insecure. *Rigidly bureaucratic* censorship regimes, in which the rules are known and enforced, tend to flourish where the intelligentsia is still relatively small, but important for the functioning of the economy, and pampered, where any complexity in the domestic economy is imported and where the governing class feels relatively secure. *Flexibly bureaucratic* regimes, where the censorship rules are applied unevenly reflect the growth and internal differentiation of an intelligentsia required to sustain an economy whose increasing complexity is internally driven. This intelligentsia needs and is able to assert its several, sometimes competing, interests, and puts pressure on the governing class to open avenues for that competition. In these states the governing class loses cohesion and censorship becomes part of the political process. Regimes in which censorship is *mainly implicit* flourish where the governing class has no alternative but to allow the highly-differentiated intelligentsia, on which its wealth and power rests, to share influence and therefore speak with a relatively untrammelled and discordant voice. Ironically, this type of regime shares many charactersitics with the arbitrary regimes – what is permitted in normal circumstances is subject to the hazards of private prosecution and legal interpretation, to the vagaries of self-censorship and to the pressures to conform that build-up within a highly-differentiated, competitive and mutually-dependent priviligentsia.

States were classified by way of a rudimentary Delphi route: independent observers with experience of the state in question and a sensitivity to the topic were polled directly or indirectly for their judgements. Consensus views were generally adopted, with exceptions made for changed circumstances. Where judgements differed, which they frequently did, particularly as between the two bureaucratic categories, and between 'arbitrary' and 'mainly implicit', I have tended to the more rigid, and the arbitrary (but not in the case of Egypt). There are further cases where elements of more than one censorship regime coexist in one state without any clearly predominating, as in Yugoslavia in the first months of 1991. Subtlety has always taken second place to clarity. Some countries' inclusion within the 'arbitrary' category reflect the anarchy associated with civil war, as in the Lebanon, Liberia or Suriname. In others it reflects an unfinished settling down process after a sharp change in political regime, as in Hungary.

All categories freeze the categorized and so offend against reality, against Heracleitos ('All is flux, nothing stays still') – and against my Delphi panelists. They, quite properly, drew attention to the flux at the time they pronounced: deterioration in Costa Rica, Ecuador, El Salvador, Guyana, Mexico, Panama; improvements in Chile, Haiti, Paraguay, much of Eastern Europe. Their reservations have, regrettably, been overridden. The symbol on the map covers prisoners of conscience as defined by Amnesty International: people detained for their beliefs, colour, sex, ethnic origin, language or religion who have not used or advocated violence, as well as people considered by Amnesty as possible prisoners of conscience; it includes conscientious objectors to military service; as well as prisoners adopted by PEN International.

Sources:
Article 19, *World Report 1991*, London: Library Association, 1991 (seen in draft form); Committee to Protect Journalists (CPJ), *Attacks on the Press 1989*, New York: CPJ, March 1990; Freedom House, *Freedom in the World 1989-90*, New York: Freedom House, 1990; *Index on Censorship*, London: Writers and Scholars International Ltd, monthly; International PEN Writers in Prison Committee, *Writers and Journalists Reported Kidnapped, Imprisoned, Banned, Under House or Town Arrest, or Awaiting Trial*, London: International PEN, September 1990; Reporters Sans Frontières, *La Lettre de Reporters sans Frontières*, Montpellier: RSF, monthly; Smith, Anthony, *The Geopolitics of Information, How Western Culture Dominates the World*, London: Faber & Faber, 1980; Sussman, Leonard R., *Power, The Press and the Technology of Freedom, the Coming Age of ISDN*, New York: Freedom House, 1989; Zymon, John, Paul Sieghart & John Humphries, *The World of Science and the Rule of Law*, Oxford University Press, 1986; press reports.

Acknowledgements:
Many people in a number of organizations, and in a personal capacity, pooled their knowledge: Stephen Ellis and Gill Lusk at Africa Confidential, London; Richard Carver at Africa Watch, London; Nell Butler, Liz Cleary-Rodriguez, Said Essoulami, Carmel Redford, and Frances De Souza at Article 19, London; Tim Given, Adawela Maja-Pearce, Ursula Rushton, Philip Spender, and Lek Hor Tan at Index on Censorship, London; Adel Darwish, London; Maurice Frankel, London; François Misser, Brussels; and Joan Williams, Kingston, Jamaica.

36 THE BILLION-DOLLAR CLUB

Big is brutal but, in today's world, inevitable. Impelled by instant communication and cheap transport and travel, business has broken through the narrow confines of domestic markets to graze in the world at large. One hundred and ninety-five transnational corporations, just short of half of the 400 for which data are available, garnered more than a quarter of their sales abroad in the mid-1980s; 69 of them sold more abroad than at home. At the end of the decade they were growing at five percent per year in real terms in a sluggish world economy.

This picture accords with the one presented in **5. Market Muscle** where sales and net physical exports are compared (the graphic 'Corrected Vision'). It is a picture of the transnational corporation as the essential foreign legionary for today's national economy, the main enforcer of changes in world economic power, the ultimate instrument for concentrating that power in fewer and fewer states and, within them, in fewer and fewer hands.

The transnational corporation presents a constantly-shifting target to the observer; the tracking trails far behind the tracked. Even the identity collapses under scrutiny: 150 of the top 500 named by the UN Centre of the Transnational Corporation in 1985 did not make it onto *Fortune*'s equivalent list only four years later – they had succumbed to merger; to breakup or unbundling; to failure or sluggishness; to the effect of changes in currency exchange rates; or to changes in the accounting conventions used at different stages in the business's own development. Victims too, perhaps, of the different information environments in which they operate, for the corporations analyzed are essentially secretive, hiding their activities, in so far as they can, from each other, from governments at home and abroad, from employees, shareholders, the general public – and from their would-be analysts.

Commonly neglected in all the analyses are the number of potential Billion-Dollar Club members – of enormous bulk and potential influence – such as the giant Russian corporations, from Aeroflot, the world's biggest airline, to the aerospace, military, mining and heavy industrial corporations which sustain that state's considerable, if fumbling, manufacturing power. As the Russian economy finds its place in the world, this neglect is unlikely to persist.

Sources:
UN Centre on Transnational Corporations (UNCTC), *Transnational Corporations in World Development, Trends and Prospects*, New York: UN, 1988; *Fortune Magazine*, 30 July 1990.

Acknowledgements:
Karl Sauvant, Head, UNCTC, New York, made light of, and in, sharing his considerable experience; and Graham Vickery, Directorate for Science, Technology and Industry, OECD, Paris, responded patiently to inquiries and requests.

37 GOING, GOING ... GONE

If it can be defined and protected it can be owned. Land has been enclosed almost everywhere, privately and by the state. The oceans and seas are on the way to being similarly expropriated from the common heritage – by the state mainly, but also privately (see **1. The World of States** and **2. The Claimant State**). The air looks to be going the same way, at least in the imaginings of the apprehensive. *Gasping*, a play by Ben Elton on the privatization of air, ran for eight-and-a-half months in London in 1990. And life itself is being claimed for private appropriation: during the current Uruguay round of international trade talks in which the extension of GATT rules to intellectual property is a key item, governments are coming under increasing pressure from private companies to entrench the new forms of life manufactured in their laboratories – products of genetic engineering – behind patents, copyrights and trademarks.

Privatization is a quick, seemingly safe route to increased profit, presence and power for the purchasing companies. For the divesting states, the motives are more complex. Some see it primarily as a necessary adjustment to new economic circumstances: ever-pressing world markets are subjecting state monopolies to ever-closer and more critical scrutiny, revealing them to be corporate coelocanths, unable to move freely in an increasingly competitive environment, and inferior in most respects to the (mostly private) transnational corporation (see **36. The Billion-Dollar Club**). Others see in privatization a way to relieve budgetary stress in the transition from state interventionism to non-interventionism. Yet others use it to gain relief from the importunities of rich, foreign uncles who might adorn their pleasure with loans or aid of some kind. And others use privatization to spread the charms of possession beyond the political class, and so to widen its base in society (see **26. Are You With Me?**).

None of these aims is pursued to the exclusion of the others: relieving budgetary stress is a normal component of a strategy for increasing competitiveness as well as a standard argument for, and from, external agencies. Structural adjustments, however tiny, are dressed up for the benefit of such agencies, while being used to staunch budgetary haemorrhages.

Nor are these aims pursued with clinical purity: a clear view of the advantages to be gained from geographical mobility and greater market opportunism is often occluded in practice by condoning, or conniving at private monopolies that turn out to be as hidebound and immobile as their state predecessors. An attempt to furnish or replenish Treasury coffers is more likely than not to be compromised by giveaway prices that will attract support from the protopriviligentsia while defrauding the public at large. It is, after all, in the nature of public representation in the market system to be also a private possession, a source of personal profit, presence and power, and by the same token, it is in its nature to muddle public purposes.

Even assuming that the aim of privatization is clear and uncorrupted, there are natural limits to its progress everywhere, except in the very heartlands of the market system. The state has built its business – badly in most cases, madly in some – where the domestic private sector was unequal to the task of fending off or challenging foreign economic might. The state has commandeered enormous resources in the process, further weakening, where it did not altogether extinguish, private enterprise. Now that the major state commercial bodies are seen to be at best awkward players in world markets, and at worst clear losers, there is usually no one left on whom to unload them except – cruel, cruel irony – the foreign private enterprises that they were designed to resist in the first place.

Seen from Mars, privatization is a primrose path to an unprecedented concentration of economic power in ever-fewer, ever-larger hands, and to its equal and opposite – an unprecedented loss of economic power by an ever-larger number.

Sources:
Centre for Privatization, *Privatization Survey for Developing Countries*, prepared for the United States Agency for International Development, Bureau for Private Enterprise, Washington DC, March 1990; Kikeri, Sunita, *Bank Lending for Divestiture, A Review of Expenditure*, World Bank Working Paper, WPS 333, May 1990; *Privatisation International*, London, monthly; private communications; press reports.

Acknowledgements:
Rodney Lord, Editor, *Privatisation International*, London, and Diana Lord were helpful, and generous, hosts; Michael Field, Centre for Privatization, Washington, solved a problem of resources; Margaret Sadard, Privatization Council, **149**

Washington, pointed me in the right direction; Geoff Lamb, External Relations Division, and Michael Ward, then of the International Economics Division, the World Bank, added their mighty mites.

38 THE TOP LINE

Compensation, as pay is called when it runs into six or more figures, is far too complex and important to be God-given. It is the gift of compensation committees. In the USA where 90 percent of public companies have such committees, three-quarters of their members are current or former executives, more often than not the boss's cronies. The rest are mostly from peer companies or the business services that are the boss's clients. It is a rare compensation committee which can sport a truly independent member.

These committees base their deliberations – when they do deliberate – on reports from 'compensation consultants' appointed by the company's main board which is chaired, generally, by the chief executive officer whose salary is being fixed. Some CEOs have the grace to withdraw when their worth is being assessed. Others ... well, they are powerful people.

There is no science, little need, not a little hocus-pocus and settling of mutual debts, and much greed, in fixing top pay. And the outcomes are sometimes bizarre: for every $1000 fall in shareholders' value in Navistar International (formerly International Harvester), James Cotting, its CEO, is reported to have become richer by $1.41. More generally pay and performance are simply not related to each other: in a sample of 1000 companies, also in the USA, CEOs' pay changed by just two cents for every $1000 change in their stockmarket value. This was in 1990, and there is no reason to believe that anything has changed since.

The market in which top managers operate is fractured by linguistic, cultural, political and security barriers internationally, and by racial, cultural, community and friendship barriers nationally. Being a very imperfect market, it allows huge disparities in pay to persist between managers doing equivalent work in different places and even larger disparities in the chasms that everywhere separate the exalted and the lowly in business.

The figures on which both the main and the inset maps rest are for 'total cash', that is the annual base salary including all fixed bonuses plus all performance-related bonuses (both company and individual). They do not include the 'perks' or payments in kind which are almost universal in the upper reaches of business – company housing, company cars, company health insurance, company contributions for children's education, company pensions, company golden parachutes, company non- or quasi-business travel, company communications, company connections, company contacts, company this, company that and company the other. In the UK, these perks add 10 percent to a chief executive's pay, nothing to that of a supervisor. The figures also do not allow for the effects of taxation.

One important 'perk' is financial security, which is considered, in part, in 'Sorry to See You Go'. The figures in the main map relate to companies with an annual turnover of US$200-300 million. For purposes of international comparison, the original numbers in national currencies were converted into US dollars at the rates given in the *Financial Times*' Guide to World Currencies of 6 August 1990, and then converted into dollars of equal purchasing power on the basis of values derived from the United Nations Development Programme's *Human Development Report 1990*.

The caption quote comes from Jaclyn Fierman's article, 'The People Who Set the CEO's Pay' in *Fortune*, 12 March 1990.

Sources:
Hay Management Consultants, personal communication; The Wyatt Company, personal com-munication; TPF&C, a Towers Perrin company, *Worldwide Total Remuneration, 1988*; press reports.

Acknowledgements:
Claudia Kulatunga, Hay Management Consultants, London, created the clearing; Michael Dixon, *Financial Times*, London, pointed in its general direction; and Rachel Baker, Wyatt Personal Financial Services Limited, Dillis Viney, Towers Perrin, and Sue Winterbottom, Employment Conditions Abroad Limited, all of London, were reassuring staging posts and supply depots on the way.

39

GOLDEN FIX

Coca and poppies are easy to grow, easy to refine into cocaine and heroin, easy to transport and easy to use. Once used they are hard to give up.

As consumer products projected onto a global market they have a lot going for them: committed consumers – perhaps 50 million habitual users worldwide; a mass of suppliers and other employees – distributors, enforcers, salespeople, agents numbering 1.5 million in Peru, Colombia and Bolivia alone; and some of the most chilling – and rich – business operators in the world – made members of the Sicilian Mafia and its offshoot, the US cartel that goes by the same name, and the owner-members of the rival Colombian cocaine cartels, numbering no more than a couple of thousand.

They also find grudging support among the enlightened and informed, increasingly exasperated and appalled at the waste involved in prohibition – it cost the US Navy and Coast Guard $120,000 to impound one kilo of cocaine on average in 1988 – and by the corruption of judiciaries, whole governments and the very notion of law and order in the producing, transit and money-laundering states. A drug bust on the scale of the US invasion of Panama in 1989 might be excused if it worked. But has it?

Difficult as it is to wean people from drugs, it is proving even more difficult to wean the world financial system from dependence on drug money. A Group of Seven (rich states) Task Force reporting in April 1990 recommended that money laundering be made a criminal offence, only to find that eight out of fifteen states involved in preparing the report had no such law. The Vienna Convention, sponsored by the United Nations in 1988, which makes money-laundering an extraditable crime, has been signed by 80 states, but ratified by only four.

Sources:
Ardila, Patricia, *Beyond Law Enforcement: Narcotics and Development*, Alexandria, Va: The Panos Institute, February 1990; Hawkes, Nigel, *The International Drugs Trade*, Hove, East Sussex: Wayland, 1988; Lyman, Michael D., 'Gangland', *Drug Trafficking by Organized Criminals*, Springfield, Ill.: Charles Thomas, 1989; Sterling, Claire, 'The Mafia', *The Long Reach of the International Sicilian Mafia*, London: Hamish Hamilton, 1990; US Department of Justice, *Drug Trafficking, a report to the President of the United States*, Washington DC, 3 August 1989; US Drug Enforcement Administration (DEA), *Money Laundering and the Illicit Drug Trade* (DEA Sensitive), Washington DC, September 1988; press reports.

Acknowledgements:
Kay Frederick at the Institute for the Study of Drugs Dependence (ISDD), London.

40

THIS LITTLE PIGGY

In a market economy anything that sells has value and all the effort that goes into its creation is worthwhile, 'productive', labour. In the pure light of established ideology, financial futures, fantasies, funerals share equal status with fish, frocks and furniture.

But the market is intrinsically fickle. It can vanish overnight, annihilating the work involved in its supply, devaluing the sense of individual worth that derives from social connectedness, and with it undermining the moral foundations of society.

This ambiguity at the very heart of the market system has sponsored a search for a more enduring criterion of value, one which focuses on the ultimate destiny of the human effort. In this light, if the goods and services produced are used in further production, are recycled, the people providing that labour can legitimately derive a sense of self-worth. If these goods and services are not recycled or, in the extreme case, not recyclable, the labour associated with them is wasted, however skilled, intense or intrinsically interesting it may be, and the expenditure of effort a source of moral disaffection.

There is a strange coalition ranged behind this concept of worth. There are the utopian revolutionaries dreaming of – and sometimes organizing for – a society based on individual needs and desires, rather than on profit-generating demand. There are the ecologists whose worst nightmares depict a world with three billion cars, 400 million tons of meat devoured a year, 40 million gigawatts of electricity and 12 billion tons of oil. And strangest of all, there are the theorists of the unthinkable, the military strategists charged with preparing for total war. Their task is, or perhaps was, to target offensive nuclear weapons, and position missile defenses, in such a way that whatever survived a nuclear holocaust in the enemy camp would be below the threshold of an integrated, self-expanding core economy, and whatever survived at home would be above that threshold. Essential to that concept of a bedrock, surplus-producing economy is the notion of recyclability.

On this interpretation all the goods and services provided by the military, and by most of the state bureaucracy, a large part of the people engaged in finance and insurance, real estate and rental services, business travel and entertainment, and a significant part of the labour force in many other industries, is worthless. And all the goods and services used by them personally and professionally, are also waste, the product of unproductive labour.

Since analysis on these lines is either a top military secret or utterly repugnant to prevailing attitudes, or indeed both, it is not surprising that there is next to no empirical data on which to base a map. Official statistics are unhelpful where they are not confusing, and private attempts to grope through them to the underlying realities have been few and underpowered. In consequence, the map provides no more than the crudest impression of the proportions between productive and unproductive labour in the various states and, by inference, of the moral security of the incumbent regimes.

The map assumes, precariously, that military spending and central government expenditure on salaries consume half of all waste spending (compared with 13.3 percent in the USA in 1970); that central government salaries as a proportion of gross domestic product in the rich (OECD) countries is equal to the unweighted average of the proportions ruling in Austria, Finland, France, Germany, the Netherlands and Sweden; that in Asia (other than Japan) and the Arab countries it is equal to the average figure for Bangladesh, India and Pakistan; in Africa – to the average for Mauritius, Sudan and Zimbabwe; in Latin America and the Caribbean – equal to Colombia's figure; and in Canada – to the USA's. It assumes, further, that waste spending as a proportion of GDP, however hazy that concept is (see notes to **6. National Income**), is a reasonable proxy for waste working as a proportion of all working; and that all recycled output is productive whether or not it is subsidized.

It need hardly be said that these are audacious, if not foolhardy, assumptions. Their cumulative effect is to reduce the proportion of wasted work in most states. In the USA, for example, the sole country for which the comparison can be made, the resultant figure – 28.1 percent – is under half of what it was in a closely supported study relating to 1970.

Readers, be warned: the concept is in far better shape than the model.

Sources:
Kidron, Michael, with Elana Gluckstein, 'Waste: US 1970', *Capitalism and Theory*, London: Pluto Press, 1974; International Labour Office (ILO), *World Labour Review 1989*, Geneva: ILO, 1989; US Arms Control and Disarmament Agency (USACDA), *World Military Expenditures and Arms Transfers 1989*, Washington DC: USACDA, 1990; World Bank, *Social Indicators of Development 1989*, Baltimore and London: Johns Hopkins University Press, 1989.

41 VALUE ADDED AND TAKEN AWAY

It is difficult to think of a more value-loaded concept in economics – or in any field for that matter – than 'value', or one that is more difficult to quantify. If the market is the ultimate touchstone, any activity that is paid for, or payable in principle, adds value to the final product or service, warfare and arms production included (see notes to **6. National Income**). If sustainable consumer welfare is the guiding principle, any activity that results in output that can serve as ingredients of further output, in other words any activity that results in goods or services that are recyclable, adds value. Choose a vantage point, and an appropriate definition comes into view.

Labour's problem is that it cannot easily make such a choice. It is precluded from attaching value to productive activity in the sense used above because so many of its number are non-productive workers (see **40. This Little Piggy**). Equally, it is precluded from seeing value in *all* market-oriented activity because such activity is related only fitfully and by chance to the long-term welfare of its people. So confusion reigns, and value, added or subtracted, is what you say it is.

Most mainstream economists, the ones empowered to measure, uphold a market
view of value. They do not, in consequence, differentiate, analytically or statistically, be-

tween productive and unproductive activity, recyclable and non-recyclable output, essential and inessential processes. The results are a nightmare: labour's share of value added in the rich states appears generally to be higher than in the poor states (although India appears amongst the plump!). Could that be because a privileged, highly paid management cadre, including even owners, are generally classed as employees in the rich, rather than because labour has bargained successfully for a larger share?

For the shares of other stakeholders in added value, the state's and management's, see **25. First Bite of the Cherry** and **38. The Top Line**.

Sources:
International Labour Office (ILO), WEP Indicators Database, 18 January 1991 and 26 February 1991; ILO, private communications.

Acknowledgements:
Tita Prada de Mesa, Employment Department, International Labour Office, Geneva, was a copious – and serene – source of advice and materials, published and not.

42 WORKPLACES

The number and proportion of people engaged in the transmission of commercial information would be a good indication of an economy's strength in the world market. Communications are, after all, at the leading edge of the fast expanding service sector worldwide (see **12. Service Power**). Unfortunately, the few figures that exist are gathered haphazardly and are not mutually comparable. A weaker indication is provided by the statistics on employment in commercial services, that is in finance, insurance, property or real estate, and business services. They too are faulted, not least because they lump services to the consumer with services to business, because they exclude commercial services provided by the state, and because – as compiled and presented by the International Labour Office – they leave out the largest labour forces in the world, namely those in China, India and the USSR. Nonetheless, this is all that was available for the main maps.

The two inset maps, 'Presence of the Past' and 'Presence of the Present', would also benefit from a finer statistical mesh, one that separates commercial from subsistence agriculture, for example, or differentiates between low- and high-tech manufactures, or between utilities for business and utilities for the home. But that again is too much to ask of the cumbersome bureaucracies currently engaged in the collection of national data and in their international harmonization and tabulation.

Source:
International Labour Office, *Year Book of Labour Statistics 1990*, 49th edition, Geneva: ILO, 1990.

Acknowledgements:
Tita Prada de Mesa, Employment Department, ILO, Geneva, convinced me that the statistical peaks could not be climbed in present conditions, and that we must make do with pictures from afar.

43 CLASS STRUGGLE

A struggle for the soul of the modern worker has been going on ever since that fractured creature was split from the land and forced to sell its creative energy in order to eat. The struggle continues today – between those who would assimilate workers fully into the market economy, as sellers of a service, labour, and those who would not, who highlight the workers' distinction in being, at one and the same time, a means of production and, as key consumer, its primary object. Neither side has won. The assimilators might claim tactical advantage in the USA, for example, but they would have to concede temporary defeat in, say, Poland or South Korea.

The main map focusses on the workers' collective experience of apartness, as expressed in strikes or through lockouts. The indicator is extremely crude. In reality, strikes and lockouts can express high commitment in either or both of the contending sides, or simple convenience; they can be contract-end set-pieces, or spontaneous explosions of exasperation; they can be demonstrations measured in hours, or long **153** open-ended battles; of general interest, or of significance to only a handful of people; isolated, or supported from outside; fought on bread-and-butter issues, or on issues of principle or politics. They can be almost anything you imagine, but arguably their very existence is a symptom of irritation, an indication that the fit between worker and market is not entirely snug.

The uncomfortable space between the workers and the employers, private or state, who preside over the market, is inhabited by the trade unions. They too come in many forms and fulfil many functions, from spearheading protest to containing it. All do both, but some do more of the one, some more of the other, as the inset map, 'In the Crossfire', illustrates. Again, there is little that holds true of all trade unions, except perhaps that none is truly free and none totally a creature of the state (so judgements are bound to differ); and for that reason alone, their very existence, even in the most controlled, corrupt and spineless embodiment, and even if their members are press-ganged into them by party, state or employer promotes amongst these members a sense of distinctiveness.

The inset map – 'Penetration' – is based on membership claims made by the unions themselves. Some of these claims are wild, some more than sober. They are all shallow in that they represent numbers, not commitment or loyalty. But the argument holds: their very existence points to activities that promote a sense of apartness amongst workers, a sense that they the workers constitute a class with discernible interests distinct from those of the market's administrators.

Sources:
International Labour Office (ILO), *Year Book of Labour Statistics 1989-90*, Geneva: ILO, 1990; Harper, F.John, ed., *Trade Unions of the World 1989-1990*, A Keesing's Reference Publication, Harlow: Longman, 1989; private communications; press reports.

Acknowledgements:
Dan Gallin, International Union of Foodworkers, Geneva, squeezed time out of a busy schedule to help. Other officials in international trade union organizations contributed out of their abundant knowledge and insights, generously and – as must be evident – self-effacingly. Richard Kuper, London, dusted off his bookshelves to noticeable effect.

44 GOBAR KA KAM

Gobar ka kam ('shit work' in Hindi) refers to the fuel patties which it has been the Indian woman's lot to form out of cow dung from time immemorial. The phrase is now properly applied to women's work in general.

Less is measured than is known about the work women do, and little enough is known. It is known, for example, that women work. One would have thought that the number who work should present no problem. Wrong. The World Bank manages to give a figure for women's share of the labour force that is six times the one given by the International Labour Office (ILO) for Niger (47 percent as against 7.9 percent), and more than ten times for Guinea-Bissau (41.2 and 3.6 percent respectively). The ILO figure has been adopted in most cases of discrepancy. It is known too that women work longer hours than men – one third more in twelve rich, industrial countries where men spend one-fifth more time in paid work but only one-third the time women spend on household tasks – but how much more in the world at large is unknown: personal time budgets are a rare statistical luxury.

It is also known that women are generally restricted to a narrower range of jobs than men – typically to those that reaffirm their ancillary, responding role: nursing, child care, primary school teaching, personal and domestic service, sales, and routine assembly – and are largely confined to the bottom of the earnings scale but the statistical coverage is meagre and opaque: pay rates, hourly earnings, weekly earnings, annual earnings are all significant for different purposes, as is the ratio between subsistence and typical male earnings, or the proportion of women who are sole providers, but they are never all given and the selection is capricious. The graphic, 'Working for Less', carries the scars of this scrappiness. It presents for a small minority of states male-female pay ratios outside agriculture, unadjusted for the number of hours worked, both of which naturally favours the comparison.

The underlying problem is that the (mainly male) priviligentsia does not want to know much more than that women exist and are in attendance (see **24. The Lesser Equal**) – women are fine so long as they remain a hidden presence.

Sources:

International Labour Office (ILO), WEP Indicators Database, 21 January 1991; ILO, *Yearbook of International Labour Statistics*, various years, Geneva: ILO, annual; Seager, Joni, and Ann Olson, *Women in the World, an international atlas*, London and Sydney: Pan Books, New York: Simon & Schuster, 1986; World Bank, *Social Indicators of Development 1989*, Baltimore and London: Johns Hopkins University Press, 1989.

Acknowledgements:

Tita Prada de Mesa, Employment and Development Department, International Labour Office, Geneva, patiently pointed out important statistical blind spots, and filled some of them in. Wouter van Ginneken,*World Labour Report*, ILO, Geneva, was more than helpful in opening avenues – in my mind and in his institution.

45 MILEX

Money alone cannot measure the cost of the military – in lives lost, in spirits broken, in imaginations and ingenuities disfigured. And the amount of money spent on the military is not easy to gauge – it is shrouded in secrecy for reasons of state security; prices of the military goods and services which it buys are wildly approximate for lack of a free market in them; and the conventional unit of measurement – the US dollar – is volatile and not universally accepted.

The figures that lie behind the shares of world military expenditure in the main map are predominantly those produced by the Stockholm International Peace Research Institute (SIPRI), the most dispassionate and reliable source available, for 1990. Where the latest year's expenditure was lacking, as in the significant cases of Sweden and Libya amongst others, the trend of real expenditures over the previous five years was extrapolated to 1990. The military budgets of the two parts of Germany (and of Yemen) were merged in anticipation of unification later that year – admittedly a rough and ready procedure. And the military expenditures of states not included in SIPRI's estimates, notably the USSR, China, Afghanistan, Vietnam, Cambodia and Laos, are as estimated for 1989 in *The New State of War and Peace*, in a manner explained there.

Sources:

Kidron, Michael, and Dan Smith, *The New State of War and Peace, an international atlas*, London: Grafton Books, New York: Simon & Schuster, 1991; Stockholm International Peace Research Institute, *SIPRI Yearbook 1991, World Armaments and Disarmament*, Oxford: Oxford University Press, 1991 and *SIPRI Yearbook 1990, World Armaments and Disarmament*, Oxford: Oxford University Press, 1990; US Arms Control and Disarmament Agency, *World Military Expenditures and Arms Transfers 1989*, Washington DC, October 1990; press reports.

Acknowledgements:

Saadat Deger and Somnat Sen at SIPRI, Stockholm, answered questions, fended off importunities and supplied essential materials in good spirit as and when required; Ingvor Wallin, also at SIPRI, kept channels open with great good humour.

46 ARMED FORCE

Humans are not the only species which dedicates some of its number to destroying its members. Ants amongst others do the same. But humans are unique in not being pro-grammed genetically to behave in that way.

Included in the cartogram, 'Under Arms', are all military servicemen and women on full-time duty; full-time active members of paramilitary forces whose training, organ-ization, equipment and control suggest that they are used in support or in lieu of regular military forces; and active internal opposition forces (see **47. Hot Spots**) that come into these categories. Excluded are all Reserves, even in those states such as Israel or Switzerland where they constitute a prime ingredient of military strategy. Also excluded are national guards, civil defence forces, people's militias, secret services and all the other covert and overt forces that are employed in safeguarding the security of the state. In China, for example, all but 1.85 million Peoples Armed Police, out of the 12 or so million under the Ministry of Public Security, are in these categories. The Lebanon where the militias are in reality fully fledged sectarian armies is an exception here. Finally, all states whose armed forces amount to less than 0.01 percent of the world total – 4700 people – have been excluded. These include Belize, Jamaica, Guyana, Luxembourg, Papua New Guinea, Suriname and Switzerland.

Comparing the numbers in the armed forces with the number of men between the ages of 18 and 22 overstates the military tax on productive employment (see **40. This** 155

Little Piggy) because the military, particularly where service is voluntary, employ many people beyond the prime soldiering age. Iraq, for example, had twice as many men under arms as in that age bracket (before the Gulf War of 1991), and North Korea 14 percent more. In another sense the comparison understates the military burden because the military have first claim on the healthiest and most active of the 18 to 22 age group.

The extent of the tax on potentially productive activity constituted by military and military-type employment sometimes beggars the imagination. In a rare historical moment when East Germany was preparing to become once again part of a united Germany and some state secrets popped out, it became known that fully one in fifteen of the entire population, infants and crones included, worked under military discipline of one sort or another: for the Stasi (secret police), the army, the border guards, customs authorities, police, the Communist Party militia, and the paramilitary Society for Sport and Technique. Although less exposed to scrutiny, there are surely more than a handful of states in a similar position.

It says something about the tilted Manicheism pervading the world that soldiers outnumber doctors to the extent they do, and so widely. Out of the 165 states surveyed for the inset map 'Dr Love and Dr Strangelove' 158 deployed more potential killers than potential curers.

Sources:
International Institute for Strategic Studies (IISS), *The Military Balance 1990-91*, London: Brassey's for IISS, Autumn 1990; Sivard, Ruth Leger, *World Military and Social Expenditures 1989*, 13th edition, Washington DC: World Priorities Inc, 1990.

Acknowledgements:
John Montgomery, Librarian, Royal United Services Institute, London, lent succour when it was most needed.

47 HOT SPOTS

The first United Nations humanitarian mission to visit Iraq after the Gulf War, in February 1991, found that the US bombing had resulted in such damage to the water supply and the sanitation services that diarrhoeal diseases amongst children had quadrupled and an epidemic of cholera was in prospect. The inescapable conclusion is that you do not have to resort to bacteriological weapons in order to wage bacteriological warfare.

The main map records the states involved in armed conflict, abroad or at home, in which the fighting is organized centrally, at least on one side, and in which there is some continuity between armed clashes. It is not a register of wars. These outnumber the states at war. In India, for example, there are three distinct wars in progress – in Kashmir, the Punjab, and Assam; and Ethiopia, Indonesia, Myanmar (Burma), the Philippines and South Africa can present a similar array. It is also not a tally of states formally at war: the USA mustered a coalition of 29 states against Iraq, many of which were members in name only and which talked (Czechoslovakia) or bought (Germany, Belgium and Japan) their way out of the fighting; the two Koreas are still officially at war more than thirty years after they ceased fighting. Only those states which were reported as being actively engaged in armed hostilities in the first three months of 1991, or which, it could be reliably assumed, were continuing an established pattern of armed hostilities at the time, feature on the map.

Wars would not be what they are were they not sustained by arms. Little is reliably known about arms sales, and less about their international trade. But thanks to the Stockholm International Peace Research Institute (SIPRI) not all is shrouded in darkness. The inset map, 'The Armourers', shows the relative success of the world's competing arms producers in a period before the Gulf War, that is before their most advanced products were tested in action. The practical lessons of that war are already having their affect on arms shopping lists.

Sources:
Stockholm International Peace Research Institute (SIPRI), *SIPRI Yearbook 1990, World Armaments and Disarmament*, Oxford University Press, 1990; press reports.

Acknowledgements:
Philip Chrimes at the press library, Royal Institute of International Affairs, London, contributed experience and knowledge as he unfailingly does.

48 THE SCORCHERS

Atmospheric gases trap heat which builds up into what is known as the greenhouse effect. There are relatively more of these gases in existence now than there have ever been, at least in the last 160,000 years, and their concentration is rising at an unprecedented rate. If the United Nations Intergovernmental Panel on Climate Change is to be trusted, average global temperatures will have risen by about 2°C above pre-industrial levels (1.1°C above today's levels) by the year 2030, and by 4°C (3.3°C above today) by 2090. The Maldives, Tuvalu and Kiribati will disappear. Vast areas of coastland in Egypt, Bangladesh, India, China and Indonesia will be permanently inundated. Important industrial sites in the USA and Japan will be threatened. Famous landmarks – the white cliffs of Dover – will go. Deserts will advance into large parts of the Mediterranean, Africa and America. Northern Russia will be flooded. Tropical diseases will spread to northern latitudes, and the cost of food production will rise by a tenth. Populations will shift in colossal migrations, and roads, railways, pipelines and mines will be disrupted. And that's only for starters.

Since wind currents ensure that every molecule of greenhouse gas, wherever generated, joins the common store, in a real sense we fry together although we light up separately.

The greenhouse gases are carbon dioxide, half the current total, arising primarily from the use of fossil fuels, cement making and deforestation; chlorofluorocarbons, 20 percent, arising from refrigeration, the manufacture of solvents and foam products, and mainly responsible for the depletion of the ozone layer; methane, 16 percent, from wet rice cultivation, factory farming and the production and transport of natural gas; tropospheric ozone eight percent; and nitrous oxide six percent.

The greenhouse gases differ hugely in potency. Molecule for molecule, methane traps 20-30 times as much heat as carbon dioxide, and the human-made chlorofluorocarbons no less than 20,000 times as much. To balance their proportionate distribution in the atmosphere and their different heat-trapping characteristics the Washington-based World Resources Institute together with the United Nations Environment Programme and the United Nations Development Programme constructed a Greenhouse Index for the three major gases responsible for 86 percent of the heat-trapping potential directly attributable to human activity. It measures their effect in carbon dioxide equivalent converted into tonnes of carbon. It is the measure adopted for the cartogram 'Global Warming'.

Belching into the atmosphere is one thing. Good manners – conservation in the energy field – is another. We may assume that conservation, as a relative newcomer to state or private policy making, could build on the substantial differences in energy use that exist between states. The colours on the cartogram, and especially 'How Much is Enough?', give a rough indication of these differences – rough because the unit of output, GDP, is a hazy concept (see notes to **6. National Income**) and no distinction is drawn between energy used for productive and unproductive purposes (see notes to **40. This Little Piggy**), or between consumer and producer use.

Sources:
United Nations (UN), *1988 Energy Statistics Yearbook*, New York: UN, 1990; World Energy Council (WEC), *Report 1989: International Energy Data*, London: WEC, 1990; World Resources Institute, *World Resources 1990-91*, New York and Oxford: Oxford University Press, 1990; press reports.

Acknowledgements:
Richard Sandbrook, Director, International Institute for Environment and Development, London, pointed to the material; Dan Lundy, Oxford University Press, New York, supplied the crucial bits in time; Fred Dixon, assistant to the General Secretary, WEC, London, identified and produced a key item.

49 DIRT'S CHEAP

The torching of Kuwait and the saturation of the northern Persian Gulf with oil by the

Iraqi (and US) forces early in 1991 were only the most recent, most wanton and most visible of a long line of intended and unintended atrocities committed by people against nature since the birth of time. Pollution has always shadowed human society. If now it threatens to overwhelm its creator, that is because even the celebrated resilience of the human planet might be reaching its limits. For whatever earth is – a thing possessed by living beings or a being in itself – it is not a bottomless trashcan. Yet it is widely treated as such.

Air pollution is chosen as the marker for environmental degradation on the map not because it is worse or more dangerous than water or soil pollution, but because more people come into continuous, and unavoidable, contact with it.

Air quality is not easy to gauge. Although there are reasonable guesses about the amount of chemical muck spewed out of chimneys and exhausts (which form the basis for colour in 'Air Pollution'), only the vaguest notions exist about where, and on whom, it falls. Few habitations are monitored by the Global Environmental Monitoring System (GEMS), the main source of information. Amongst major cities, Los Angeles, for example, notorious for its ozone pollution ('photochemical smog') is not listed. Nor is Mexico City, where oxygen pay-booths have been installed downtown to protect people from 'smog attacks'; nor is Krakow in Poland where even the stone is dissolving in the acid air; nor are Tehran, Manila, Seoul, Sao Paolo – all well-known cough cities; nor are the dozens of industrial tenement-cities in the USSR where the air is more spiked with poisons than the cheapest moonshine vodka; nor the hundreds of anonymous others that house half the world's population (see **19. Critical Mass**).

The few cities that are listed are barely touched. Most have a single monitoring station for millions of inhabitants, positioned haphazardly, not necessarily where people are most densely concentrated. And the pollutants that are monitored form a small part of the chemical concoction that goes for urban air. Carbon monoxide, for example, is ignored; ozone too.

Cleaning is possible, and has been done. Total energy consumption by industry in the rich (OECD) countries, the source of most pollution, has fallen by about 40 percent since 1970 while its contribution to gross national product has remained stable. In Sweden, the paper industry's use of water halved between 1960 and 1980 while output doubled. But to achieve cleanliness you need to pay the laundry bills – perhaps $5 billion a year in the USA, $5-7 billion in the European Community, just to halve sulphur dioxide emissions, one of many poisons – and few states believe they can pay that sort of price. Desperate to increase output now, dazzled by the example of the rich, they feel compelled to follow the litter path to 'development'.

The accident at the nuclear reactor at Chernobyl, near Kiev in the Ukraine, USSR, was a calamity just waiting to happen. The reactor in use – an RBMK – was built to a faulty design. It failed its safety tests but was cleared for operation nonetheless – many careers and bonuses were riding on its licence. Much of its housing was built of inflammable material banned for use in industrial buildings. No fire drill was ever held at the plant, the fire-fighting crews had no radiation-monitoring instruments and inadequate equipment.

The results of the accident, the largest industrial accident in history, were, and are still, terrifying. 130,000 people were resettled; 600,000 were classified as having been 'significantly exposed' to radiation; one million people were covered by a 'zone of special control'; 3.7 million still live on badly contaminated land. Huge volumes of topsoil were removed; forests and bushland destroyed: dams constructed to isolate the most polluted areas. An exclusion zone of 30 square kilometres was fenced off and turned into an experimental park for radiologists, radiobiologists and experts on the use of radiation in agriculture. It is not entirely fanciful to see the accident at Chernobyl as the final nail in Stalinism's coffin.

A few technical words: caesium-137 is only one of the many radioactive nuclides released by an explosion such as the one at Chernobyl. It is conventionally chosen to represent them all because it is the best indicator of recent fission and so a clearer pointer than others, such as iodine-131, to an unexpected source of radiation. At a dose of about 800 micro-sieverts we pass from a zone in which an increase in the incidence of cancer is currently undetectable and genetic effects are statistically insignificant to a zone in which they become apparent.

Sources:

Medvedev, Zhores A., *The Legacy of Chernobyl*, Oxford: Basil Blackwell, 1990; United Nations Scientific Committee on the Effects of Atomic Radiation (UNSCEAR), *Sources, Effects and Risks of Ionizing Radiation*, 1988 Report to the General Assembly, New York: UN, 1990; World Resources Institute (WRI), *World Resources 1990-91*, New York and Oxford: Oxford University Press, 1990; press reports.

Acknowledgements:

Zhores Medvedev, National Institute for Medical Research, London, was generous with guidance and materials; Burton Bennet, United Nations International Centre, Vienna, helped with information and materials; and Alan Morton, Curator of Physics, Science Museum, London, helped to circumvent technical pitfalls.

 EXIT

Tropical rainforests which cover six percent of the world's land area have a crucial role in regulating the global climate. They also harbour half of all living species. Yet they are being destroyed at a rate of 20 million hectares (50 million acres) a year – 38.5 hectares (95 acres) a minute. Even if they were replanted as a matter of course, which generally they are not, they would take up to a century to regrow and many hundreds of years to mature fully – a forest area cleared at Angkor, Cambodia, five and a half centuries ago has still not regenerated fully.

The destruction of the rain forests is merely the most celebrated and documented of the environmental wounds inflicted on all types of forest cover. 5,000 years ago, half the world's land area was wooded. It remained like that, with some local exceptions, until the industrial revolution and European colonial expansion of the 1800s when forest clearing became pandemic. By 1988 only a third of the land area remained under forest and woodland – an average loss of 4000 square kilometres a year since 3000 BC or, more telling, a loss of 105,000 square kilometres a year since 1800.

The wetlands whose significance for the world's ecological well-being is not as well understood, have a similar, although badly documented, history.

Some branches of the human family have lost out in the environmental mayhem: over 95 percent of Brazil's 6.9 million forest people have disappeared in the last three hundred years, as have all of Southern Africa's nomadic Bushmen. But most humans have avoided its worst consequences so far. It is the other species that have paid – in extinction and near-extinction: the 1700 mammal species listed as endangered by the International Union for the Conservation of Nature, the 2200 species of bird, the 850 species of reptile, the 133 species of amphibians and the vast, uncounted species of insects and plants.

Information on the number of species and on their relative security is more abundant for the rich states than for the poor, but the bias is the same. For that reason, the percentages depicted in 'The Way Out' represent the human pressure on other forms of life more accurately than absolute numbers could.

Lisa Taylor died unexpectedly in her sleep of heart failure on 26 August 1990. She was 31. Deeply mourned, and joyously remembered, her friends published her poems privately to coincide with a show they staged in her honour in London, February 1991.

Sources:

World Resources Institute, *World Resources 1990-91*, New York and Oxford: Oxford University Press, 1990; press reports.

Acknowledgements:

Andrea Ballard, Communications, World Wide Fund for Nature, Godalming, Surrey; and Maria McLaughlin, Library, Zoological Society of London, provided information expertly and expeditiously when it was most needed; Guy Parker-Rees, London, was forthcoming and brave.

Other Pluto Projects Available from Touchstone Books

WOMEN IN THE WORLD: AN INTERNATIONAL ATLAS
by Joni Seager and Ann Olson

With vivid maps and graphs, the global status of women is detailed in economic, political social, and educational terms--an indispensable reference source for all those concerned w women's issues.

0-671-63070-9, paper, $12.95

"WOMEN IN THE WORLD: AN INTERNATIONAL ATLAS *is wonderful! It focuses on the rig areas, asks the right questions, and the answers to those questions are instantl available because of the format."*

--Marilyn Fren

THE STATE OF THE EARTH ATLAS
Edited by Joni Seager

With 37 incisive full-color maps and cartograms, this concise and timely survey of social political, and economic forces is an invaluable multi-purpose reference covering a broad spectrum of topics from air quality and acid rain, to toxic waste, tropical forests, and touris

0-671-70524-5, paper, $13.95

"Worldly wise...the author's achievement is to present an abundance of facts in ; readable, sometimes even breezy style."

--The Econom

THE NEW STATE OF WAR AND PEACE
Edited by Michael Kidron and Dan Smith

Concise and up-to-the-minute, with 37 full-color international maps, this completely new ar indispensable military atlas provides an easy-to-understand survey of the arsenals, armies and alliances around the globe.

0-671-70103-7, paper, $14.95

Simon & Schuster/Touchstone, Simon & Schuster Building,
1230 Avenue of the Americas, New York, NY 10020

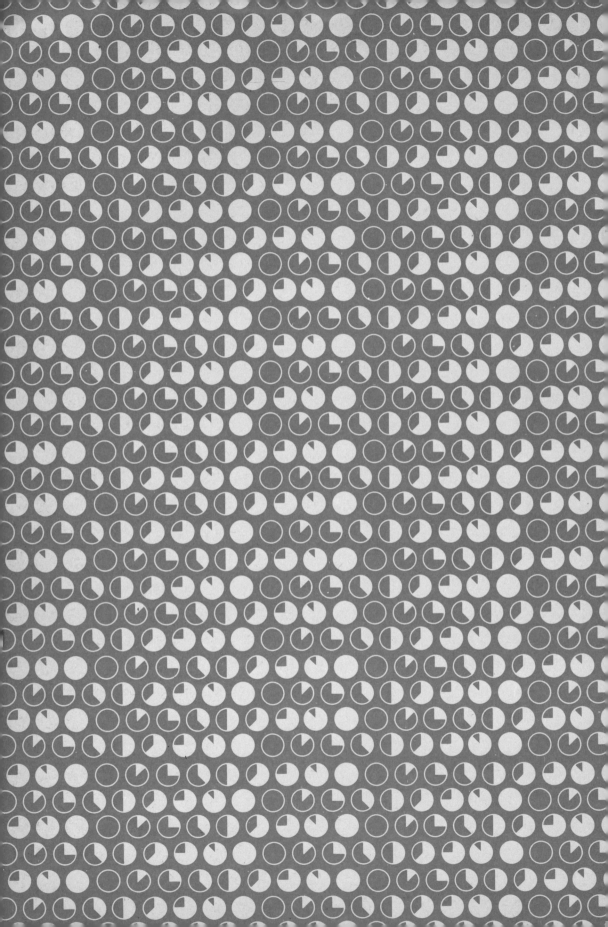